Recovering Our Ancestral Foodways

The publisher and the University of California Press Foundation gratefully acknowledge the generous support of the Ahmanson Foundation Endowment Fund in Humanities.

Recovering Our Ancestral Foodways

INDIGENOUS TRADITIONS AS A RECIPE FOR LIVING WELL

Mariaelena Huambachano

UNIVERSITY OF CALIFORNIA PRESS

University of California Press
Oakland, California

© 2024 by Mariaelena Huambachano

Library of Congress Cataloging-in-Publication Data

Names: Huambachano, Mariaelena, 1978- author.
Title: Recovering our ancestral foodways : indigenous traditions as a recipe for living well / Mariaelena Huambachano.
Description: Oakland, California : University of California Press, [2024] | Includes bibliographical references and index.
Identifiers: LCCN 2024013575 (print) | LCCN 2024013576 (ebook) | ISBN 9780520396159 (cloth) | ISBN 9780520396166 (paperback) | ISBN 9780520396173 (ebook)
Subjects: LCSH: Indigenous peoples—Food—Peru—History. | Māori (New Zealand people)—Food—History. | Food sovereignty—Peru. | Food sovereignty—New Zealand. | Food security—Peru. | Food security—New Zealand. | Indigenous peoples—Peru—Social life and customs. | Māori (New Zealand people)—Social life and customs.
Classification: LCC F3429.3.F65 H826 2024 (print) | LCC F3429.3.F65 (ebook) | DDC 978.00498—dc23/eng/20240409
LC record available at https://lccn.loc.gov/2024013575
LC ebook record available at https://lccn.loc.gov/2024013576

33 32 31 30 29 28 27 26 25 24
10 9 8 7 6 5 4 3 2 1

Para mis abuelitos

Para Larita y Agustín

And to the younger generation, who are the future leaders of the global movement for environmental and social justice. I know you will strengthen the pathway toward revitalizing Indigenous traditions, values, language, and food sovereignty.

Contents

List of Illustrations ix

Acknowledgments xi

Introduction: A Meeting of Two Different Worlds: Camote and Kūmara   1

1. Indigenous Food Sovereignty   12

2. The Weaving of the Khipu Model: An Indigenous Knowledge-Based Research Framework   32

3. Together, We Grow: Quechua and Māori Understandings of Well-Being and Shared Similarities to Sustainable Food Systems   71

4. Allin Kawsay and Values and Principles for Sustainable Food Systems   102

5. Well-Being through a Māori Lens: Māori Principles and Values Linked to Sustainable Food Systems   116

6. Rematriating Holistic/Collective Well-Being: The Chakana/Māhutonga, an Indigenous Food Sovereignty Framework   131

Conclusion. We Want Foods That Tell Our Story: Reclaiming and Celebrating Indigenous Food Sovereignty   157

Glossary of Māori and Quechua Terms   167
Notes   171
Bibliography   195
Index   221

Illustrations

FIGURES

1.	A khipukamayuq (Khipu-Master) holding a Khipu	33
2.	The Andean Khipu	35
3.	The Andean Khipu and its main horizontal cord	39
4.	Long vertical cords reflecting the being/ontology phase of the Khipu Model	40
5.	Research methods	43
6.	Quechua research partners with potatoes, corn, and beans	75
7.	Māori food growers Mate and Sonny Heitia growing kūmara	79
8.	Pātaka kai	89
9.	Seed-saving	92
10.	Andean agrobiodiversity	93
11.	Main entrance to the Valley of Lares	103
12.	Quechua famer holding native potatoes	105
13.	The Whareponga marae	118
14.	Tikanga practices in Māori food systems	122

15.	A Māori gardener holding a kūmara	129
16.	The Chakana/Māhutonga	135
17.	Women of Choquecancha wearing the llikllas (shawl)	142
18.	A welcome lunch with the women of Choquecancha	143
19.	A despacho [offerings] to Pachamama	144
20.	The logo of the Papatūānuku Kōkiri Marae	148
21.	Fresh produce from the Papatūānuku Kōkiri Marae	149
22.	Signing the Hua Parakore Korowai	151
23.	A Hua Parakore sign	153
24.	Quechua and Māori signs about food and resilience	166

MAPS

1.	Peru and study communities	45
2.	Aotearoa and study communities	46

Acknowledgments

AÑANCHAKUY (QUECHUA)—HE MIHI (MĀORI)

Ehara taku toa i te toa takitahi, engari he toa takitini. (Māori)
Hukninchik allish kaptinqa, llapanchikmi allish kanchik. (Quechua)

My success is not mine alone; it is the success of the collective.

—Māori whakataukī (proverb)

The proverb above holds true to me. This book has come to life through the support of many people who have encouraged, supported, and guided me while I researched and wrote this book, beginning over ten years ago. You all helped me immensely, and I want to acknowledge all of you.

First, I want to express my profound gratitude to the Quechua peoples of Peru and the Māori of Aotearoa for sharing your culture and foodways knowledge unreservedly. Whether we were working the land in the māra kai (food garden) and chakras (land sown by seeds), seed-saving, going on food-foraging expeditions, or just cooking and sharing a meal together, our time together has been joyful and precious to me. I am eternally grateful for the love, direction, patience, and endless support you have given me and for all your efforts in restoring Indigenous foodways, bolstering the food and environmental justice movement, and creating a just and sustainable world. In Peru, I specially want to sulpayki (say thank you) to Maria Ttito, Crisostomo Quispe, Lino Mamani, Sonia Quispe, Marisol Quispe, and Petronila Quispe; I am truly grateful to you for sharing your stories, foods knowledge, food recipes, and laughter and for always welcoming me warmly and providing shelter during my long periods researching deep in the highlands of Peru.

I am grateful to my dear Tarcila Rivera Zea: sulpayki! for all your love, encouragement, and teachings about Andean culture, resiliency, and Indigenous foodways and for keeping me grounded in my culture. Your warrior spirit, strength, and commitment to elevating Andean and Indigenous knowledge to build healthy and self-sufficient communities empower and inspire me. Also, sulpayki to my Indigenous sisters and brothers at the CHIRAPAQ organization for your love, friendship, and support. When I asked you for information for the book, you were always willing to help when needed, answering my emails almost instantly from across the ocean.

In Aotearoa, in particular, I acknowledge the wisdom and guidance of Uncle Percy Tipene, who is no longer with us. This book is in part a monument to him—to his dedication, kindness, and resilience. Uncle Percy took me under his wings, not only connecting me to Māori in the food sovereignty movement but sharing with me something as valuable as his wisdom and aspirations for knowledge networks across the Pacific and beyond and to living a life grounded in our foodways, which I aim to honor. I want to extend my deepest kia ora (thank you) to Māori kamatūa (Elder) Rereata Makiha, for always being there for me as my cultural/spiritual Māori mentor and friend. You inspire me with your wisdom, kindness, humility, and committed spirit to elevate Mātaraunga Māori. To Lionel Hotene and Valerie Teraitua from the Papatūānuku Kōkiri Marae (urban food garden) and Fred Tito and Buchanan Beech-Cullen from the Wai A Ariki Onerahirahi (Food Forest) garden, so many thanks. Also, warm thanks to Mate and Sonny Heitia and Fiona Wiremu. You all welcomed me as whānu (family), let me work the māra kai, let me cook with you, and shared many meals and laughter, and always sent me home with my arms full of healthy food grown in the māra kai. I am truly grateful to you.

Robert Whitbourne shared resources, Māori and Peruvian stories, and contacts in Peru, which allowed me to strengthen my comparative research. He kindly welcomed me to stay in his house the many times I was doing research in Whakatāne, and I had many chats, meals, and walks to the beach with him and his beautiful family. Kia ora mate! A heartfelt kia ora to Kiri Dell and her mum Hinetu Dell, who welcomed me into their tribe of Ngāti Porou, and connected me with Māori Elders and food growers whose voices appear in this book. Kiri, your aroha (love), strength, true friendship, and commitment to achieve Indigenous aspirations inspires me. Special thanks to Trish Beamsley from the Te Puna Mātauranga o Aotearoa (National Library of New Zealand) in Wellington, who was very generous with her time assisting me in finding significant archival material for this book.

I express my sincere gratitude to friends, colleagues, and institutions who have offered significant support for this book. My deepest gratitude to Kyle Whyte, who has always been there for me since he met me as a graduate student in Aotearoa, offering guidance and support as I navigated the challenging academic waters. Kyle has been my mentor, colleague, and friend. A special shout out to you for having invited me as a graduate student to present work from this book in a seminar in a US university. The feedback I received there proved to be valuable for what would have become a key chapter of my book on the Khipu Model. Your kindness, humility, and vision sustain me and inspire me. I am honored and thankful to look up to you as the brother I never had.

My heartfelt thank you to my dear friend, colleague, and mentor Hannah Wittman. Your friendship, kindness, guidance, and expertise sustained me. I am indebted to you for being so generous with your time checking on me, energizing discussions, reading entire drafts, and offering detailed and generative comments. And the talk on Indigenous Food Sovereignty that you and your graduate students at the Centre for Sustainable Food Systems at the University of British Columbia organized, and our productive book workshop in Vancouver, helped me see my way through lots of directions and ideas. Thank you! I couldn't have done it without your support. A warm kia ora to my dear Krushil Watene for your aroha (love) and manaakitanga (hospitality) and for finding ways to support my work, whether I needed a laugh or advice, and for inviting me to discuss my work in seminars and offering financial support for a writing retreat. You gave me strength and inspired me in countless ways.

I express my gratitude to my friend and mentor, Gabriel Eweje, who pushed me during my graduate studies to think more deeply about sustainable development and food systems and was always there for me, whether I needed advice, laughter, or homemade food, which he prepared and enjoyed with his lovely family. My most profound gratitude to Māori scholars Manuka Hēnare, Rachel Wolfgramm, Chellie Spiller, and Carla

Houkamau, for your aroha and korero (discussions), and for engaging with my thinking and critiques as I began to think more deeply about Indigenous foods, sustainability, and global indigeneity. I am grateful also to the KIN group that we as young Indigenous scholars established in 2015, which continues to this day. To Kiri Dell, Abigail McClutchie, Dara Kelly, Amber Nicholson, and Manuhiri Huatahi: our conviviality during our writing retreats up North of Aotearoa sparked insightful discussions that allowed me to understand more about Māori concepts. Your welcoming me with open arms every time I returned home to Aotearoa from the United States meant so much.

In the United States, I remember June 2016, as I was approaching the end of my doctoral studies in Aotearoa, when Vice President for Institutional Diversity and Equity Liza Cariaga-Lo notified me that I had received a Presidential Diversity Postdoctoral Fellowship in the Department of American Studies at Brown University. The time and mentorship I received at Brown were key to developing the book manuscript. I am grateful to Liza for her encouragement and Elizabeth Hoover for her hospitality during my time there. Robert Preucel's guidance and support as well as that of the Haffenreffer Museum of Anthropology at Brown were instrumental, especially the public lecture Robert organized to discuss the Khipu Model. It wasn't until I arrived at Brown University in late 2016 that I considered publishing this manuscript, which led me to research and write this project in earnest. My deepest gratitude to Tricia Rose, Stéphanie Larrieux, and Caitlin Murphy at Brown University's Center for the Study of Race and Ethnicity in America, which, during my tenure there as a postdoctoral research associate, supported my book through research seminars and writing groups, and has always been there offering guidance, a sympathetic ear, and laughter.

Brown is just one of the institutions that has been instrumental in this book's development since the beginning, and institutions provided vital context for conversations with friends, and colleagues in workshops, public lectures, and conferences. I am grateful to the 4W Leadership Circle at the University of Wisconsin, especially to Lori DiPrete Brown, for gifting me your time in reading early drafts of the book's manuscript, providing in-depth feedback, going for walks and swimming in Lake Mendota while chatting about my book, and all your love and encouragement. In addition to the Presidential Diversity Fellowship at Brown, I am grateful for the Research in the Humanities Center at the University of Wisconsin-Madison for the academic year it funded to finalize research and key chapters of the book, and the Humanities Center at Syracuse University for the teaching release to finish the various stages of the manuscript's production from copyediting to printing.

Over the years, there were so many friends and colleagues who were willing to organize campus brown bag presentations or community meetings both in person and online where I was able to present my book's framework, goals, and aspirations, and to talk through my findings. Others offered encouragement, connected me to someone new, and invited me to be part of international environmental justice and public policy reports to engage the topic of Indigenous cosmovision/worldview, traditional ecological knowledge and food sovereignty at a broader and meaningful international level. You know who you are, and to all of you, I am grateful! Special mention to Patricia Balvanera (National University of Mexico, UNAM) and Aroha Mead, who advocated for me to be part of the Intergovernmental Science-Policy Platform on Biodiversity and Ecosystem Services (IPBES). Joining over one hundred scientists from around the world tasked with writing the report on Diverse Values and Valuation of Nature proved rewarding. I am grateful to you, Patty, for offering me the international space to discuss Indigenous philosophies and research methods, extending my intellectual inquiry into global indigeneity and environmental justice and knowledge about policy making. A huge thank you goes to my compañeros Gabriel Nemogá Soto (University of Winnipeg) and Tuyeni Heita Mwampamba (UNAM and Sokoine University of Agriculture, Tanzania) for your support, laughter, hard-working attitude, research resources, and inspiring chats about Indigenous worldviews, biocultural heritage, climate justice, and research methods in support of my research ideas.

Many colleagues read and offered important feedback on portions of this manuscript at different stages: Hannah Wittman, Gail Hamner, Krushil Watene, Kyle Whyte, Ben White, Pierre Bélanger, María Elena García, Jennifer Gómez Menjivar, Lori Diprete Brown, Kate Marshall, Tuyeni Mwampamba, and Jessica Hutchings. I am grateful to all of you! A heartfelt thank you to my dear friend and colleague Pierre Bélanger, for all your support and generous offer to design the maps, and many thanks to

Peruvian scholars Alex Paredes and Brenda Teruya at Syracuse University, who helped me with the bibliography. Special thanks to Kate Epstein of EpsteinWords and Megan Provost, who assisted with manuscript editing, for being generous with your time by accommodating all my writing deadlines even to the last moment. At the University of California Press, my deepest gratitude to Kate Marshall who believed in this project very early on and Chad Attenborough who was so diligent in the production process. Your help was vital and thank you for being the best editor and editorial associate I could hope for.

I feel very lucky to be able to write and collaborate with colleagues who are not only incredible scholars but are also just really kind people. A warm thank you to my dear Latinx friends, Almita Miranda, José Villagrán, Kevin Escudero, and Iris Montero, for organizing in-person and virtual writing groups, supporting each other by offering to write together, stimulating chats, and lots of laughter. The road towards completion of this manuscript would have been longer and a lot less cheerful on my own. I am glad you were there with me. To my Abiayala hermanas, Jennifer Gómez Menjívar, Sue Haglund, and Marisa Aki'Nene Muñoz, I feel very fortunate to have brilliant, thoughtful, and kind women who have supported my work, organizing virtual chats to check in on me, offering me feedback, and sharing much laughter with me. Your love, encouragement, and sisterhood have meant so much to me.

A warm thank you to my lifetime friend Christian Kasprowicz, who despite the distance was always there for me from the beginning of this book. Your friendship, love, stimulating discussions, advice, traveling together, trying delicious new foods, and making me laugh helped me to stay inspired and determined when things got tough during this book's research and writing process. It all has meant so much to me and I am forever grateful to you. A big thank you to my school friend Gina Aprile, her partner Adam O'Brien, and her son Raito, for your love, for offering me a nourishing meal and welcoming me at your place in the sacred valley of the Inkas, the times I arrived very late from fieldwork, and for letting me stay at your home when I needed a quiet place to reconnect with Pachamama, to restore and recharge.

My family is also present in these pages in multiple ways. Some of my beloved relatives have passed away but have left me with precious memories and teachings about Peruvian culture and foodways. To my beloved grandparents Agustín Huambachano and my bundle of munay (love in Quechua), my grandmother Manuela (mi mami Goyita), who passed away when I was in the last writing stage of this book: you are always with me. Sharing these stories helps keep both of you in my heart. To my beautiful mother Elena and sister Patty: together you are my rock. I would not have done this book were it not for you both. Being on the other side of the world, away from you, is hard. Despite this, you were there with me every step of the way. Thank you for your love, for making me laugh, for reminding me "you can do it," and for sending me lovely bouquet of flowers when things got tough. They lifted me up, bringing joy to my heart and giving me strength. Your love kept me grounded, humbled, and walking firm on this fascinating book journey—it has been our journey. To my lovely niece and goddaughter Larita: you always kept me on my toes by asking, "Madrina, how is your book going?" Your kind and joyful demeanor filled my heart with happiness and motivated me to finish this book successfully, with the hope you'll someday read it and find it inspiring. My gratitude to Uncle Julio Bringas Huambachano for spending many long hours tracing our Indigenous family tree and for the many chats talking about our family food traditions, stories, and history. You are undoubtedly the historian of the family, and I am grateful to have you! To Aunties Carmen, Chela, Uncles Tato, Lalo, and Mickey, and cousins Mili, Boysito, Victor, Janito, and Paula: I am truly grateful for your love, delicious Peruvian food, and always checking in on me to ensure I am doing okay. I am profoundly grateful and love you all immensely!

Lastly, sulpayki to all the food growers, gardeners, seed keepers, food sovereignty advocates, academics, and grassroots activists from around the world I have met in this book journey. To my Indigenous food sovereignty and environmental justice sisters and warriors, Charlotte Coté, Melissa Nelson, Dawn Morrison, Rowen White, Krushil Watene, Fiona Wiremu, and Mate Heitia: your passion, determination, and vision to creating pathways for building healthy and resilience communities will continue to invigorate me and fill my heart with love, joy, and enthusiasm as I continue with my research and writing. Sulpayki and kia ora all for sharing in my journey!

Introduction

A MEETING OF TWO DIFFERENT WORLDS

Camote and Kūmara

My journey into the study of Indigenous food systems started, like any hearty and fruitful endeavor, in the ground—more specifically, with a sweet potato.[1] Western-trained ethnobotanists call it *ipomoea batatas*, but it is known to me and my community in Peru as camote. Camote is native to South America but has traversed the world; so have I. I was born and raised in Chorrillos,[2] Peru, a seaside town near the postcolonial capital city of Lima. Although Chorrillos was a relatively urbanized environment, my family instilled in me a deep appreciation of my Indigenous[3] Quechua heritage, kept alive through oral traditions, traditional foods, and festivals passed from generation to generation. I loved the mid-year holidays I took to the remote highland town of Acarí in the Department of Arequipa,[4] where my paternal Quechua grandmother owned a chakra[5] (agricultural field). As a child, I was fascinated by the many varieties of potatoes, sweet potatoes, and corn seeds growing there. The colors and textures of these food crops differed markedly from those I ate regularly in coastal Peru. I would spend days in the chakra drawing the different shapes of the camote/sweet potato and recording the names of various local fruits.

Back in Chorrillos I regularly took part in the Indigenous agricultural celebration of yunza,[6] a tradition of Indigenous farmers and the campesinos (peasants) who immigrated to Lima over many generations.[7] The festival signifies that the harvesting season is approaching and offers gratitude to Pachamama (Mother Earth) for gifting us with an abundance of food from the sea and land. While my family and I lost yunza and many other communal food traditions when the political instability, economic crisis, and social unrest of the 1980s and 1990s brought us to Aotearoa New Zealand (hereafter Aotearoa) when I was a teenager, I quickly realized that I was not alone in my love of ancestral foodways.[8] In the interaction that would ultimately lead to this book, during a road trip in the North Island of the country, my younger sister Patty and I had stopped for a coffee break in a small Māori town of Tokoroa,[9] and we got to talking with some of the patrons. Upon learning that we came from Peru, a local man asked me if I had heard about the kūmara,[10] a starchy and sweet-tasting tuber similar to the potato that grows below the soil.

"Ah yes," I replied joyfully, "that's camote!" With his evocative description of this tuber, I knew well, my new friend had brought me right back to my grandmother's chakra. I told him of the importance of camote in my own traditions. I explained that like potatoes, corn, and other native food crops, camote is a vital source of food and nutrition in Peru. It is a staple of Peruvian cuisine and a reminder of the country's vibrant biodiversity[11] and millennia of cultural heritage.

"Ah, we are related!" the man replied. "We are related because we both share the whakapapa [genealogy] and gift of the kūmara." This unexpected encounter got me interested in the many unheard stories of the deep-rooted cultural connections that exist between Indigenous peoples—in this case, between my Peruvian ancestors in South America and the Māori in Oceania. This interest soon became a journey into the study of Quechua and Māori peoples' "foodways," that is, the food systems of Indigenous peoples grounded in their holistic philosophies of life, science, and traditions as they feature within particular eco-cultural landscapes. The camote/kūmara provided me with a starting point for exploring the richness and breadth of Māori and Quechua peoples' culture and social and ecological wisdom as a member of both communities, one by birth and the other by bond.

A primary goal of this book is to demonstrate how to ethically conduct research in Indigenous communities through a research methodology that

I call the Khipu Model. A core part of the model is the need to establish relationships within a community before starting a study, identify the community's needs and interests, and co-design projects that benefit the community. The research for this book took place in two distinct places that I have chosen to bring together because I believed these were the sites where I was most able to undertake these steps. My connections to Peru and to Aotearoa allowed me to bring context-specific cultural knowledge, language skills, and longevity to my research. I was able to establish long-lasting relationships with food growers, gardeners, seed keepers, food sovereignty advocates, academics, and grassroots activists. One outcome of my work was the establishment of a knowledge-sharing network between these two Indigenous communities. Given their distance they would likely have otherwise been unconnected, yet they share similar epistemological, ontological, and ethical philosophies of food sovereignty. Ultimately, my friends on both sides of the Pacific gave me the context in which to model what I believe to be the most ethical way to do research in Indigenous communities. Building an Indigenous knowledge network across an ocean for the benefit of both communities was one of the triumphs of this project.

FOSTERING A HEALTHY FOOD SYSTEM: THE POWER OF TRADITIONAL ECOLOGICAL KNOWLEDGE

Metaphorically speaking, just as the kūmara/sweet potato crossed the Pacific Ocean to arrive in Aotearoa, and spread out rapidly around the country, laying roots in environments where it could flourish, I, too, had crossed oceans to reach Aotearoa. I had arrived first in Napier, a beachside city on the eastern coast of the North Island of Aotearoa, where I began building kinships with the people who tend it, the Māori. Over time, long-lasting relationships stretched to various cities where I lived, visited often, and did the research for this book—Tāmaki Makaurau (Auckland), Te Papa-i-Oea (Palmerston North), Taupō, Whangārei, Tūranga-nui-a-Kiwa (Gisborne), and Whakatāne—all in the North Island. In all these cross-cultural exchanges, I learned personal stories from my Māori friends, reveling in learning about a culture rich in storytelling, myths, legends, and proverbs. My connections with Māori were upheld with our shared history of colonization, disruption of our ancestral foodways, and intergenerational trauma. Our shared experiences generally, and our love and respect for the kūmara/camote specifically, brought us closer together and reinforced our determination to protect and restore Indigenous philosophies, languages, ancestral knowledge, and food systems.

My cross-cultural experience in my homeland of Peru and my new home of Aotearoa was crystallized in the chance encounter connecting over the kūmara/camote/sweet potato that shaped my intellectual trajectory. It motivated my interest in pursuing international comparative research on indigeneity, food systems, environmental justice, sustainability, and public policy, especially between Peru, Aotearoa, and, in the past seven years, Turtle Island (North America). I began my academic trajectory in Aotearoa in 2000, studying international business and trade, sustainable development, and the globalization of the food system in my undergraduate years, earning a bachelor's degree in 2004, a postgraduate diploma in 2009, and a master's degree in 2011. As a graduate student, I conducted studies on Peru's and Aotearoa's agricultural sectors from 2007 to 2012, assessing their sustainability, environmental policies, and traditional ecological knowledge (TEK).[12] TEK is the context-specific wisdom and practices of Indigenous peoples that is dynamic and constantly evolving and culturally transmitted from one generation to the other.

This initial work revealed that the connection I had perceived between Aotearoa's and Peru's Indigenous peoples' cosmovision/worldview was real. It is based on a kinship-centric system wherein all community members, human and non-human (deities, rivers, mountains), have duties and responsibilities to respect Nature[13] and care for one another. Beyond the kūmara/camote/sweet potato, their foodways share a similar Indigenous cosmovision about preserving soil health, agrobiodiversity, and traditional agricultural knowledge. Peru and Aotearoa are rich in biodiversity, are major agricultural exporters, and their Indigenous populations still sustain and celebrate the ecological and cultural value of their foodways.

However, both Peru's and Aotearoa's Indigenous populations face high levels of food insecurity, which reflect their history of colonization. Colonial orientations are palpable in the dominant capitalist food system, which keeps the costs of producing food, such as labor, to a minimum, making food cheap and accessible at the expense of human and environmental health.[14] Because of their access to food that is not nourishing, Māori people suffer the highest rates of type 2 diabetes and cardiovascular diseases of any ethnic group in Aotearoa.[15] Indigenous people of Peru share a similar fate. In Cusco, in the rural Andean region of Peru, 18 percent of Indigenous children are chronically undernourished; their daily diets have insufficient calories, nutrients, and proteins for healthy growth, a rate almost twice that of the most privileged comparably aged group in Peru.[16]

The loss of Indigenous lands, disruption of their foodways, racial discrimination, and policies increasing the presence of processed foods into their diets are some of the key drivers of Indigenous food insecurity and nutrition inequities.[17] Thus, efforts by both Māori and Quechua people to preserve their TEK and cultural heritage—and with them their cultures, languages, lands, and foodways—to beat back food insecurity and undernourishment are vital. They are also increasingly successful.[18] Research on how Indigenous ideologies and traditions shape sustainable food systems is likewise vital, but it is not yet abundant. This book emerges from this gap in the academic literature and asks how Indigenous peoples' philosophies—in this case, those of the Quechua and Māori—can contribute to fostering a more inclusive, equitable, and healthy food system in their own communities and at a broader scale.

To best answer this question through my study, I developed the "Khipu Model," an Indigenous-based research methodology. I provide a detailed explanation of the conceptualization and application of the Khipu Model in chapter 2; here, I will note that I developed it by adapting the configuration of the Andean Khipu, a complex and colorful knowledge-keeping system containing knotted cords to use it as framework of knowledge creation.[19] The Khipu Model is rooted in the ways of knowing, values, and principles of Quechua and Māori; incorporates a community-based participatory action research approach; and engages traditional ecological knowledge theory. The Khipu Model also draws from a substantive literature review of the Kaupapa Māori, a Māori research framework, and the body of scholarship addressing postcolonial research methods.

This book draws from a wide range of research literature, including on subjects such as food sovereignty, settler colonialism, food security, and environmental justice. It gives special attention to how research has engaged with food sovereignty, that is, having autonomy and control over the food you (as an individual or group) consume as both a social movement and conceptual framework. An extensive body of food sovereignty scholarship focusing on human rights-based approaches to food and nutrition points to the deficiencies in today's industrial food system.[20] While the industrial food system has supplied large volumes of food to global markets, it destroys ecosystems, exacerbates the exploitation of farmers and farm workers, and compromises the health and well-being of the eaters and the harvesters alike. We need a "food system" that produces healthier and more sustainable diets and provides decent pay and working conditions.

Global food systems scholars and practitioners increasingly go beyond questioning the unsustainable methods of industrial agriculture to seek the development of a healthier and more equitable food system model. Indigenous scholars, too, have highlighted the connection between food sovereignty and settler colonialism, pointing to the negative socio-ecological and economic impacts of settler agrarian systems on Indigenous land and people. They offer an essential corrective in the literature on food systems and food sovereignty through arguments for the need to understand and support *Indigenous* Food Sovereignty—access to traditional foodways, the reclamation and affirmation of Indigenous food-related knowledge, eco-cultural values and practices built up over thousands of years—to drive global sustainability transitions.[21]

Building on more than a decade of research, this book traces two examples of the political project of practicing and defining context-based Indigenous philosophies of food sovereignty. My comparison of the Quechua and Māori recounts how they are employing their collective practices toward mending human-Nature relationships that have been disrupted due to colonization, the capitalist food system, and alarming rates of environmental degradation. Quechua and Māori research collaborators' collective organization to stay culturally and spiritually connected to their land exudes a context-specific holistic ideology of living well, strengthened by values and principles like reciprocity, solidarity, and intergenerational TEK. These holistic philosophies of life assert their Indigenous cosmovision and control over the resources of their lands. Such assertion of control is itself a political act in support of a radically holistic approach to food systems that would supersede any specific Indigenous community.

This book describes the creative and constructive ways in which both the Quechua and Māori are reclaiming, revitalizing, and upholding Indigenous philosophies of well-being and food sovereignty. I recount the Quechua and Māori foodways and TEK of sustainable food systems stories, positioning both these foodways and TEK as core strategies of Indigenous communities, strategies that aim to move beyond the ameliorative task of "Indigenizing" existing industrial food systems and toward the radical reshaping of global food systems through Indigenous-based frameworks. In this book, when I use the term "food system" or "food systems," I am referring to all actors and institutions involved in the producing, processing, consuming, selling, transporting, or otherwise managing of the food upon which humanity depends. The focus on Indigenous-based frameworks of food sovereignty is crucial for disentangling food systems from Eurocentric, capitalist norms and practices. Such a reorientation to these Indigenous-based frameworks is essentially a political act and an important step toward healing our ancestral lands and our bodies and living in harmony with one another and with Nature.

In line with such arguments, this book centers on stories, philosophies, and practices of Indigenous Food Sovereignty actors—specifically Quechua and Māori—in pursuit of more equitable, health-promoting, and ecologically resilient food systems. Additionally, through a lens that validates Indigenous science, I explore the TEK and place-based discourse centralized in Indigenous philosophies and foodways to broaden the meaning of Indigenous philosophies of food sovereignty. In conducting research for this book, I learned again and again that the shared ancestral kūmara/camote was just one of many connections between Quechua and Māori research collaborators. These two Indigenous communities that are geographically far apart share various epistemological and ontological similarities, not the least of which is a similar Indigenous cosmovision. I am grateful for the chance to, with permission, tell Māori and Quechua stories in a way that is original and true to them, though certainly not definitive. In telling their stories, I do not claim to speak for my own Quechua ancestors or for Māori people. Rather, I draw on the grounded knowledge that each research partner generously shared with me to explore the relationship between foodways, holistic philosophies of well-being, and food sovereignty. I also draw on the knowledge I attained from my lived cultural experiences as an Indigenous woman of Peru and resident of Aotearoa.

Come with me, then, on a journey through the South Pacific Ocean from Peru to Aotearoa. You will learn how the Quechua and Māori are bolstering the resilience and resurgence of their foodways and Indigenous Food Sovereignty by holding fast to their traditions, ancestral wisdom, cultural heritage, and values for a sustainable future. The painful and complex history of colonization and settler colonization in Quechua and Māori territories is an inevitable part of this journey. A modern driver of colonialism is industrial food production, which insists that we embrace mechanized farming to feed the world. It mistakenly assumes Indigenous science or TEK are unscalable and ignores TEK's crucial role in sustainable agricultural systems. This book looks at this painful history and its contemporary consequences. Its two synergistic case studies from Peru and Aotearoa offer a counter-narrative that elevates the significance of Indigenous TEK and holistic Indigenous philosophies of well-being in achieving sustainable food systems.

As we travel on this alternative path, unearthing the beautiful and millennia-old foodways and traditions of Quechua and Māori, I recognize that Indigenous societies are distinct and diverse, and that knowledge is place-based. Therefore, no single Indigenous philosophy or Indigenous Food Sovereignty framework will serve all contexts and situations. However, my research points to epistemological and ontological similarities between the Quechua and Māori, noting foundational values, principles, and methods of Indigenous philosophies of food sovereignty. These food sovereignty philosophies, I suggest, provide a pathway toward flourishing livelihoods. They may resonate with other Indigenous societies and thereby contribute to the restoration of cultural foodways and working landscapes on the local and global scale.

The central aims of this study are threefold. First, I seek to reposition the significance of Indigenous peoples' philosophies of well-being, Indigenous Food Sovereignty, and TEK at the core of innovative solutions to make global food systems more sustainable. By bringing the Indigenous foodways and holistic philosophies of well-being of the Quechua and the Māori into conversation with one another, I demonstrate the synergies of TEK as well as its attentive flexibility toward local land differences. The significance of Indigenous-based frameworks of foodways is not their homogeneous approach to food production (which Western scientific practices at a high price) but their common disposition toward the interconnections of life, soil health, and well-being. Second, I offer an exploration of how the two communities on which I focus developed their own research-based frameworks and philosophies of food sovereignty, drawing from their TEK. This exploration clarifies how different communities align foodways and TEK with their cosmovision and use this alignment in their political strivings toward food sovereignty. Third, I aim to support building global/planetary connections between Quechua and Māori and other Indigenous communities globally. What became clear through my research was how important it is for these two Indigenous communities and others to reconnect and strengthen their relationships with their ancestral foodways and philosophies of well-being. Demonstrating how food binds communities across generations and the importance of building synergies and knowledge sharing about Indigenous Food Sovereignty, TEK, traditions, and methods to make growing, hunting, and gathering food possible, save seeds, and feed ourselves and wider networks that lack food. I hope that this book will link Indigenous people, farmers, seed keepers, activists, academics, and allies at the local level and internationally in transnational advocacy networks to scale up knowledge about and methods of food sovereignty.

The kūmara/camote/sweet potato and other Indigenous food crops are not forgotten in colonial lands in which mass-produced, processed foods reign. Indigenous foodways still exist as living proof of the value of Indigenous traditions, resiliency, and the powerful means of Indigenous reunification not only bringing Indigenous communities together against settler colonial violations but providing a framework for living well and healing the land. If Quechua and Māori can still find that kinship at the intersection—the sweet, starchy heart of their ancestral foodways—centuries later, so can other Indigenous peoples. Geography might keep us apart, but shared traditions can bring us together.

STRUCTURE OF THIS BOOK

The book begins with an account of Indigenous Food Sovereignty in chapter 1. I provide a historical context of the dominant Anglo/Eurocentric way of thinking about food systems, followed by describing settler colonialism and how it has disrupted Indigenous lifeways and foodways. I then turn to a discussion on the revival of Indigenous Food Sovereignty and the role of Indigenous philosophies in "rematriating" cultures of well-being.

In chapter 2, I provide an in-depth account of the Khipu Model in practice, including its theoretical background and how I use it to deeply understand the historical and contemporary political, cultural, and food struggles of my Quechua and Māori research partners. I also discuss how the Khipu Model represents an innovative research model for studying food systems transformation.

Through rich narratives that emerge from the Khipu Model, chapter 3 explores the foundations of an Indigenous philosophy of well-being within Quechua and Māori peoples' traditional settings. Then, I present common philosophical principles that emerge from this analysis, such as spirituality and relational well-being, self-determination, and intergenerational equity, justice, and accountability. Finally, I discuss the role of Indigenous thinking in driving a well-being agenda in the twenty-first century.

Chapters 4 and 5 outline and analyze core values and beliefs entrenched in Quechua and Māori philosophies of well-being, which are not merely a matter of philosophical inquiry: they have profound implications in developing food security and food sovereignty policies to strengthen sustainable food systems.

Chapter 6 provides in-depth accounts of how shared ontological and epistemological similarities emerging from Quechua and Māori research partners support the development of an Indigenous-based Food Sovereignty framework as a pathway toward sustainable food systems anchored on rematriating "holistic/collective well-being" philosophies. I do this through a relational case study of the Papatūānuku Kōkiri Marae (Māori urban community garden) and the Andean seed keepers, or "women of Choquecancha," a subsistence farming community in the highlands of Peru. These case studies are emblematic of how Indigenous peoples are asserting their right to food and Indigenous Food Sovereignty.

They reveal the reclamation of Indigenous agricultural roots, traditions, food autonomy, self-determination, self-sufficiency, and Indigenous peoples' rights to grow culturally relevant foods despite living in a patriarchal and capitalist society.

I conclude the book by highlighting Indigenous resilience and resurgence in advancing Indigenous Food Sovereignty and rematriating holistic/collecting well-being philosophies. Because this book is in part a celebration of all efforts undertaken by Indigenous peoples and local communities globally in restoring traditional food systems and food sovereignty, the conclusion focuses on the voices of people on the ground. Thus, we close with the seed savers, food foragers, fishers, community organizers, educators, and chefs who facilitate and witness this movement firsthand.

1 Indigenous Food Sovereignty

> Food sovereignty is an affirmation of who we are as Indigenous peoples and a way, one of the most surefooted ways, to restore our relationship with the world around us.
>
> —Winona LaDuke

The rise of today's Indigenous Food Sovereignty movement is part of a long history of resistance to elements endemic to colonialism, settler colonialism, and capitalism: violent dispossession, exploitation, and struggles for land, water, seeds, natural resources, labor, markets, and disruption of cultural lifeways of Indigenous peoples. Indigenous peoples living in settler colonial societies, such as the Māori, face acute food insecurity; in Aotearoa, for example, Māori are twice as likely to suffer from a diet-related disease than non-Māori.[1] Peru's rich biodiversity and vast agrobiodiversity is well-known for its contribution to regional and global food baskets.[2] It is a paradox of Peru that despite the rich variety of crops existing in its territory and mastery of ancestral agricultural practices, Quechua communities in the country's highlands are among the most vulnerable groups in the world in the matter of food insecurity.[3] Grappling with the root cause of this social injustice requires understanding history. It also requires understanding why Indigenous farmers, seed keepers, chefs, and activists, like the Quechua and Māori who appear in this book, are moving toward radically reshaping global food systems by developing Indigenous-based frameworks informed by their cosmovision, philosophies, and traditional ecological knowledge.

This chapter brings the reader's attention to the structural root causes impacting the health and well-being of Indigenous peoples like the Quechua and Māori. Legacies continue today in practices and norms that make the lives of human and non-human kin precarious. I discuss the origins of colonialism and the global capitalist food system, as well as the rising food justice movement and the United Nations' 2030 agenda for sustainable development. I explore the significant influence of Indigenous foodways and traditional ecological knowledge (TEK) of environmental stewardship on the lifeways of Quechua and Māori and the broader Indigenous populations globally. I conclude by discussing the revival of Indigenous Food Sovereignty and "rematriating holistic/collective well-being."

COLONIALISM AND SETTLER COLONIALISM: DISRUPTION OF INDIGENOUS LIFEWAYS

The global context of colonialism, settler colonialism, the rise of food injustices, and the global emergence of the 2030 agenda for sustainable development provide vital context for my case studies. The roots of colonization can be found in the Christian Doctrine of Discovery (DoD). The DoD asserted the superiority of the European Christian states and provided a legal rationale for expropriating territory and violating the rights of Indigenous peoples. The concept was initiated with a series of fifteenth-century papal bulls (edicts) that justified enslavement, land theft, and resource extraction, initially by Portuguese and Spanish explorers who were raiding Africa and the American continent.[4] The DoD continues in the long wake of the racist (or anti-Indigenous) practices, policies, attitudes, and norms of settler colonialism.

Settler colonialism is the systematic elimination of Indigenous peoples through a land-centered dispossession project, which destroys kinship relations and interdependent ecologies in politics, cultural knowledge, and sovereignty of Indigenous peoples.[5] Understanding it helps us to recognize the full impacts of colonialism and ongoing settler colonialism on Indigenous lifeways. For example, when the Spaniards conquered Peru in 1532, they established the encomienda policy designed to seize control of Indigenous Peruvians' land and labor. This law drastically altered Quechua peoples' traditional sociopolitical, ecological, and economic institutions and destroyed many of Peru's Indigenous populations.[6] In Aotearoa, land dispossession can be traced to British duplicity in the crown's 1840 Te Tiriti o Waitangi (Treaty of Waitangi) with Māori leaders.[7] In the Māori-language version signed by chiefs, the treaty acknowledges crown governorship of lands, but Māori retain sovereignty. In the English-language version of the treaty, Māori cede the sovereignty of Aotearoa to Britain. The treaty began a slow and ongoing process of settler colonialism based on segregating Māori from the land and, hence, from access to traditional foods.[8] The long history of dismantling the knowledge and values of Indigenous life ways exudes the equally long—and continuing—legacies of colonialism and settler colonialism. The effects of these legacies on the food practices of Indigenous communities remains today. Indeed, settler colonialism continues to form the incontrovertible logic of today's capitalist food system, which this book and the Indigenous communities I love aim to overturn.

THE RISE OF A CAPITALIST FOOD SYSTEM

"Development"—progress, modernity, and industrialization—is consistent with the struggles of Indigenous peoples for preservation of their cultural identity, rights, fundamental freedoms, and survival. In a Western economic development paradigm, higher production is a means of capitalizing on an opportunity to profit through more vigorous application of modern scientific and technical knowledge.[9] Two significant historical periods define the Anglo-Eurocentric theory of development. First, the Enlightenment and European imperialist periods of the seventeenth and eighteenth centuries marked the initial period of large-scale interaction between Indigenous and European peoples. A hierarchical Eurocentric worldview based on perceived cultural, political, and economic supremacy was established at that time among European peoples. Second, the post–World War II period saw the reframing of this civilized/uncivilized dichotomy. At that time the United States emerged as a superpower that redefined the global order politically, economically, militarily, and ideologically. Central to this Anglo-Eurocentric development narrative is a binary and hierarchal classification of nations and peoples that treats the homogenized "other" as deficient in all aspects of life.[10]

The discourse of the Anglo-Eurocentric theory of economic development reached a tipping point in the twentieth century when US President Harry S. Truman declared that the world was divided between the "developed" (the United States and its wealthy allies) and the "undeveloped" (the poor nations of Africa, Asia, and Latin America). He asserted that the undeveloped must enter a path to development, as defined by the United States. Much of the industrialized world enthusiastically seconded Truman's views of development. The new international organizations emerging from the postwar dynamic—the United Nations, the World Bank, and the International Monetary Fund—eagerly adopted it. In the more than seventy years since Truman's declaration, international commitment to the development project has only intensified.[11]

In the 1960s and 1970s, capitalism and modernization gained prominence in the developed world as the rubric for addressing economic development and maximizing food production and trade for an expanding global population. It is unsurprising that industrial agricultural systems, founded on the capitalist concept that the main objective of a business is to maximize profits, manufactured a new demand for cheap food during this period. Nor is it surprising that they ultimately established a monopoly control over food systems, reasserting the dominant position of industrialized countries.[12] In the 1980s, the election of Prime Minister Margaret Thatcher in the United Kingdom and President Ronald Reagan in the United States signaled the consolidation of the neoliberal paradigm, grounded in advocacy of free-market capitalism. The neoliberal paradigm maintained that markets need to be free from government control. Theorists of neoliberalism claimed that regulation of any sort inhibits free trade and compromises wealth production. They argued that only the unfettered movement of capital, goods, and services would deliver prosperity. Neoliberalism not only disregarded the different economic structures of industrial versus nonindustrial nations, but preyed on the latter through economic policies that exploited these differences and landed nonindustrial nations with massive burdens of debt.[13] For example, structural inequalities arise from the industrialized food production model, which draws on food, cheap labor, and raw materials produced elsewhere. Then, through technological know-how, industrialized nations have the ability to set prices to retain a much higher share of the value created in these exchanges. These food security inequalities are salient in developing countries, to the detriment of vulnerable communities such as minority and low-income populations, migrant farm workers, and refugees and displaced persons.[14]

FOOD INJUSTICE: INDIGENOUS STRUGGLES TO ACCESS TRADITIONAL FOODS

The capitalist food system and its modern colonial driver of industrial food production threatens the loss of Indigenous foodways and the potential of these foodways to rescue our global food systems. The industrial food system disrupts the land-rooted teachings that Indigenous peoples obtain from food-related activities. Examples are teachings of respect, consent, gratitude, and reciprocity in tending crops or farming fish. These practices renew familial, communal, cultural, political, and social relationships that balance the binding process between Indigenous peoples and their human and non-human relatives. Deprivation of these experiential practices and lived experiences causes what Potawatomi philosopher Kyle Whyte calls a "food injustice": "The violation of [a people's] collective self-determination to grow food as a collective in ways that do not limit another group's capability to do so."[15] The prevalence of food injustice is evidenced by Māori people's elevated rates of type 2 diabetes and cardiovascular disease, which is the highest of any ethnic group in Aotearoa. Rural Peruvian communities, where many ethnic groups such as Quechua and Aymara live, are among the most exposed to chronic hunger and malnutrition.[16] The same fate is experienced by other Indigenous peoples living in settler-colonial societies, such as Australia's Aboriginal and Torres Strait Islander people, who experience food insecurity at a disproportionate rate. More than 26 percent of Indigenous households ran out of food at least once in 2019, and the rate is even higher, at 43 percent, in remote Indigenous communities.[17]

Underlying all of these chronic yet heightened injustices are racist, patriarchal, and settler-colonial structures endemic to capitalism. These structures create conditions that strip people and communities of their ability to build equitable and sustainable food systems.[18] Enmeshing food in systems of oppression threatens the well-being of people everywhere. Food injustice affects not only Indigenous peoples but also urban communities of color, migrant farmworkers, members of minority and low-income populations, and many others around the globe. As Potawatomi Robin Kimmerer puts it: "Something is broken when the food comes on a Styrofoam tray wrapped in slippery plastic, a carcass of a being whose only chance at life was a cramped cage. This is not a gift of life; it is a theft."[19] Clearly, changing the industrial food system requires a paradigm shift. We must reconnect with Nature and restore the fragile ecosystems that support human life. Equitable and just food systems found in Indigenous philosophies of well-being and their intersections with sustainable food systems are key to that shift. In chronicling efforts to preserve the long-term sustainability of Earth's natural resources from the 1980s to 2023, I learned that Indigenous theories of well-being have reached beyond academic circles and civil society to influence global development agendas. The notion of sustainable development adopted by the United Nations closely resembles and draws on these Indigenous philosophies.

THE EMERGENCE OF THE 2030 AGENDA FOR SUSTAINABLE DEVELOPMENT

In 1983, the United Nations tasked the World Commission on Environment and Development with chartering a global agenda for change into the twenty-first century. This resulted in "Our Common Future," also known as the Brundtland Report, which popularized the concept of sustainable development (SD) in 1987. More recent years have seen a fierce debate about how to advance an SD agenda. In 2015, the United Nations member states convened in New York to adopt the 2030 Agenda for Sustainable Development. This universal policy agenda puts forth a global plan of action to achieve SD by focusing on a set of seventeen interrelated sustainable development goals (SDGs) and 169 associated targets.[20] The SDGs are part of a global agenda in which governments are tasked with developing pathways toward social, economic, and environmental dimensions of sustainability to eradicate poverty, among other indicators of well-being for people and the planet, by the year 2030.[21] SD and Indigenous philosophies of well-being have numerous shared values. As former UN Special Rapporteur on the Rights of Indigenous Peoples Victoria Tauli-Corpuz stated in 2020, Indigenous philosophies of good living "promote biocultural conservation, social equity, and the recognition of rights of Nature, offering alternative pathways toward more just and sustainable futures."[22] As this book illustrates, the Quechua and Māori have long effectively implemented and practiced SD through the pursuit of holistic ideologies of well-being. These communities have prized SD as a critical component for optimal relationships between humans and the natural world, traditional food-growing, and achieving intergenerational equity and justice. SD literature and policymaking of food security and food systems have not explicitly included Indigenous theories of holistic well-being, a failure this book seeks to remedy.[23]

UNDERSTANDING INDIGENOUS PHILOSOPHIES OF WELL-BEING

If the land is healthy, our foods will be healthy, and our physical and spiritual bodies will be healthy.

Throughout this book, I contend that one of the shared similarities of Quechua and Māori research partners is a cosmovision that foregrounds a holistic and relational philosophy of life wherein human and more-than-human beings work together as stewards of the land. Quechua and some Māori research partners use the terms "allin kawsay" and "mauri ora," respectively, for this philosophy. Similar philosophies exist throughout the Indigenous world. In South America, "sumak kawsay" in Kichwa/Quechua, "suma qamaña" in Aymara, and "sumak ñandereco" in Guaraní are all generally translated as "living well." Turtle Island (North America) has "mino-mnaamodzawin" (good life)[24] and "Nuu-chah-nulth" (everything is interconnected) in the Anishinaabe and Nuu-chah-nulth (nuučaan̓uɫ) languages respectively.[25] In South Africa's Zulu language, "Ubuntu" is a relational human values approach to living.[26] These Indigenous concepts, sometimes broadly translated as "good living" or "living well," refer to an Indigenous cosmovision about how we ought to live in harmony with Nature. These philosophies long predate the 1987 coinage of the term "sustainable development" to refer to "development that meets the needs of the present without compromising the ability of future generations to meet their own needs"[27] to address the unhealthy state of the planet. And yet, the guiding principles of SD are also those of Indigenous peoples' enduring philosophy of life. This Indigenous philosophy requires ongoing attention to maintain the organic balance between the ecological, economic, and social systems that are constantly nurturing one another.

As this book's ethnography will reveal, Quechua and Māori collaborators' respective philosophies of life—allin kawsay and mauri ora—are designed to achieve mutually respectful and beneficial relationships between humans and between humans and Nature. These philosophies are intended to promote and preserve cultural knowledge and the sustainability of ecosystems for generations to come. In the cosmovision of Māori and Quechua communities, life is a continuous rebirth in all its manifestations. Life is a cycle connected to human and non-human ancestors who work together to create the material and spiritual conditions to build and maintain a harmonic life, which is in permanent construction. I theorize this fundamental Quechua and Māori commonality as "holistic/collective well-being." I use this term to underscore that from the perspective of Māori and Quechua research partners, well-being is not only about *human* well-being, including the human right to healthy diets and access to cultural foods. It is also about the well-being of the *collective*, which includes the well-being of non-humans such as land, rivers, and forests that have the right to be respected, nourished, and preserved by their human kin. The former is linked to the human rights-based approach to food, and the latter is akin to environmental personhood, a legal concept that recognizes and assigns ecological entities such as rivers, mountains, and lakes the status of a legal person and guarantees these entities rights, protections, and responsibilities. The Right of Nature/Mother Earth is a movement to protect land and resources for future generations by bestowing legal personhood to Nature. The river, mountains, lakes and other non-human beings belong to no particular person, so no particular person can assert rights over them; the premise of environmental personhood as a legal concept is to address the fact that Western legal systems are based on such rights. For example, the Māori tribes that live along the Whanganui River in Whanganui revere the river as a tupuna, or ancestor. In this they recognize that its waters have physically and spiritually nourished them for generations. However, recognition of their deep relationship with the river has been a battle since the 1840 signing of the Te Tiriti o Waitangi, known in English as the Treaty of Waitangi, Aotearoa's founding document. Furthermore, farming, forestry, dams, and development projects compromised the health and well-being of Māori tribes and the Whanganui River. One hundred and sixty years into the Māori battle with the British Crown to preserve the physical and spiritual life force of the Whanganui River, in 2007 it became the first river in the world to be granted the same legal rights as a human being.[28] Fourteen years later, the Magpie River became the first river in Canada to be granted legal personhood.[29] I discuss Quechua and Māori thinking of holistic/collective well-being as linked to personhood rights and provide examples in chapters 3 and 6.

The Quechua and Māori research partners who participated in this study uphold a kinship tradition that they employ in diverse ways in food systems to safeguard holistic/collective well-being. Kyle Whyte uses the term "time as kinship" to describe the way in which many Indigenous peoples view kinship "as an ethic of shared responsibility."[30] For many Indigenous communities, this means that responsible human-Nature-spiritual relationships must first be established or restored to have healthy soils and foods. I witnessed how this kinship tradition reverberates in Quechua and Māori traditions wherein Mother Earth—Pachamama in Quechua and Papatūānuku in Māori—is the embodiment of a "female being," a living entity with personhood rights. Water is the very lifeblood of Pachamama/Papatūānuku. The land and soils, as the tribal stories tell, represent the skin of Pachamama/Papatūānuku, supporting the growth of all biological organisms (birds, insects, animals, trees, seeds, and human beings) who have a soul and energy. Pachamama/Papatūānuku gives birth to all things and binds all natural entities together, including humans.

Just as a mother nurtures her children, Pachamama/Papatūānuku nourishes those who inhabit her with an abundance of food. Pachamama/Papatūānuku is revered as the giver of life.

The well-being of everyone —human and non-human— is achieved through the establishment of healthy relationships with Nature, between the waters and soils that provide the food; the people and communities that grow, prepare, consume, and recirculate it; and the non-human beings who guard the energy that flows into this bounty. In this way, Indigenous foodways respect and foster traditions, ancestral knowledge, values, and self-determination and is a critical component of their histories, identity, sovereignty, spirituality, intergenerational knowledge, and heritage. Additionally, Quechua and Māori collaborators' philosophies of well-being underpin cultural, spiritual, and ecological values that flow into one philosophical strand. I understand this as: *if the land is healthy, our foods will be healthy, and our physical and spiritual bodies will be healthy*. I came to understand this philosophy, and how my Quechua ancestors and the Indigenous Māori understood the value of foodways and well-being, through spending time with knowledge holders of traditional foods, horticulturists, farmers, seed savers, and activists, as described in chapters 4 and 5.

INDIGENOUS SCIENCE AND EXPERTISE IN FOOD-SYSTEM TRANSFORMATION

The dominance of Western science in global food production is evident in the large amount of food that is produced with high technological and scientific methods such as post-harvest technology and biotechnological techniques. While a common perception of Indigenous food systems is that they are less productive than industrialized/high-input systems, evidence shows that traditional food systems produce high yields and more nutritious foods.[31] In this book, I demonstrate that Indigenous peoples have unique knowledge systems or traditional ecological knowledge (TEK), articulating diverse perspectives of communities' epistemologies and ontologies and promoting sustainable methods and practices to pursue sustainable food systems and food sovereignty. The tensions and ambiguities between Indigenous and Western science are underscored by the fact that the predominant conceptualization of TEK comes from Eurocentric scholarship.

In the book *Sacred Ecology*, Western scholar Fikret Berkes explains that TEK is a singular body of Indigenous knowledge.[32] It includes skills, practices, and innovations of Indigenous peoples acquired primarily through oral traditions from one generation to the next over thousands of years. Indigenous scholars debate this Western view of TEK, pointing out that traditional knowledge is place-based and therefore cannot be confined to a singular source of knowledge.[33] Anishinaabe scholar Deborah McGregor eloquently articulates this: "To understand where TEK comes from, one must start with Indigenous peoples and our own understanding of the world."[34] This study supports the Indigenous view of TEK, and proposes that Quechua and Māori have their own TEKs reflecting their ways of knowing and being. Consequently, using the "Khipu Model," an Indigenous-based research methodology, I explore the TEKs of Quechua (yachay) and Māori (mātauranga). While each is distinct, I found important parallels in how these two bodies of ancestral knowledge and practices shaped their food systems through oral history and experiential learning from one generation to the next. These sets of understandings, interpretations, and meanings of the environment manifest unique and context-specific Indigenous philosophies of life discussed in chapters 3, 4, and 5 and support an Indigenous-based food sovereignty framework that this book describes in chapter 6.

Bodies of Indigenous science such as the Quechua yachay and the mātauranga Māori have only recently been recognized as having a critical role to play in international conversations about environmental sustainability and building sustainable food systems. But they have been embedded in Indigenous cultures for centuries. These TEK-based systems promote ancestral food methods and practices in pursuit of food sovereignty and environmental justice. These include its applicability in the realization of the human right to food.[35] This is "a right to all nutritional elements that a person needs to live a healthy and active life, and to the means to access them,"[36] namely traditional knowledge sharing to promote self-sufficiency, healthy diets, and well-being. Examples of the scaling up of TEK in sustainable agriculture and food systems are found in the work of agroecology and food sovereignty scholars such as Miguel Altieri, Clara Nicholls, Hannah Wittman, Steven Gliessman, Maywa Montenegro de Wit, Alastair Iles, and Ivette Perfecto, among others. These scholars have provided research-based evidence from Mexico, Brazil, the United States, and Costa Rica of the vital role that agroecological practices imbued in Indigenous TEK play in expanding food sovereignty and food security.[37]

There is increasing interest in grassroots, academic, and policy circles in Indigenous science as a potential solution to pressing global concerns about food insecurity and climate change. In December 2022, US President Joe Biden released "first-of-a-kind Indigenous knowledge guidance for federal agencies"[38] with the goal of including Indigenous knowledge in US federal research, policy, and decision-making. This guideline responds to the call from tribal nations to recognize their agency, expertise, and input in addressing climate change. There is also work by social movements, intergovernmental organizations, scholars, and civil society actors to increase recognition of agroecology as a science that can play an essential role in solving the food and environmental crisis in ways that prioritize social justice.[39] Defined by Miguel Altieri as "the application of ecological concepts and principles to the design and management of sustainable agroecosystems," agroecology centers the role of Indigenous TEK in sustainable agriculture.[40] It has garnered support from international farmers' organizations and the United Nations.[41] As Michael Pimbert argues, the transition to more sustainable food systems requires the democratization of ways of knowing, allowing the co-creation of knowledge to develop forward-thinking food security, food sovereignty, and agroecological policies.[42] The acknowledgment of agroecology as a science provides an opportunity for the recognition of Indigenous TEK as a valid knowledge system and moves toward the democratization of knowledge production.

Much of the literature on TEK deals with similarities and differences between Western science and traditional/local knowledge.[43] Yet empirical research has not addressed the inherently collaborative approach of TEK. Thus, researchers know little about the linkages between TEK, Indigenous Food Sovereignty, health, and well-being. To address this knowledge gap, this book offers the first comparative research of Māori and Quechua peoples' TEKs and their respective contributions in healthy and ecologically sustainable food production methods. I also extend knowledge of TEK's collaborative approach by describing an Indigenous philosophy of food sovereignty within Quechua and Māori contexts. In so doing I focus on their shared core values of restoring disrupted sustainable food systems.

FOOD SECURITY, FOOD SOVEREIGNTY, AND THE REVIVAL OF INDIGENOUS FOOD SOVEREIGNTY

In my time with Quechua and Māori communities, I saw how physical and spiritual well-being depended on nourishing foodways. The stories outlined in this book began when I recognized the work of Quechua and Māori farmers, gardeners, chefs, and activists confronting contemporary, colonial-rooted food struggles by reviving Indigenous Food Sovereignty. The Indigenous Food Sovereignty movement across the world—predominantly in North America, Latin America, and Oceania—is expanding. Communities are reclaiming their agricultural roots and cultural foodways in order to restore and preserve tribal sovereignty and intergenerational knowledge. As scholars, civil society members, activists, and practitioners of agroecology, agrarian change, and international development move forward with discussions of Indigenous Food Sovereignty in safeguarding sustainable food systems, it is imperative to point out the distinctions between food security, food sovereignty, and Indigenous Food Sovereignty.

Food Security

Food security is a global policy objective that has evolved, developed, and diversified over time. According to the United Nations Food and Agriculture Organization, food security occurs when all people, at all times, have physical, social, and economic access to sufficient and nutritious food that meets their dietary needs for a healthy and active life.[44] More recently, the four previously identified dimensions of food security—availability, access, utilization, and stability—have been extended to include agency and sustainability, and the right to food has been acknowledged as central to food security.[45] Such inclusion underscores that previous definitions of food security had not adequately engaged with the conditions within which food was produced or distributed, nor with who was hungry or malnourished and why. It calls for radically transformed systems that are "empowering, equitable, regenerative, productive, prosperous" and that "boldly reshape the underlying principles from production to consumption."[46]

The debate about the best approaches to food security often focuses on the current industrial agricultural model characterized by high-technology approaches with the objective of increasing productivity and efficiency. Although this approach has produced large volumes of food, problems of hunger, degradation of land, unhealthy ecosystems, and lack of access to food persist.[47] Philip McMichael uses the term "globalizing food regime" to describe the intensification and expansion across borders of the industrial model of agriculture that favors large-scale production and is often oriented toward export markets.[48] As he underscores, industrial food production has adversely impacted human and environmental health. Agribusiness, predominantly in Europe and North America, has taken the lead in the ongoing transformation of agriculture and food production. It has produced massive amounts of unhealthy processed foods stripped of nutritional value and tainted with pesticides that pose risks to our health. It has endangered Indigenous farmers, peasants, pastoralists, and their traditional livelihoods. It threatens local food systems and undermines people's capacity for self-sufficiency and autonomy over what food is produced, how, and by whom.[49] Scholars of food studies, the environment, agroecology, and Indigenous peoples have long criticized this omission of concern.[50]

Food Sovereignty

Unlike food security, the concept of food sovereignty emerged as a response to food injustice, resulting from the industrialization of agriculture that has dominated global farming over the past half century.[51] Food security focuses on individualized health and nutritional status while food sovereignty encompasses community well-being. The concept of food sovereignty gained prominence on the international stage in 1996 when La Vía Campesina—an international movement that brings together millions of small- and medium-scale farmers, Indigenous peoples, peasants, and agricultural workers—took a stand against the prevailing neoliberal model of agriculture and trade, defending their rights to seeds and to food-harvesting grounds. "Food sovereignty" was redefined in the 2007 Forum for Food Sovereignty in Sélingué, Mali, and referenced in the Declaration of Nyéléni as "the right of peoples to healthy and culturally appropriate food produced through ecologically sound and sustainable methods, and their right to define their own food and agriculture systems."[52] Food sovereignty places the power to control foods with the people who cultivate, tend, produce, consume, and distribute it. Thus, it is antithetical to the dominant global food security regime. As Michael Menser points out, food sovereignty is "a project for the democratization of the food system that also aims to restructure the state and remake the global economy."[53] Over the past four decades, it has grown into a social movement that demands the democratization of food systems by shifting power concentration and restoring autonomy in individuals' relationship with food. To achieve this social justice outcome, food sovereignty is framed on a language of a rights-based approach to tangible things like land and seeds. It is also oriented toward ideological concerns like the ability to define one's culturally appropriate food systems. The concept of a universal human right is generally considered beneficial to all. Yet Indigenous scholars such as Melissa Nelson, Jessica Hutchings, and Jeff Corntassel have pointed out that the framing of rights as legal entitlements entrenched in food sovereignty has de-emphasized the cultural relationships that Indigenous people have with the land, with one another, their families, and broader non-human kin. For example, Hutchings urges us to question whose land we are on and on whose land our food is grown to understand the impacts of settler colonization on soil sovereignty and most Indigenous peoples' tangible and intangible cultural connection with the land.[54] Corntassel argues that the rights-based discourse tends to "compartmentaliz[e]" "Indigenous powers of self-determination" because it "separate[es] questions of homelands and natural resources from those of political/legal recognition of a limited Indigenous autonomy within the existing framework of the host state(s)."[55] The global concept of food sovereignty focuses on the rights of peoples to choose what food is grown and where, and as a concept and movement, resonates with the aspirations and actions of Indigenous peoples on enhancing food security and environmental sustainability through ecologically sustainable methods, community self-reliance and supporting individuals in defining their own food systems. But it's worth noting that for Indigenous peoples living in settler-colonial societies, the "sovereignty" of the state over its territory and its right to impart policies without external interference has a painful history. Therefore, particularly in colonized societies, peoples' rights and countries' rights are not necessarily the same thing. There is therefore a need to formulate a distinct Indigenous Food Sovereignty concept, one that provides a continuation of anti-colonial struggles against government asserting sovereignty over food production and distribution without their interference.

Indigenous Food Sovereignty

As a concept, framework, and movement, Indigenous Food Sovereignty goes beyond food security and sovereignty. It aims to reconnect Indigenous peoples with their foodways and build flourishing communities according to their own traditions, values, TEK, and practices as discussed by Indigenous Food Sovereignty scholars such as Charlotte Coté, Melissa Nelson, Dawn Morrison, Fiona Wiremu, Mate Heitia, Michelle Daigle, and Valerie Segrest. These scholars argue that Indigenous Food Sovereignty transcends the legal aspect of the right to food and human rights-based foundation of the food sovereignty concept. Indigenous Food Sovereignty underscores a relational, ethics-of-care approach to food imbued in an Indigenous cosmovision.[56] Secwepmec scholar Dawn Morrison clearly articulates this and writes that Indigenous Food Sovereignty must uphold Indigenous peoples' "long-standing sacred responsibilities to nurture healthy, interdependent relationships with the land, plants, and animals that provide us with our food."[57] The complexities and uniqueness of Indigenous food systems are part of the reason that Indigenous Food Sovereignty falls into its own category compared to other subsets of food sovereignty.

Academics increasingly recognize that the revival of Indigenous Food Sovereignty and TEK shapes movements for Indigenous self-determination and decolonization. For example, Native American scholars including Jeff Corntassel (Tsalagi) and Cheryl Bryce (Songhees) argue that Indigenous Food Sovereignty is the result of an Indigenous resurgence in foregrounding Indigenous sovereignty, customary laws, and practices informing Indigenous philosophies for living well and establishing food systems.[58] Mushkegowuk

(Cree) scholar Michelle Daigle describes these laws and practices as Indigenous political and legal orders that frame Indigenous authority and governance.[59] Likewise, food studies scholars Hannah Wittman, Sam Grey, and Raj Patel contend that Indigenous Food Sovereignty efforts are forms of resistance against settler colonialism and its legacies, including industrial food production.[60] They also argue that Indigenous Food Sovereignty efforts reflect a resurgence of Indigenous autonomy.

In Aotearoa, the recent revitalization of te reo Māori (the Māori language), Land March protests, and pockets of māra kai (food gardens) are all examples of Indigenous Food Sovereignty revival. In Peru, one example of Indigenous Food Sovereignty in action is the Indigenous association CHIRAPAQ. The name means "flashing of stars" in the Quechua dialect of the Ayacucho region of Peru; though the organization typically spells its name in all capitals, the name is not an acronym. CHIRAPAQ is an Indigenous organization that congregates with Amazonian and Andean people and was established more than thirty-five years ago by Quechua leader Tarcila Rivera Zea. It is dedicated to defending Indigenous rights and asserting Indigenous peoples' right to food. My own efforts in the region of Lares in Cusco also qualify as Indigenous Food Sovereignty in action. I have partnered with the Quechua communities of Choquecancha, Ccachin, and Pampacorral to lead eco-cultural and climate change projects surrounding seed sovereignty and medicinal plant knowledge as a means of improving health, promoting culture, and achieving food sovereignty. Beyond Peru and Aotearoa, in Turtle Island, Indigenous seed keepers are coalescing via the Seed Keepers Network. This organization is educating tribal people about seed planting and saving and pushing for "Indigenous seed rematriation" from institutions that have collected or inherited seeds back to their communities of origin.[61]

REMATRIATING HOLISTIC/COLLECTIVE WELL-BEING:
RECLAIMING AND RESTORING INDIGENOUS TRADITIONS
AND FOODWAYS

Through the study of the revolutionary actions of the Quechua and Māori in reclaiming, restoring, and preserving their cultures of well-being and foodways based on kin ties with the land and its features, this book reveals that Indigenous Food Sovereignty is a driver of "rematriating holistic/collective well-being." In the seed sovereignty movement, we use the word "rematriation" to challenge the masculinist underpinnings inherent in the term "repatriation" (patria, "father"). The land is our mother, Mother Earth, and in this spirit, we return Indigenous seeds and foodways home to it and to our maternal communities of origin.[62] In this book, "rematriation" refers to the recovering of Quechua and Māori ancestral foodways and restoring of holistic/collective philosophies of well-being as a pathway to revitalize and foster Indigenous foodways, TEK, and well-being at the local and international scale. The earth is on the brink of depletion, and the chances for us and for future generations to live long, healthy, fruitful lives are diminishing rapidly. Environmental degradation, climate change, and global health crises continue to threaten human livelihood. Food insecurity is rampant globally. According to a report by the Food and Agriculture Organization (FAO), between 720 and 811 million people go to bed hungry each night; 40.1 million children under five worldwide are obese due in part to poor nutrition; and environmental degradation continues to threaten the basic elements that sustain life.[63] The United Nations World Food Program projects famines of devastating proportions by 2030, which will expose gross inequalities and threaten the livelihoods of some of the world's most vulnerable people: Indigenous and rural farmers, infants, low-income people, and communities of color.[64]

This book answers the call to action by putting forth the Chakana/Māhutonga, a composite Indigenous Food Sovereignty framework, which I assembled in partnership with Māori and Quechua research collaborators. It contends that building a sustainable, inclusive, and healthy food system requires diverse knowledge systems, food sovereignty methods, and an intimate understanding of the relationship between humans and the ecosystems and of the need to maintain this balance. The framework is named after the Southern Cross constellation, one of the striking astronomical associations shared between Quechua and Māori peoples, who call it Chakana and Māhutonga, respectively.[65] It is visible throughout the year in the southern skies of both countries, watching over the progress and proliferation of the communities it has guided through mystical intuition, traditions, and agricultural knowledge. The Chakana/

Māhutonga framework encompasses the key fundamental similarities that my Quechua and Māori research partners hold that are inextricably linked to and rooted in self-determination, human rights-based approach, ethics, and intergenerational equity and justice described in chapter 6.

The Chakana/Māhutonga framework is built on the principle that these shared foundational elements may resonate with other Indigenous and local communities. Therefore, it is possible to scale diverse knowledge of sustainable agricultural systems, holistic philosophies of life, and Indigenous Food Sovereignty approaches linking growers and eaters to build sustainable and equitable food systems. I use the Chakana/Māhutonga metaphorically and utilize its composition, centered on four bright stars, a little differently than my research partners do for their agricultural purposes. I frame the suggested solutions for sustainable food systems—cultural, ecological, economic, and political—in each of the four quadrants of this constellation. Each of these four interdependent quadrants reveals how Quechua and Māori understand holistic/collective well-being as linked to healthy food systems. I place *spirituality* at the heart of the model because community members acknowledged spirituality as the infuser of energy and vitality, permeating all quadrants. The *cultural/spiritual well-being* quadrant, which community members often link directly to the spiritual center of the Chakana/Māhutonga, recognizes the fundamental linkages between land, ecosystems, spirituality, and human health. This quadrant underscores "foodways for reestablishing identity and reviving cultures of well-being." Thus, this quadrant focuses on reconfiguring our human-Nature-spiritual relationship with the land, helping us become agents of social change who are actively seeking to participate in ecoculture restoration projects such as Indigenous Food Sovereignty.

The *environmental well-being* quadrant is essential for achieving the culture of well-being and for ensuring the accessibility of "culturally relevant foods." The goal of this quadrant is to promote environmental sustainability and protection of land, water, and sky, on which humans are dependent for both a healthy life and a strong spiritual connection. Achieving this requires that humans protect Pachamama/Papatūānuku from human exploitation and become stewards and protectors of biodiversity. Ultimately, it involves recentering environmental governance on Indigenous principles, practices, and the mutual caretaking between people and place.

The *political well-being* quadrant is vital for achieving environmental well-being and emphasizes "human rights-based approaches to food" and "personhood rights of Nature/Mother Earth" as necessary to ensure respect for the life essence of human and non-human actors in the food systems. This quadrant grounds calls for Indigenous peoples' right to food, which is inseparable from their right to land, resources, culture, and self-determination. Self-governance, sovereignty, and autonomy are identified as key strategies to ensure the availability and accessibility of healthy foods. It also urges recognition of the rights of Nature and the honoring of international treaties and covenants such as the United Nations Declaration on the Rights of Indigenous Peoples and the United Nations Declaration on the Rights of Peasants and Other People Working in Rural Areas.[66]

The *economies of well-being* quadrant centers on "food for thriving and flourishing communities." It is about enhancing the dignity and well-being of the land, Pachamama/Papatūānuku, as the fundamental order for how we think of trading and making transactions. Foodways and their economic aspects—cultivation, processing, preparation, consumption, and recirculation—have unique abilities to foster economies of well-being rooted in principles of gratitude, reciprocity, and solidarity that shape one's identity, relationships, and places. Thus, economies of well-being transcend economies of competition. They take into account an Indigenous cosmovision and its inherent relationality approach to Nature, its inviting in and reestablishing of relationships, and its rekindling of kinship relations that sit at the center of Indigenous ways of being.

As described in greater detail in chapter 6, one of the major contributions of the Chakana/Māhutonga framework is that it provides an Indigenous, TEK-driven food-system restorative framework. Each of the four interdependent quadrants of the Chakana/Māhutonga model reflects how the Quechua and Māori who partnered in this research understand mutual flourishing as vital to the preservation of healthy food systems. But first, chapter 2 will provide an in-depth account on the development and operationalization of the Khipu Model, an Indigenous-based research framework that I developed to explore Quechua and Māori philosophies and knowledge of sustainable food systems.

2 The Weaving of the Khipu Model

AN INDIGENOUS KNOWLEDGE-BASED
RESEARCH FRAMEWORK

Te manu ka kai i te miro, nōna te ngahere. Te manu ka kai i te mātauranga, nōna te ao. Te whai au te tira haere. (The bird that partakes of the miro berry reigns in the forest. The bird that partakes of knowledge accesses the world.)[1]

Here nothing remains static. This is why a theory of the world, or a methodology, does not belong here. Here the only thing that belongs is an open and continuous conversation, with the active participation of all those who are in the Andean World.[2]

—Māori whakataukī (proverb)

"Allillanchu, noqaq sutiymi Mariaelena Huambachano, Peru suyumantakani." (Greetings, my name is Mariaelena Huambachano, and I am originally from Peru.) Following Quechua and Māori Indigenous protocols, I am reintroducing myself here. I am a woman with Indigenous Quechua ancestry of Peru and also a mestiza[3] raised in Chorrillos, a fisherman's town in Southern Lima-Peru, who had the opportunity to live and further my education in Aotearoa. On my mother's side, my grandmother is a mestiza, and my grandfather is of Andean lineage that stretches back to the ancient Indigenous Andean civilization of Wari, which flourished on the northern coast and the south-central Andes of modern-day Peru between 500 and 1000 CE. On my father's side, my Quechua-speaking grandmother is from the rural town of Acarí in Arequipa in Southern Peru, and my grandfather is a mestizo with African heritage from Northern Peru. My ancestry and experiences are vast and varied. I hold

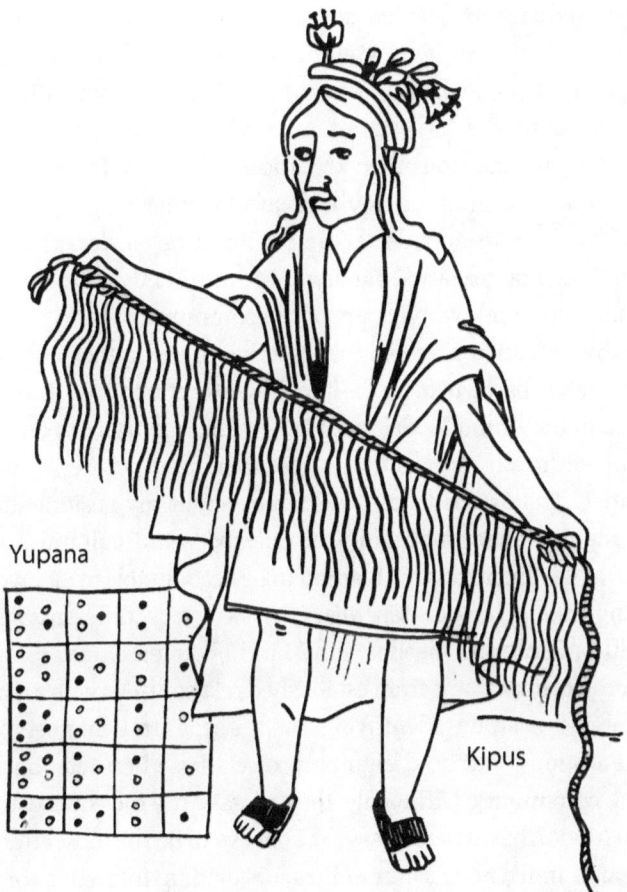

Figure 1. A khipukamayuq (Khipu-Master), who in Inka times had the role of reciting information encoded in the Khipu to the Inka, holding a Khipu, and a Yupana, an Inkan counting device. Illustration: Sam Bradd.

within me Indigenous identity but also Anglo-Eurocentric[4] academic knowledge, which I have at times found overwhelming to reconcile.

I was never wholly of my Indigenous identity, as I am not fluent in Quechua. But I always knew and valued my Indigenous lineage. Discrimination against Indigenous Peruvians has been so blatant, especially in the capital city of Lima, that many Quechua speakers such as my great-grandparents decided not to teach their children the language. They knew their descendants might suffer for Quechua fluency. Indeed, the colonial and post-colonial government has systematically repressed Indigenous languages as part of an overall campaign to dispossess Indigenous Peruvians from their traditional cultures. In my initial visits with Quechua communities, my lack of Quechua language knowledge made me feel like an outsider at times. But I began learning Quechua from my Quechua research partners and enrolled in online Quechua lessons, and soon I felt wholly part of the community.

While this extended personal introduction of the author may seem odd within a research-based text, I offer it to draw attention to the three elements entrenched in the Khipu Model that I believe are important to do respectful, thoughtful, ethically appropriate research that centers Indigenous communities. The first is to be transparent about my positionality in this study, to highlight the importance of reflexivity and cultural humility in building long-lasting relationships, and to be accountable to all my relations. Conducting research over ten years in two very different field sites/communities, Peruvian Quechua and Māori of Aotearoa, taught me that a research project must come from established relationships with a community before starting a study, identifying their needs and interests, building research questions, and co-designing projects based on relationships that benefit the community. Ultimately, they all gave me the context to develop the Khipu Model that articulates what I believe to be the most ethical way to do research in Indigenous communities: unearthing through a comparative lens the similarity of Indigenous foodways, traditional ecological knowledge (TEK), and Indigenous philosophies of food sovereignty, and then reflecting on particular issues from different vantage points.

The need to develop the Khipu Model became clear to me at a moment when I found my scholarly self on shaky ground. How could I reconcile an Indigenous paradigm within a Euro-Western research framework without disregarding Indigenous knowledge and its role in the research? Could I integrate Indigenous and Western research methods? How will the data be analyzed? And, perhaps more importantly, will the dissemination of research bring positive change to the lives of the researched peoples? These are principled questions that emerge from my background, lived experiences, and preliminary fieldwork for this study with Māori and

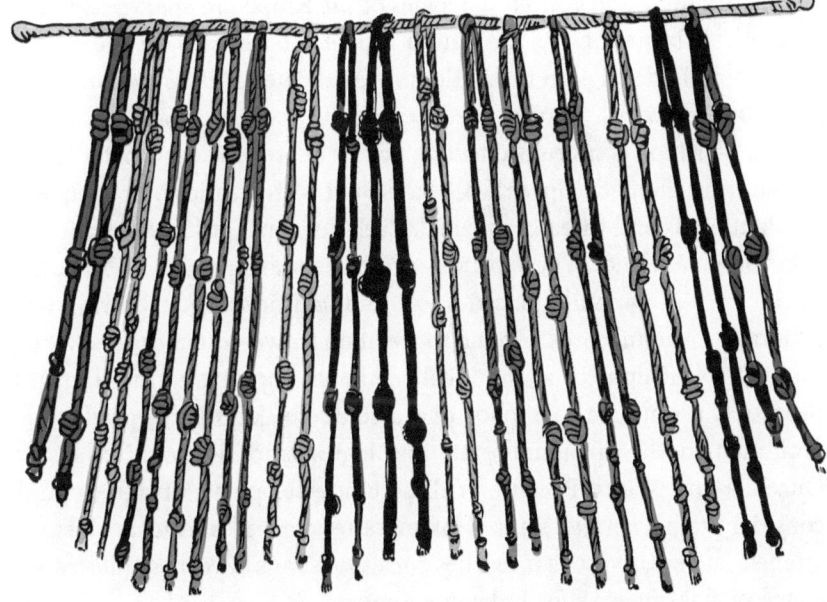

Figure 2. The Andean Khipu consists of one long primary cord, one centimeter thick, woven from llama or alpaca wool laces, with a series of subsequent pendant cords and threads attached. Each pendant cord has a particular color, spin, and knot. These pendant cords contain encoded information in the form of carefully placed knots and additional knot-bearing and subsidiary pendant cords. Illustration: Sam Bradd.

Peruvian Indigenous communities. Indigenous scholars working with decolonizing methodologies have been asking similar questions for decades.[5] Academia privileges a Eurocentric way of research rooted in centuries-old Euro-Western schools of thought that separate Eurocentric knowledge from specific geo-historical contexts. Eurocentric worldviews are regarded as universally relevant and thus applicable in Indigenous studies.[6] However, they are not suited to Indigenous research like mine, which is dedicated to elucidating and uplifting Indigenous science and values. The Khipu,[7] an ancestral method of record-keeping, became my solution to developing a methodology that resonates with Indigenous approaches to generating knowledge. The Khipu Model brings together Indigenous intellectual traditions, cultures, and imagery to inform innovative research models for food systems transformation.

The cognitive and conceptual logics of the Khipu are analogous to the theoretical framework of the Khipu Model. The Inka used the Khipu throughout their reign in the Andes to record detailed information about goods and services, natural resources, taxes, statistics, and historical events.[8] A Khipu comprises one long primary cord, one centimeter thick, woven from llama or alpaca wool laces, and with a series of subsequent pendant cords and threads attached. Each pendant cord has a particular color, spin, and knot. These pendant cords contain encoded information in the form of carefully placed knots and additional knot-bearing and subsidiary pendant cords. I found the relation between memory and visual form of the Khipu to be the ideal metaphor for shaping my thought process. I use it as a metaphor and a source of knowledge production grounded in the epistemologies, ontologies, and relational ethics of Quechua and Māori. Because of these unique elements of the Khipu, I consider it the perfect symbol of my ancestors' rich Andean history, science, and creativity, as it reaches back thousands of years to illustrate a conceptual framework for Indigenous enquiry.[9]

Just as in the Khipu, the primary horizontal and vertical pendants, cords, threads, and knots in the Khipu Model work with the others. The tapestry woven between them represents the thinking process guiding the selection of the most culturally sensitive research methods for this study. In this study, Quechua and Māori research partners are farmers, gardeners, Elders,[10] community leaders, seed keepers, food/seed sovereignty advocates and activists, and people knowledgeable about foodways, agricultural knowledge and food traditions. The Khipu Model incorporates Quechua and Māori partners' cultural values, ethics, and participatory action research methods. It also validates Native science, which in this book I refer to as TEK, by supporting Indigenous practices and promoting intergenerational knowledge transmission, and it draws from fundamental principles of the Kaupapa Māori.

Specifically, the Khipu Model incorporates five key principles and concepts of the Kaupapa Māori, the first of which is tino rangatiratanga,[11] the notion of Indigenous self-determination. The second is tikanga, a Māori concept that encapsulates customary and ethical practices or behavioral guidelines for living and interacting with others. The third concept is mātauranga Māori, a sacred, contextual, and kinship-specific ancestral wisdom.¹² The fourth is the principle of āta, which, according to Māori scholar Taina Whakaatere Pohatu, "is a vital cultural tool created to shape and guide understandings of relationships and well-being," and in the Khipu Model prioritizes the growing of respectful relationships.¹³ It is āta that requires that researchers obtain informed consent from Indigenous communities before doing fieldwork, in addition to the permission gained from their host university. The fifth is the principle of ako, which requires that research conducted with Māori peoples respect Māori culture and recognize traditional ways of learning and knowledge exchange.¹⁴ Finally, the Khipu Model takes into consideration the bodies of decolonizing methodologies that give voice to the voiceless—communities of color such as Latin Americans, Asians, and African Americans, and vulnerable societies such as Indigenous peoples within an Anglo-American and Eurocentric academia—to confront the limitations of Western methodologies.

The efficacy of the Khipu Model relied on creating it with Indigenous communities and for their benefit. This meant anchoring understandings of the value of ethics of engagement in research to yield long-lasting partnerships to frame a research topic and community-based project that resonates with the living realities of the communities being studied and that could benefit them. As a result, using the Khipu Model, this book addresses the central research question for this study: how can Indigenous peoples' philosophies—in this case, those of the Quechua and Māori—contribute to fostering a more inclusive, equitable, and healthy food system in their own communities and at a broader scale? As an Indigenous scholar, my positionality in this study is to re-center Indigenous worldviews, science, and intellectual sovereignty in order to reclaim, restore, and protect Indigenous knowledge and methodologies in academia. In alignment with my positionality, the book's research philosophy is entrenched in an Indigenous research paradigm that examines, through a comparative lens, the knowledge systems of Quechua and Māori to explore their respective philosophies of well-being as they relate to sustainable food systems.

The aim of the Khipu Model is twofold. First, it is designed to demonstrate through its creation that Indigenous-based research frameworks exist, and, if used correctly, are accessible to Indigenous and non-Indigenous researchers. Second, it is intended as a platform for both Indigenous and non-Indigenous scholars to draw from Indigenous literature, guidelines, and innovation to foster the co-creation of knowledge production more respectfully and beneficially for Indigenous and other vulnerable societies. For all of these reasons, I find the Khipu Model useful and successful in navigating the questions that dotted the "shaky ground" of my research. The process that led to the creation of the Khipu Model is a story in itself, which I share in this chapter.

In the next section, I describe the conceptualization and operationalization of the Khipu Model. I then discuss how I used it for food justice/sovereignty research. I conclude with the role of the Khipu Model in supporting the democratization of knowledge production and in transforming epistemic violence by centering Indigenous relational ethics, a collaborative and respectful engagement across differing worldviews and paradigms that could be replicated in other contexts. My hope is that the Khipu Model can be a guiding research methodology framework within and beyond the Indigenous world. In using it, I believe, scholars will forge a future of mindful, tactful, and comprehensive scholarship that confronts and supplements Western research's shortcomings.

THE WEAVING OF THE KHIPU MODEL

In this section, I describe the theoretical framework of the Khipu Model, consisting of three interrelated phases—*knowing*, *being*, and *doing*. They articulate the epistemology, ontology, and ethical principles shaping the model's foundation.

Knowing: Epistemology and Positionality

Knowing is the first fundamental phase of the Khipu because it establishes the philosophical position of this study, grounded in Indigenous ways of knowing/epistemology. This phase also underscores Quechua and Māori research partners' distinctive TEK systems, referred to as mātauranga in Māori and yachay in Quechua, as they relate to foodways, biodiversity preservation, and agricultural prowess. In the Khipu Model, the primary horizontal cord sustaining the multiple intertwined threads and knots attached to it symbolizes this phase.

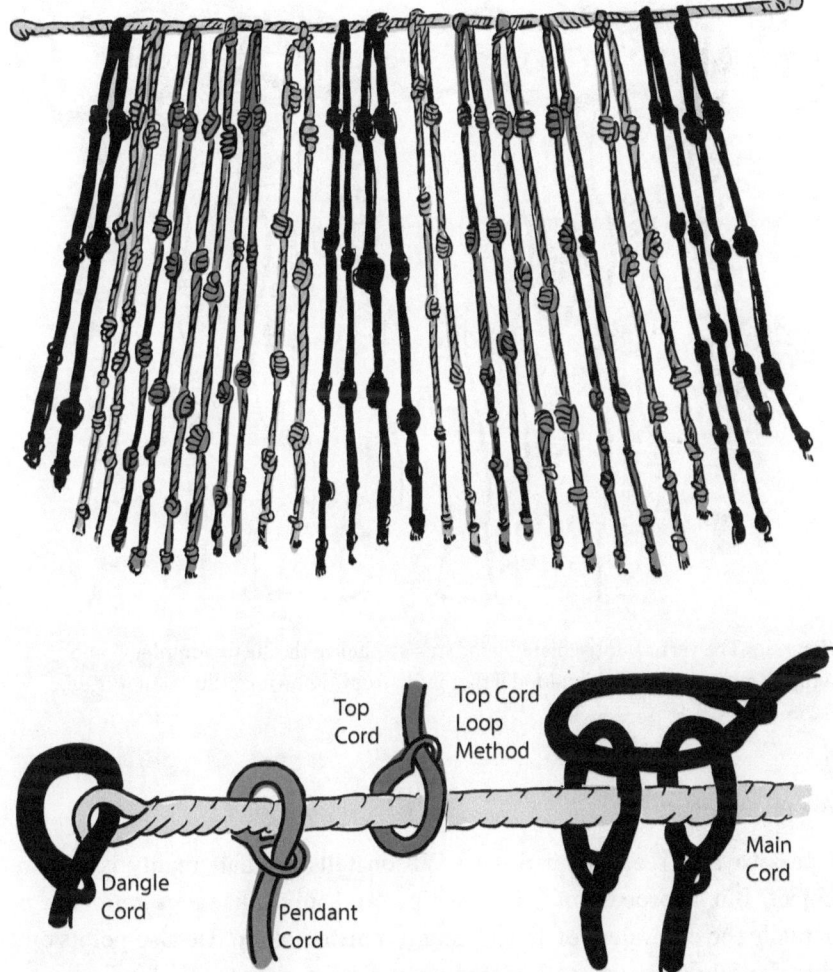

Figure 3. The main horizontal cord sustaining all the threads and knots embedded in the Khipu represents the first fundamental phase of the Khipu Model—"knowing." Illustration: Sam Bradd.

Complementing the knowing phase is the recognition of Indigenous autonomy. This recognition acknowledges Indigenous peoples' right to self-determination. For example, Quechua and Māori research partners had a very active voice in all stages of the Khipu Model and had autonomy in selecting research questions, objectives, and data sovereignty.

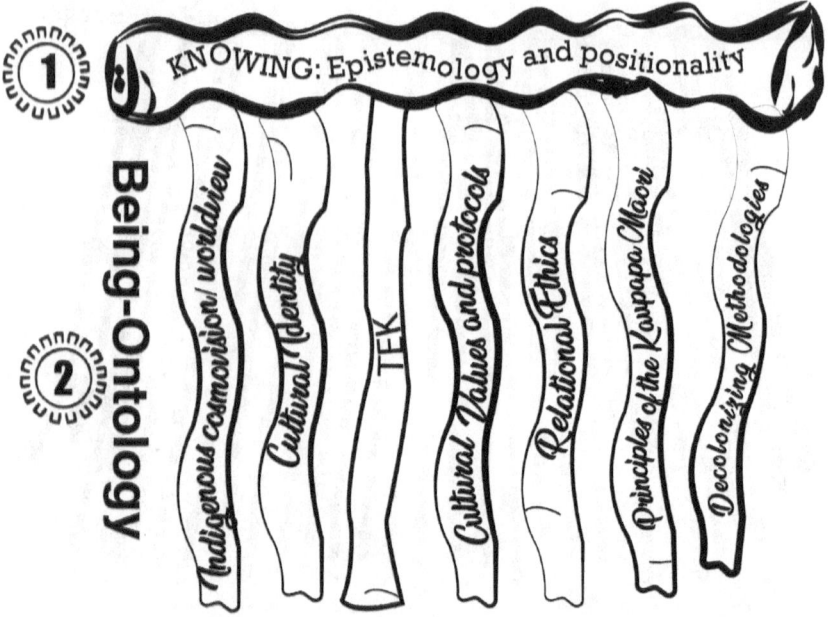

Figure 4. The vertical interrelated pendants symbolize the "being/ontology" and "ethical" phases of the Khipu Model that build from "knowing." Illustration: Paula Sarmiento.

Being: Ontology

Opaskwayak Cree scholar Shawn Wilson tells us that "reality is not an object, but a process of relationships, and an Indigenous ontology is actually the equivalent of an Indigenous epistemology." He also points out that "an Indigenous methodology must be a process that adheres to relational accountability," that is, ethics or axiology.[15] Thus, as a way to highlight the importance of foregrounding vibrant *relationships* and *responsibilities* between the researcher and study communities, I use the imagery of intertwined vertical cords of the Khipu to mean the being/ontology and ethical phases in the Khipu Model. The *being/ontology* phase in the Khipu Model encompasses understanding and respecting Indigenous relational ethics and responsibility based on Indigenous worldview, values, cultural protocols, and deeply rooted TEKs, and draws from the five fundamental principles of the Kaupapa Māori described above.

I deploy these Māori concepts in the Khipu Model to emphasize the rights of my Quechua and Māori research partners to exercise self-determination, autonomy, and relational ethics in this research study. In a similar vein, the Khipu Model incorporates key tenets engrained in Quechua culture that I observed during my visits. These include reciprocity (ayninakuy)—what is received must be paid back in equal measure; complementarity (yanantin-masintin)—an egalitarian principle found in the transmission of knowledge related to agricultural practices; and equilibrium (rakinakuy) with Nature, with Pachamama, with the sacred world, and among community members. These key principles complement *being* by establishing parameters for discussing the best approach to knowledge production within and between communities and offering understandings of cultural protocols developed by Quechua and Māori collaborators. This stage also draws from scholarship that focuses on decolonizing methodologies.

Upholding the relational-ethics research approach of this study, my investigation went through a thorough review by the Human Ethics Review Committee at my research institution. The documents I submitted to obtain this approval detailed how I would comply with Peruvian customary local laws and ethical conduct in my capacity as both an Indigenous researcher native of Peru and a New Zealand citizen. Overall, the *being* stage calls for the embracement of an ethics of engagement that incorporates personal responsibility and accountability between the researcher and study communities. It also suggests researchers must consider questions like, "Who is benefitting from the research? Am I the right person to be writing about the things I write about? How can I empower local communities and scholars? How can my work serve these communities rather than just talk about them?" I discussed and addressed these questions with Quechua and Māori research collaborators during my visits. As a result, the Khipu Model contains Métis Canadian and Cora Weber-Pillwax's three Rs of conducting research: respect, reciprocity, and relationality.[16] For example, the Khipu Model recognizes that the researcher is responsible for the research project's impacts on the participants' lives. It also acknowledges that the purpose of research is to benefit the community and its people. This means that, in choosing research methods, I had to consider carefully not only the possible effects on the study communities and Indigenous research methods, but also the effects of each specific research method on study partners.

Doing: Indigenous "Voices" Guiding the Framing of Preferred Research Methods

In coming full circle, the knowing and being threads played a crucial role in building up the last stage—*doing*—metaphorically represented in the knots attached to the threads and cords of the Khipu. Each of these elements— the epistemologies, ontologies, and ethics—inform the selection of research methods that are culturally sensitive while ensuring the rigor of research.

In the process of working closely with study communities, there emerges a natural inter-subjectivity between researcher and study partners that aligns with the goals of social justice that underpin the Khipu Model to make the research process democratic, just, liberating, and beneficial for all participants. This Indigenous way of conducting research resonates with community-based participatory action research (CBPAR),[17] though Indigenous researchers have taken CBPAR a step further to place an emphasis on moral responsibilities to communities through the adoption of decolonizing methodologies. Decolonizing methodologies focus on the best means of acquiring and interpreting knowledge about the world by confronting Anglo-Eurocentric epistemological assertions and the limitations of Anglo-Eurocentric research practices such as ethical standards and customary protocols.[18]

Recognizing a social justice component in the call for decolonizing methodologies and CBPAR, I embraced them as a way to ensure my research empowers community members and, where they have been marginalized, brings their voices to the fore. I also included CBPAR as a means of achieving broader community input and greater community acceptance of research projects; thus, this investigation incorporates CBPAR to promote dialogue and partnership trust between the researcher and researched. For these reasons, and in accordance with the Khipu Model, Quechua and Māori study partners were involved in the very early planning stages of this investigation. They had a very active *voice* in all phases of the Khipu Model, as I engaged in constant dialogue and negotiation with leaders and community members. This process was vital

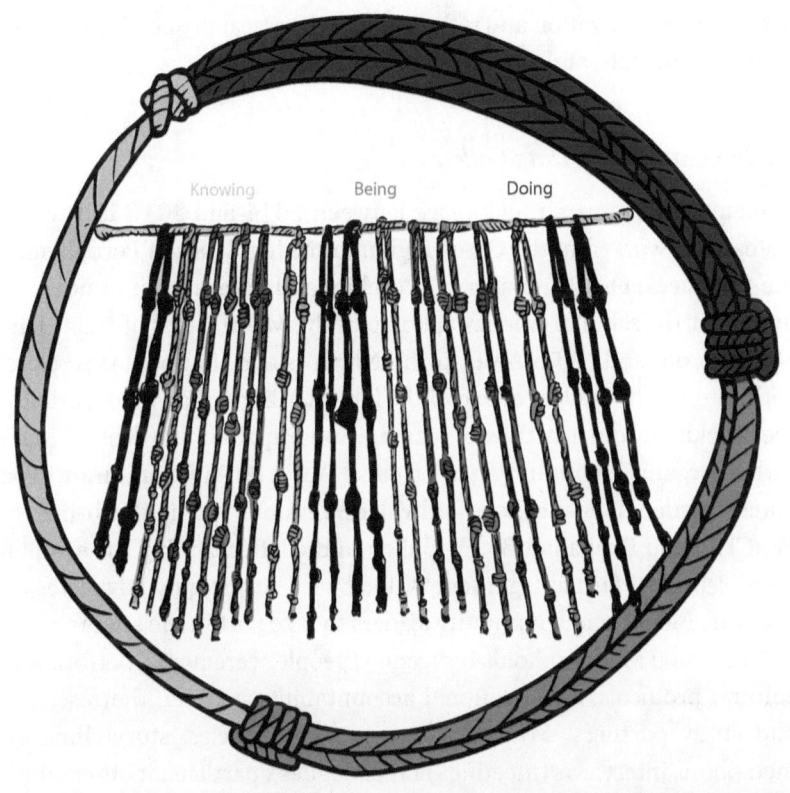

Knowing: Epistemology	Being: Ontology	Doing: Research methods
Philosophical position	Quechua and Māori worldviews and TEK	Storytelling and metaphors
Quechua and Māori Cosmovision/worldview	Kaupapa Māori approach	Community assemblies
	Cultural identity	Talking circles
	Quechua and Māori cultural values and protocols	Interviews
	Relational ethics	Participant Observation
	Decolonizing methodologies	CBPAR

Figure 5. This circular diagram shows all interrelated stages of the Khipu. In coming full circle, the knowing and being threads played a crucial role in building up the last stage—*doing* (Research Methods)—metaphorically represented in the knots attached to the threads and cords of the Khipu. Each of these elements—the epistemologies, ontologies, and ethics—inform the selection of research methods that are culturally sensitive while ensuring the rigor of research. Illustration: Sam Bradd.

to the conceptualization and refinement of the research questions, themes, cultural protocols, and validation of research findings.

Study Location and Data Collection

The empirical research took place between 2014 and 2016 in Peru and Aotearoa. I worked in the Cusco region in the highlands of Peru, home of the Choquecancha, Pampacorral, Ccachin, and Sacaca communities, and in the North Island of Aotearoa, home of the Māori tribes of Ngāti Hine, Ngāti Porou, and Ngāti Awa. In the North Island, I also worked closely with community leaders of two of the largest Māori urban food gardens in the Auckland and Northland regions: the Papatūānuku Kōkiri Marae (urban organic community garden) and Wai A Ariki Onerahirahi (Food Forest) garden. Lionel Hotene and Valerie Teraitua work in the former and Fred Tito and Buchanan Beech-Cullen in the latter. During the sampling stage, I invited farmers, gardeners, food/seed sovereignty advocates and activists, Elders, and community leaders to take part in the study.

The Khipu Model upholds Indigenous people's ceremonial performance, cultural protocols, and relational accountability between the researcher and study partners. My inclusion of talking circles, storytelling and metaphors, interviews (meetings and dialogues), participant observations, and secondary data as part of my data collection methods reflected this. In total, I recorded forty-five interviews, twenty-three in Peru and twenty-two in Aotearoa. Most of the data collection took place at research participants' chakras (agricultural fields), marae (sacred meeting place), or households. I transcribed and translated them into Spanish and English. In this process, I was able to hear and absorb the rich oral traditions of storytelling, proverbs, folktales, and customs of Quechua and Māori research collaborators, recognize their commonalities and distinctions, and test the applicability and reliability of emerging concepts, themes, ideas, and principles.

COMMUNITY GATHERINGS

Following the Khipu Model framework, before gathering any empirical data, I met with study partners in Peru and Aotearoa to discuss the research methods, refine the research questions, and translate them to Quechua,

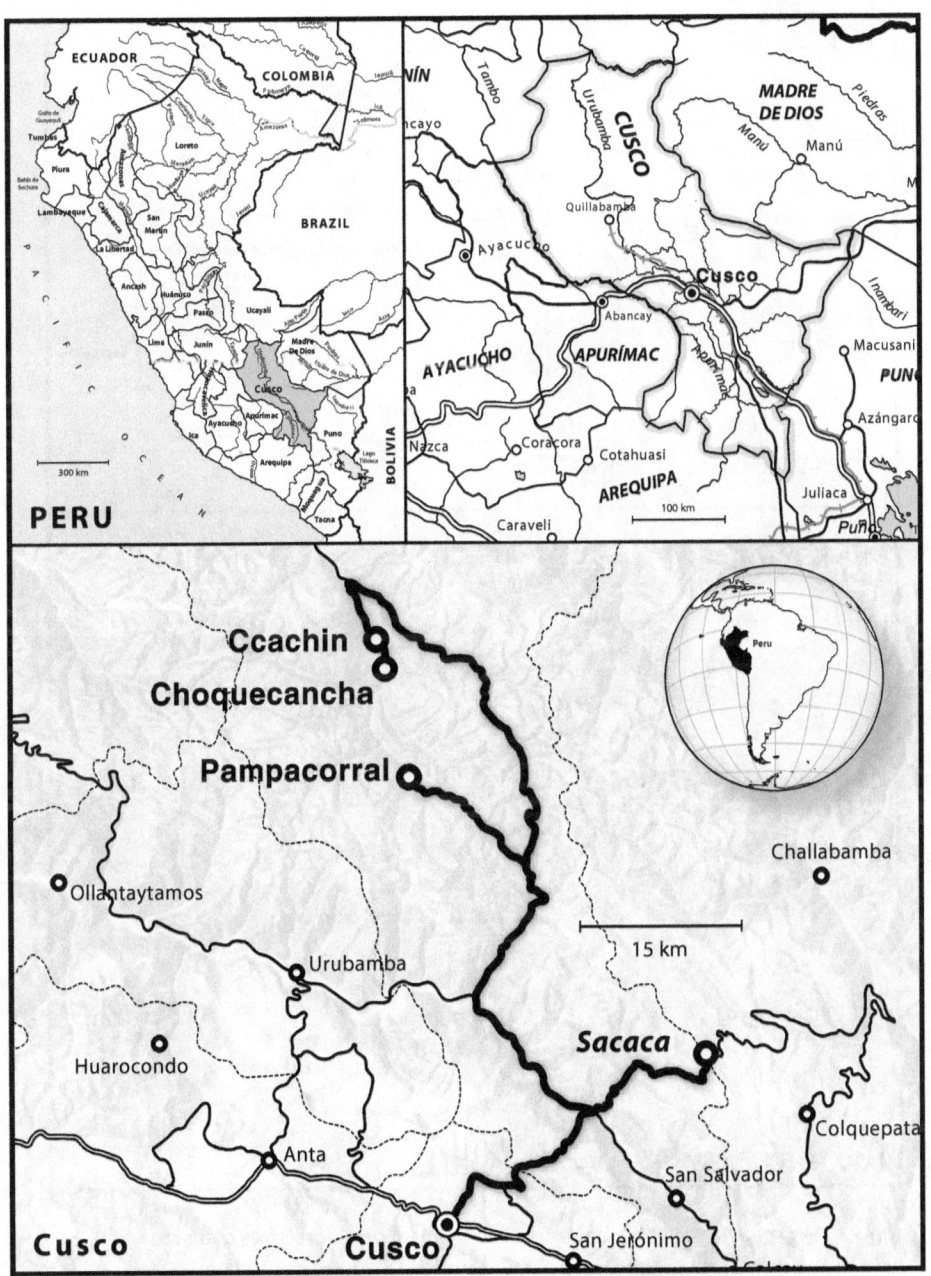

Map 1. Map of Peru showing the four Quechua communities that took part in this study: Choquecancha, Sacaca, Pampacorral, and Ccachin. Illustration: Pierre Bélanger.

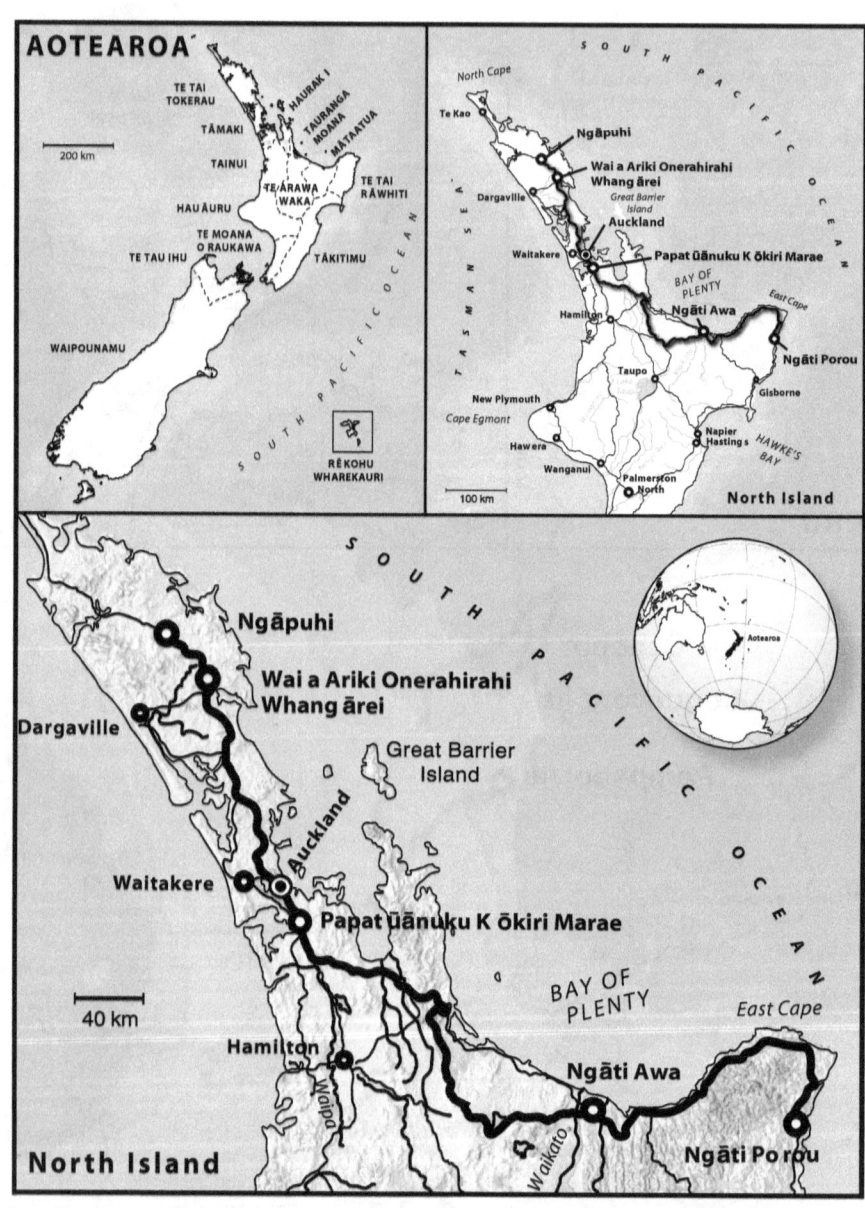

Map 2. Map of Aotearoa New Zealand showing the four Māori tribes and urban food gardens that took part in this study: Ngāti Hine, Ngāti Porou, and Ngāti Awa; Papatūānuku Kōkiri Marae (urban organic community garden) and Wai A Ariki Onerahirahi (Food Forest) garden. Illustration: Pierre Bélanger.

Spanish, English, and Māori. I held two community assemblies with each of the study communities. The aim of these gatherings was twofold. First, I wanted to build rapport with potential research participants. Second, I wanted to frame the interview protocols and questions to ensure my research was respectful of local customs. In Peru, on May 2, 2014, at an altitude of approximately 3,300 meters (11,000 feet) above sea level in the Quechua community of Ccachin, we held the first community assembly. In this gathering, which was entitled "Food Security in the Andes," attendees and I determined that open-ended questions or unstructured interviews would best facilitate collecting rich data through oral stories. The twenty-five attendees included Elders, food foragers, and community leaders from the Quechua communities of Choquecancha, Rosaspata, Sacaca, Pampacorral, and Ccachin. The second gathering, with the same number of attendees, occurred on June 5, 2014, in the Quechua community of Choquecancha in the Valley of Lares, located approximately 3,900 meters (13,000 feet) above sea level in the foothills of the Lares Mountain Range. It was entitled "Andean Philosophy and Food Systems." In it we explored allin kawsay and foodways. The twenty-five attendees included Elders, food foragers, and community leaders from all four Quechua communities. After each of these gatherings, I wrote down customary protocols and identified eight research participants who exhibited ample knowledge of traditional agriculture, seed saving and preservation, the Andean agricultural calendar, and traditional medicine for follow-up interviews. Each research partner was compensated for their time with food baskets.[19]

In Aotearoa, on April 9, 2015, the first gathering was held in Gisborne at Whareponga in the tribal lands of Ngāti Porou. The subsequent gathering was held on May 23, 2015, in Whangarei at the Wai A Ariki Onerahirahi (Food Forest) garden. The objectives of these community gatherings were the same as those I organized with Quechua communities. The first gathering was called "Māori kai" (Māori food) and "He kai kei aku ringa" (the food is in my hand), titles that reflect local and global perspectives on Indigenous food security within the context of climate change. Following these gatherings, I recorded my observations about marae (meeting place) etiquette rooted in Māori ethics and cultural values. These included the pōwhiri (welcome ritual) and manaakitanga (hospitality) vital in strengthening relationships with Māori. I asked attendees to participate in the research, which ultimately yielded nine research participants from Ngāti Porou and nine from Ngāti Hine. I gave a food basket to each research partner in gratitude for their time.[20] Also, in resonance with the principle of manaakitanga, each meeting was followed by eating the midday meal together. I then engaged in in-depth, unstructured, one-on-one interviews with each research participant on topics such as sustainable farming, climate change, seed sovereignty, traditional rituals, food practices, and food security strategies. The similarities between the Indigenous gatherings I organized, and "typical" Western-culture informed workshops, are not insignificant. However, the Khipu Model gatherings and talking circles are distinct in that they feature the rituals and protocols underpinning Indigenous ceremonial performance and acknowledge ethical research relationships and accountabilities. I explain how below.

TALKING CIRCLES: TALKING AND LEARNING TOGETHER

Talking circles are an Indigenous method for elucidating and sharing knowledge with a collectivistic and spiritual approach.[21] Two talking circles were conducted in each country, and six research participants in Aotearoa and seven in Peru formed them. Like focus groups, talking circles consist of a selected group of people who are brought together to discuss a particular topic and whose responses can be used as a representation of the group.[22] Conversations explored key research themes, including the cosmovisions of the Quechua and Māori peoples, biodiversity, food security strategies, traditional food practices, and the future of traditional food systems. Unlike focus groups, talking circles employ place-based cultural and spiritual tribal traditions such as ceremonial welcome rituals, blessings of food, and ending the session with prayers. For example, in Aotearoa a kaumātua would begin the talking circle with a karakia (prayer) and blessing of food. In Peru an Elder would perform the k'intu at the beginning of each talking circle. They would take a bunch of coca leaves from their chuspa (a bag designated for the purpose) and carefully choose three to symbolize the three dimensions of the Andean cosmovision: Janaq patsa (upper world or cosmos), Kay patsa (real, visible world), and Ja-wa patsa (intangible world, darkness, invisible forces). The Elder then raised the leaves, facing them towards the east, in the direction of the sun and the community's apu (spirits of the sacred mountains). Facing the coca leaves in the direction of the sun and the apu are signs of respect for the ancestors and seeking permission to share knowledge during the talking circles. The Elder then blew over them in a gesture referred to as phukuy (gratitude) and said a prayer in Quechua. K'intu signifies "connectedness and relationships" between the social, natural, and spiritual worlds; such rituals sharply distinguished the talking circles from conventional focus groups.[23]

STORYTELLING AND METAPHORS

Traditional ecological knowledge is rooted in Indigenous peoples' worldviews and is shared through oral stories and teachings and acquired from their intimate relationship with both living and non-living beings (mountains, rivers, sun, moon) as well as from personal experiences. It is akin to what some Indigenous researchers refer to as "native storytelling" and "metaphors."[24] Within Quechua and Māori knowledge structures, storytelling and the use of metaphors are methods of gathering, preserving, and interpreting the voices and memories of the ancestors, passed down from one generation to the other through oral history. In this way, storytelling and the use of metaphors are recognized as valid and reliable by virtue of their relationality. Thus, the storytelling and metaphors that emerged from the data collection process were analyzed and their meaning was validated with the help of research partners.

INTERVIEWS

Fifteen individual interviews were recorded in both countries. The overall aim of the interviews was to explore "data on understandings, opinions, what people remember doing, attitudes, feelings and the like, that people have in common."[25] Interviews are generally considered the best method of data collection when the researcher's main purpose is to gain rich accounts of a phenomenon.[26] An unstructured interview approach was used in this study because it favors open-ended questions, allowing for more flexibility and freedom to seek knowledge.[27]

PARTICIPANT OBSERVATIONS

I acted as a participant observer in line with the CBPAR approach from the time of my preliminary ethnographic research through the conclusion of the study. The aim was to gain a close and intimate familiarity with study participants and their sustainability practices, traditions, and agricultural techniques in food production. Most of the gatherings, interviews, and talking circles where I gathered data took place at the community leaders' chakras, family homes, community gathering halls, homes, and marae (sacred meeting place). I recorded my observations using different tools, including notes, descriptions of activities, charts, sketches and diagrams, photographs, maps, and personal reflective journals.

SECONDARY DATA

I obtained secondary data in the form of archival text records and journal articles documenting Indigenous peoples' knowledge, traditional agriculture, history, and cultural values, among other topics related to my research. Much of this was obtained in trips to Peru and Bolivia's national libraries in 2014 and 2015.[28] I was able to find information about the Andean philosophy of allin/sumak kawsay and about Peruvian Andean history prior to and during the post-colonization period, as well as information on the food culture of Andean people, food preparation and preservation techniques, and recipes. In Aotearoa, I visited the Alexander Turnbull Library at the National Library of New Zealand in Wellington in 2013, 2015, and 2021. There I accessed the archival collection of images, manuscripts, and audio about Māori history and traditional food practices in precolonial and modern times.

Data Analysis

I used a thematic analysis method comprising five steps, as summarized below. I also used the NVivo 10 software to capture a large volume of narratives and verbatim data—such as long interviews and field notes—to organize them, and to refine the coding. As the inter-subjective researcher, I undertook an ongoing, reflexive dialogue throughout the analytical process.

Stage 1: First, I familiarized myself with the empirical and secondary data collected in Peru and Aotearoa. I transcribed and translated the recordings and immersed myself in the data by constantly listening to the recordings and reading the transcriptions, field notes, and desktop research literature on an ongoing basis. This helped me to get familiar with all aspects of the data and explore initial ideas and thoughts. The goal was to enable knowledge to emerge and evolve organically throughout all phases of the data analysis.

Stage 2: Next, I began to code the data corpus and data sets systematically and across both sets according to a particular topic. I used tables and mind maps to code and group all interesting verbatim data for this phase. "Data corpus" refers to all data gathered in this investigation, and "data sets" are all data from the corpus used for analysis. My analysis approach depended on whether a particular pattern was present and my interest in investigating that specific topic. For instance, when I was interested in how the Indigenous agricultural calendar worked, my data set consisted of all information across my entire data corpus that had some relevance to Māori and Quechua seasonal harvesting systems. I read complete data sets several times before I began the coding process. I then started searching for meanings and patterns to elicit the voices of the ancestors through the interviewee's responses, storytelling, and metaphors, which I found enlightening. I started perceiving, feeling, and seeing their realities through the data, so I started taking notes and marking ideas for coding with different colors.

Stage 3: I searched for themes by refining, re-grouping, and gathering all data items and extracts into potential themes and meta-themes. "Data item" refers to each piece of data that I collected through all research methods of this study, which together form the entire data corpus. For example, data items in this research included talking circles, metaphors, individual interviews, historical information, or journal articles. A "data extract" refers to an individually coded data set identified within and extracted from a data item. A theme captures a common, recurring pattern or meaning across data sets, in this case from steps 1 and 2. Using inductive coding, I then started sorting the codes into potential themes and collated all the relevant coded data extracts within the identified themes and sought meaning in them. In essence, I started to analyze my codes and consider how different ideas might differ from an overarching theme. Initially 138 themes emerged from the data gathered in Peru, and 128 emerged from the data gathered in Aotearoa. In this phase, I also ended up with a set of codes that did not seem to belong anywhere, and so I created a theme called "miscellaneous" to capture those codes.

A meta-theme is a theme that acquires meaning through the systematic co-occurrence of two or more other themes. One meta-theme was "We learned to live with the rhythm of the tides and moon, but it got disrupted with the colonization of time." Based on Māori responses, this meta-theme alludes to a theme about the Māori lunar calendar for planting and fishing— Maramataka Māori, which has been very influential in advising the agricultural, fishery, and hunting activities of Māori to procure food. It also draws attention to the repercussions of European settlement for use of the Māori Maramataka. Another important meta-theme is "Earth is our mother," which captured both Quechua and Māori's ontologies of land. This meta-theme also provides insights into the Māori and Quechua research partners' struggles with land dispossession and forced migration that stripped away their cultural and spiritual connection with Pachamama/Papatūānuku (Mother Earth). Also, using a manual system, I noted initial ideas and patterns, and I classified every pattern found in the transcripts within code. I used highlighters and colored pens to indicate possible patterns, and post-it notes to identify the segments of data in the entire data corpus.

Stage 4: In the fourth stage, I refined the meta-themes through a mind map analysis of the 138 initial themes found in Peru, and 128 in Aotearoa, to avoid repetition and choose the final themes and meta-themes to understand the overall story of the study's analysis. I began to reduce the themes by reviewing every code in my data corpus. Consequently, I realized that there were repetitive and irrelevant themes. Some themes I collapsed into each other; for example, land claims in Aotearoa in the 1970s and the self-governance of ayllu formed one theme. Others had to be broken down into separate sub-themes. This stage concluded with my identification of seven meta-themes: (1) food is sacred: it is our right to food; (2) strong cultural identity: customs and traditions; (3) self-determination and land rights; (4) TEK; (5) ethical principles for food security; (6) Indigenous innovation systems; and (7) sustainability.

Stage 5: I carefully reviewed, defined, and named the final themes in stage 5. Then, I gave each a specific meta-theme name. I developed a narrative of five to twenty-five single-spaced pages related to each of these three meta-themes. Then, I constructed a set of twenty-seven narratives describing traditional Indigenous practices for food production by tracing through all the chronologically ordered raw data for each interview that was identified every time a given issue arose. Also, I recorded the values that underpinned such traditional practices through quotations from a combination of interviews, meeting transcripts, archival documentation, secondary data, and field notes. At the end of this phase, I had a substantial amount of empirical data informing the initial themes and how they fitted together, providing me an overall story of this investigation. Once I had sets of narratives for all themes, I then examined historical accounts, secondary data related to the themes, activities, stories, and metaphors for each of them. For example, the narrative below suggests a difference between traditional and organic food production practices from a Māori perspective:

> We are bringing back our traditional practices slowly, but we are. We are practicing spirituality in the māra kai [food garden] because we need to acknowledge our tupuna (ancestors). In my deep analysis and use of the practice of organic food production, there were still something lacking, and what I couldn't sort of capture at the time. So, I did some compatibility in terms of the Māori traditional ways and practice of organic food. And based on my analysis, then I was asked to be part of a process of setting up the New Zealand Minimum Standards, you know, for organic food in Aotearoa.

I analyzed this narrative with secondary data about organic and industrial food production in Aotearoa. I engaged in an iterative, cross-case study analysis, building broader meaning to the quotations and metaphors between these two groups. For example, I examined the key traditional practices of Māori agricultural systems and the Quechua people and the implications of their Indigenous knowledge for food security. Finally, secondary data on the main topics within each meta-theme, such as the history of Quechua and Māori people, traditional food practices, Indigenous rights, food sovereignty, and industrial food production, aided the analysis. The process of transcribing, translating (from Quechua to Spanish and then Spanish to English), writing field notes, and other related administrative matters was at times overwhelming due to the large amount of data that I had gathered. However, this qualitative data analysis method proved to be an invaluable tool that provided me with robust empirical data and findings, which I validated with research collaborators.

In addition to initial interviews, further validation was gained by way of follow-up conversations (in person and by email) on key themes such as soil health, seed sovereignty, and environmental governance. I also participated in a series of events about Indigeneity, specifically about Māori and Quechua culture, traditions, and international food security/sovereignty initiatives. For example, in July 2015, at the invitation of Uncle Percy Tipene of Ngāti Hine and members of the Papatūānuku Kōkiri Marae, I witnessed the certification of the Papatūānuku Marae as a Māori urban garden producing natural food without chemical inputs.

In March 2016, I attended the Mātauranga Māori workshop organized by the Ngā Pae o te Māramatanga (New Zealand's Māori Centre of Research Excellence), and in May I travelled to Turtle Island to take part in the Food Sovereignty Summit in New York City. In addition, in June 2016, I organized a food security workshop entitled "He kai kei aku ringa (there is food in my hands)" in collaboration with the Mira Száscy Research Centre and held at the University of Auckland in Aotearoa. There, I presented and discussed initial findings of my study at the local level with Māori research partners, academics, and community members and at the international level with Indigenous food sovereignty scholars from Turtle Island, such as Potawatomi Citizen Kyle Whyte. I took notes on responses and discussions, which helped me significantly with the continued revision and crystallization/validation of my results.

Final empirical results were validated with research collaborators. I did so in gatherings in both countries, where I presented a summary of the major research findings to tribal members. In 2018, as community members had requested, I made visits to both countries to share the results of the study. In June 2018, I presented the results of this study at the Papatūānuku Kōkiri Marae in South Auckland and in December 2018 at the Wai A Ariki Onerahirahi (Food Forest) garden, Aotearoa. In July 2019, I presented results in the Quechua community of Choquecancha and in August 2019 in Pampacorral in Peru. This extra layer of validation of findings with research partners supports the fundamental relational ethics of the Khipu Model, underscoring the importance of establishing long-lasting, trusting, and reciprocal relationships with study communities to ensure the legitimacy of the research.

USING THE KHIPU MODEL FOR RESEARCH ON FOOD JUSTICE/SOVEREIGNTY

In this section I discuss how I use the Khipu Model for research on food justice/sovereignty. I also describe how I deployed "ethics of engagement in research" and the "value of long-lasting relations" that foreground voices and thought processes of Indigenous communities as fundamental principles in framing the Khipu Model. I aim to demonstrate how Indigenous research paradigms and imagery can yield innovative research models that advance the inclusion of Indigenous perspectives in transformative, action-oriented research in the study of food systems.

The Khipu Model framework originates from within the research space built by postcolonial methodologies, and a key example of it is the Kaupapa Māori. The scholarship work of esteemed Kaupapa Māori scholars such as Linda Tuhiwai Smith, Graham Hingangaroa Smith and Lione Pihama—and personal discussions with them—were invaluable in my learning of it. Kaupapa Māori was born out of the recognition of the need for a research praxis that can redress concerns about disrespectful Eurocentric research methods and biases, as well as the perpetuation of neocolonial representations and neocolonial power structures that undermine the local knowledge and experiences of marginalized groups. The Kaupapa Māori movement grew during the 1970s and, by the late 1980s, it had developed among Māori people as a political consciousness that continues to this day. As Māori scholar Graham Hingangaroa Smith explained,

> Māori communities armed with the new critical understandings of the shortcomings of the state and structural analysis began to assert transformative actions to deal with the twin crises of language demise and educational underachievement for themselves.[29]

The intention of the Kaupapa movement was to achieve "increased autonomy over their own [Māori] lives and cultural welfare."[30] This call for autonomy was operationalized within a Kaupapa Māori approach as self-determination (tino rangatiratanga in Māori), which asserts Māori autonomy to do research *by* and *for* Māori people.[31] Decolonial scholars argue that Western scientific research is explicitly linked to colonialism because data gathering with Indigenous peoples is conducted through an objectivistic research approach.[32] Thus, they serve the colonizers' interests of disenfranchising Indigenous peoples from their culture and ways of knowing. Global coloniality effectively excluded Indigenous peoples and their knowledge from systems/bodies of research. Peruvian sociologist Aníbal Quijano defines coloniality as epistemic hegemony over geographical areas and as a racial classification project proposed to legitimize Eurocentric structures of power.[33] Examples of postcolonial research methodologies include feminist methodologies[34] that challenge the pervasive patriarchy of Western knowledge, anti- and postcolonial approaches,[35] and critical race theory. These alternative methodologies are attentive to living realities, the history of colonization, power relations, and ethics in the field.

This counterhegemonic work has been fundamental to advancing theories and methods for addressing unequal power relations in field research and achieving ethical practices for researching social justice and emancipation for oppressed groups. Indigenous and minoritized groups that have been rendered vulnerable to research are working towards the building of decolonizing research methodologies. Within Indigenous contexts, Indigenous research methodologies and approaches are a contestation of the dominant, Anglo-Eurocentric philosophies of knowledge. They constitute a direct act of reclamation of Indigenous intellectual sovereignty, Native/Indigenous science, equal power relations, and social justice.[36] They are also relevant to groups historically vulnerable to research who have been challenging Eurocentrism in knowledge production for decades, opening new spaces, discussion, and solidarity among them.

The need for healing, social justice, self-determination, cultural revival, and decolonizing methodologies provided critical motivation for the development of the Khipu Model. At the core of the Khipu Model are two fundamental considerations: *ethics of engagement in research* and that the research must come from established relationships *with a community* from the outset. Studying secondary literature about research topics of interest in order to frame my research study is important, but it is not enough. My research project showed me this. In what follows, I describe how my research topic and approach emerged based on my positionality and trusting relationships with Quechua and Māori communities.

Ethics of Engagement: Setting the Research Agenda to Understand Indigenous Reality and to Identify and Define a Specific Research Topic

Shawn Wilson (Opaskwayak Cree) describes an Indigenous research paradigm as one rooted in the fundamental belief that knowledge is *relational*—it is shared in the relationship among humans and non-humans and the cosmos. His explanation foregrounds the principle of respect instilled in the adage, "I am accountable to all my relations."[37] This relational accountability pivots around the understanding that researchers need to fulfill responsibilities to an extended relational network that includes the natural and the spiritual world. In line with my understanding of relational ethics and accountability, the Khipu Model embraces an "ethics of engagement" approach that embodies key concepts: cultural humility, positionality, reflexivity, and relational accountability. Vivian Chávez describes the concept of cultural humility as "a life-long practice that requires social inclusion practitioners and researchers to be aware of who they are and who they are not. Human beings are uniquely different, with personal stories, contexts, and frames of reference."[38] In essence, she states that cultural humility is an active and reflexive process that researchers should consider within their work. Chávez explains that developing mutually beneficial partnerships is fundamental to cultural humility. Without openness and modesty, it is impossible to effectively merge the strengths of different ways of knowing. Paolo Freire also called for such attention, claiming that "dialogue cannot exist without humility"[39] and therefore that work with communities must be integrated and interactive at the most elementary level. Cultural humility resonates with my research philosophy on developing meaningful research frameworks to elevate historically silenced voices and recognize their expertise in the co-creation of knowledge production. Being intentional about cultural humility made it imperative for me to reflect on the various instances in which some "partnerships" perpetuate harmful and exploitative practices because they exist within the epistemological parameters of the Western university system and do not acknowledge even the possibility that types of knowledge never verified by a university scientist could be valid.

A key aspect of practicing cultural humility involves acknowledging positionality when working with or for historically marginalized groups.

Yaqui/Chicana scholar Marisa Duarte states that "the methodology of positionality requires researchers to identify their own degrees of privilege . . . before seeking the epistemological basis of their intellectual craft." She further argues that the purpose of recognizing such positionality is to help researchers to understand "how their way of making meaning, of framing research, within their conceptual universe is tied to their positionality within an unjust world."[40] I will further this argument by saying that positionality in research is especially important for Indigenous researchers as we have both "insider" knowledge within the Indigenous communities to which we belong and "outsider" knowledge since we make inquiries from a perspective outside of the community being studied. Consequently, reflexivity[41]—examining one's own positionality, being aware of how our field research experience and emotions affect us as researchers, and being mindful of the power relations involved and our influence on the people or topic being studied—became an integral part of my research framework.

Cultural humility also proved helpful to me in understanding and overcoming the nuances and issues of the politics of knowledge production and the challenges of complying with respective institutional ethics formalities in the different contexts of Aotearoa and Peru, which are different from each other. For example, before the empirical research portion of this study took place in 2014, open discussions about Indigeneity with research partners in both countries made me aware of the histories of colonization and local realities. I also learned that Indigeneity is a contested term. It brings attention to the complex suite of experiences, identities, and knowledge, as they are related to the lived experiences of Indigenous groups and other oppressed societies.

Long-Term Relations Foregrounding Indigenous Voices and Thought

In my work, cultural identity and relationality always intersect. As Wilson writes, "relationships do not merely shape reality; they *are* reality."[42] This statement draws attention to the importance of *relational accountability* in Indigenous research methodologies. I was aware of how intersecting cultures, social locations, and complex power dynamics impact my lived experiences and, therefore, my worldview. This helped me to continually reassess how both my Indigenous and Western worldviews influenced the research process. It also helped me to understand how I navigate the complexities of power relations and how those influence interpretations and methods. I recognized the need to pay attention to the role of culture, spiritualism, gender, and sexuality as dimensions of intersectionality in Indigenous forms of inquiry. Also, I sought to understand power dynamics between insider and outsider knowledge, study contributions, and ethical considerations when researching with Quechua and Māori communities. I found that having an in-depth understanding of these core elements greatly helped me in approaching communities with integrity.

Understanding Indigenous Reality to Identify and Define a Research Topic

Desktop research on Peru's and Aotearoa's urgent challenges in 2012 indicated that climate change is a pressing concern for both countries. Climate change threatens biodiversity hotspots such as the tropical Andes of Peru and the island nation of Aotearoa. The loss of biodiversity, such as the decline of native plant species, not only threatens the Earth's natural resources but also jeopardizes the sustainability of food crops. Also, my previous studies conducted between 2007 and 2012 on the sustainability, environmental policies, and traditional agricultural knowledge of Aotearoa and Peru underscored the value of Indigenous knowledge in biodiversity preservation and the limited inclusion of their expertise in both countries' environmental and food security affairs.[43] Recognizing this, I halted my desktop research and went out into the field to connect and build relationships with Indigenous Peruvians and Māori to understand their ancestral legacies, histories, struggles, and aspirations while seeking to make room for their voices in developing the research framework of my study.

Because I was working full-time before joining the doctoral program, I was able to self-fund my trip to consult with my communities. My interest in working with the Awajún (Indigenous peoples of the Amazonian region of Peru)[44] and Quechua grew out of my personal experience of having visited the Amazon and Andean regions of Peru in my childhood and during my undergraduate studies, allowing me to learn first-hand about their ways of life, food traditions, and food security struggles. Upholding my research philosophy of working with and for the benefit of Indigenous communities, between April 2013 and August 2013, I made two visits each to the Quechua and Awajún communities in the Andean and Amazon regions of Peru, respectively. The aim was to understand their lived realities and struggles and explore the possibility of collaborating with them in a study project that could benefit them. On March 19, 2013, I departed from Auckland City in Aotearoa to embark on a five-month preliminary field trip in Peru to visit with the Awajún people living in Moyobamba, the capital city of the Amazon region of San Martín, and with Quechua peoples residing in the highlands of Cusco.

In October 2012, prior to these initial visits, I began making connections with grassroots organizations such as Slow Food Peru; non-governmental organizations (NGOs) such as the Association for Nature and Sustainable Development (ANDES), a Cusco-based NGO; and international development organizations such as Conservation International. I engaged in food security, land-based movements, and sustainable-development projects in Peru. In January 2013, I contacted Ulla Helimo, who was working for Conservation International (CI)-Peru as the project coordinator of the BioCuencas project, an integrated watershed management approach whose primary objective is to promote the conservation of the Amazon basin through ecosystem management. After several months of correspondence we met at the end of March 2013 at the organization's office in Lima, Peru. In this meeting I also met Dr. Claudio Schneider, senior technical director of CI. Weeks later, I travelled with Ulla from Lima to the Amazon region of Peru to visit with the Awajún Native Community of Shampuyacu for a week. The trip involved flying into the Amazonian city of Tarapoto and then driving about three hours, deep into the forest, to reach the Alto Mayo protected area. During this visit, I met with Huamán Espino, a community leader of the Shampuyaco tribe, his family, and other community members. Huamán told me that about six hundred native families live in Shampuyaco in the upper part of the Alto Mayo River. They rely primarily on hunting, fishing, and tending native crops, such as sweet potatoes and yams, for sustenance. Despite Huamán's warm welcome, the Shampuyaco community's apprehension at my presence was apparent from the first assembly meeting I attended. Shampuyaco community members, leaders, and Elders expressed their distrust towards researchers and, as a collective, decided to take a stronger stance on researchers wanting to study their ways of life. I tried to overcome these reservations by helping them work the land. Helping in working the land became the vehicle for developing a relationship with the Shampuyaco people. I learned that yacón, a root vegetable domesticated by the Indigenous peoples of the Andes and grown by farmers at mid-elevations on the eastern slopes of the Andes descending toward the Amazon, is a staple food for the Shampuyaco people. Because it is a juicy tuber, yacón also provides a welcome source of refreshment during fieldwork. In addition to yacón, I enjoyed camu camu, which contains a high concentration of vitamin C. I also recorded medicinal plants such as chambira that reduce fever. During my visit, I noted that children under the age of ten were experiencing malnutrition and anemia. The Shampuyaco people attributed this to a decline in the cultivation of traditional foods caused by clearing land for cash products, such as coffee and cacao, and climate change impacts, such as drought.[45]

I also connected with Víctor Mardonio Del Castillo Reátegui, then-mayor of Moyobamba, the capital of the San Martín Amazonian region in northern Peru, and Cesar Montoya. Cesar was director of the organic coffee cooperative CAPEMA, one of the largest in the provinces of Moyobamba and Rioja in Peru, providing employment to Awajún people, their families, and the community in general, during this trip. Braulio Cáceres, the regional coordinator of CI-Peru in Alto Mayo, discussed with me pressing issues impacting Awajún people, such as the lack of access to a diverse and nutritious diet. I also met with Lourdes Villegas Merino, who was then CAPEMA's regional coordinator of food security. These visits with Awajún people offered me insight into their ways of life, struggles, and opportunities. They helped me identify food insecurity and climate change as significant threats to their well-being.

In early October 2012, I contacted Tammy Stenner, then interim-director of ANDES. We remained in touch for the next five months over Skype and email. In June 2013, I traveled to Cusco City, where I met Tammy and then made several visits to the Quechua communities of Chawaytire and Paru Paru, which are two of the five Quechua communities that form the Potato Park, an area dedicated to the conservation of Peru's agrobiodiversity located within the Cusco Valley. In this preliminary field work in Cusco, I worked with community members of Chawaytire and Paru Paru in the chakra, growing potatoes, corn, medicinal plants, and wild foods. Sometimes, we made chicha de jora, a drink made from fermented corn, and drank it as community members shared stories about growing ancestral foodways and learning together about soil health. My meetings with community leaders, food growers, and Elders were largely informal, taking place for example while I went food foraging with the women, on walks with Elders, and through discussions in the chakra. These conversations provided the context I was missing from desktop research about specific knowledge and challenges facing Quechua and Māori.

I learned, for instance, that first-hand accounts of events recounted in the literature sometimes differed from what scholars had written. For example, sumak kawsay is the predominant terminology to describe a Quechua philosophy of life in the literature. However, community members of Chawaytire and Paru Paru contested this and said that "allin kawsay" is the Quechua terminology they use for such philosophy. To avoid duplicating such errors, I determined to follow Quechua methods of knowledge production in my unfolding research, engaging talking circles and community gatherings, in addition to the more standard personal interviews conducted by researchers. Some groups, primarily the young leaders, asked me to make presentations about my findings. Knowing of my ties to Aotearoa and my relationship with the Māori, they also asked me to give presentations about Māori culture. Such presentations wove naturally into ongoing, meaningful discussions about Quechua ways of life, traditional knowledge, cultural values, and their belief system. This visit made me realize the vital role that allin kawsay plays in the lives of Quechua communities, and that it would be essential to explore the integration of this philosophy of life with sustainable food systems as part of my study.

During these visits, I strengthened relationships with Quechua and Amazonian Indigenous peoples. I listened to their concerns, needs, and aspirations. Community gatherings and conversations about the cultivation and harvesting of crops revealed the discontent and frustration of some community members toward the researchers who had visited them, learned from them, and then never made any further contact with the community. They said that researchers come uninvited to their communities, hoping to entice them to provide insight into plant breeding techniques, climate change resilience, and food security practices in exchange for money or food vouchers. These initial visits underscored that, unlike Aotearoa, where Māori have the established Kaupapa Māori, the highlands of Peru do not have an established Indigenous-based research methodology. In its absence, NGOs and community leaders sometimes instructed Quechua communities to cooperate with researchers without question. In attempts to develop a decolonial research methodology in Cusco, in 2010, the five Quechua communities that make up the Potato Park worked mostly with foreign researchers to develop the Andean Potato Park's biocultural protocol (PPBC). The PPBC is a participatory action-research approach for equitable benefit-sharing. The aim was to outline Andean values and customary laws that could facilitate the strengthening of relationships between ANDES, Quechua communities, and Western researchers. However, the PPBC is still relatively new and unknown compared to the Kaupapa Māori and was not used in the communities I was working with. This provided an opportunity for me to discuss with Quechua communities I was working with how we might develop a research framework anchored in Quechua ways of knowing and including complementary approaches of participatory and decolonizing research to inform norms and obligations. This model, we hoped, would make the researchers who follow me more responsive to Indigenous societies.

At the conclusion of all of my visits, I always offered an expression of gratitude by cooking a traditional Peruvian dish called Cuy al palo. The dish consists of a guinea pig marinated in salt, pepper, oil, cumin, garlic, and huacatay (black mint or southern marigold) and cooked on a stick, which must be turned regularly so that the whole guinea pig becomes crispy and fully roasted. I also provided books and pencils for the children and gave each pregnant woman wool baby clothes knitted by my mother, Elena Huambachano. I offered all community members of the Quechua communities of Chawaytire, Paru Paru, and the Amazonian community of Awajún my heartfelt thanks for their time and for sharing so many stories with me, and I promised to develop a research project with them and for them: one that could tell their stories and could benefit them in return. Although research for this book centered on Quechua communities and not on the Awajún, I held true to my belief and promise that my research should benefit the communities I studied. Over the years, I have remained in touch with tribal Awajún leaders such as Huamán Espino and community members like Cesar Montoya of CAPEMA. In 2015, I helped CAPEMA to develop a community-based food sovereignty project to revitalize Awajún's traditional food systems, economies, and environmental sustainability, which received funding from the Manatū Aorere (New Zealand Ministry of Foreign Affairs and Trade) in 2016.

My framing of the Khipu Model and selection of study locations continued throughout subsequent visits with Quechua peoples in 2014 and 2015. Building from preliminary visits to Cusco from 2008 to 2013, I remained in touch with Tammy Stenner and coordinated with her to travel to Peru in 2014 to work as a four-month volunteer at the Potato Park. In February 2014, I arrived in Cusco City as a research volunteer at ANDES, where I worked as a research assistant to various ANDES food security projects and performed admin-related tasks as an expression of reciprocity. As part of that work I was introduced to community leaders of the Quechua community of Chawaytire located in the Sacred Valley of the Inkas, about thirty minutes by car from Cusco City. In parallel I began making connections with food growers and knowledge holders of Andean agriculture and biodiversity preservation by visiting the San Pedro market in Cusco City, and the Calca and Pisac Markets in the Sacred Valley of the Inkas. Also, I attended workshops on seed preservation and climate change mitigation organized by the Municipality of Cusco City.

Furthermore, during my time volunteering at ANDES, I formed a friendship with Sofia Villafuerte, a food security project coordinator who had established connections with food growers and community leaders in the Lares Valley situated in the province of Calca in the Cusco Region. Sofia received permission from leaders she knew in each community to visit them and bring me along. In April 2014, she and I embarked on a week-long trip to the Lares Valley. There, I connected with community leaders and knowledge-holders of the Quechua communities of Choquecancha, Pampacorral, Ccachin, and Rosaspata. In subsequent visits, I contacted leaders I knew in each community, such as Petronila Quispe and Valentina Quispe, directly, and asked permission to visit them. I also offered to work on each interviewee's chakra. I stayed with Sonia Quispe of Choquecancha and Valentina Quispe of Rosaspata, and I visited frequently with paqo (Andean healer) Juan de Dios Cruz Silva of Ccachin and other community members.

Building Relationships in Aotearoa

Because of my Indigenous background, forging close relationships with Māori and understanding their struggles and aspirations was an organic process. I garnered knowledge about the unique cultural systems of Māori people, which varies from tribe to tribe. I learned that Māori traditions, values, and belief systems run deep in many aspects of their daily lives and are embedded in their language, food practices, and overall outlook of a good life. Having this "Indigenous" insider knowledge equipped me with knowledge of the Kaupapa Māori theory. It enabled me, an outsider, to rapidly appreciate the value of mātauranga Māori (Māori knowledge) and to be aware of deploying best practices when researching with Māori. This meant that as a non-Māori, I had to recognize and follow tikanga Māori, the ethical values and correct ways of behaving and interacting with others an in everyday Māori life.

The practice of tikanga Māori can vary between tribes and sub-tribes. For example, all Māori meet their manaakitanga (hospitality) responsibilities to host and care for their manuhiri (guests or visitors), although customs as to how they express greeting and welcome may differ.[46] In December 2012, during my first gathering, a workshop at the James Henare Māori Research Centre, as an Indigenous scholar at the University of Auckland's Waipapa Marae, I was welcomed in a pōwhiri, a special ceremony. Every stage of the pōwhiri focuses on manaakitanga (acts of giving and caring for), a key component of Māori culture, and ends with the sharing of food to help everyone move from the heightened, spiritual state of the pōwhiri back to ordinary activities. In this case it began with a kaumātua (respected Elder) blessing the food and concluded with a karakia (prayer).

Understandings of tikanga Māori facilitated my establishment of respectful and trusting relationships with Māori people—knowledge-holders of traditional food planting and harvesting practices, community leaders, business people, and academics who had tribal affiliations—in the North Island of the country. From 2012 to 2016, I attended every Māori workshop I could in relation to the Titiriti o Waitangi (Treaty of Waitangi), the maramataka (Māori lunar calendar), Māori land rights, and other related meetings held through the University of Auckland, Massey

University, University of Otago, and community events. In March 2012, I connected with Associate Professor Mānuka Hēnare, who was then associate dean and director of the Mira Száscy Research Centre for Māori and Pasifika Economic Development at the University of Auckland.[47] We started meeting occasionally to discuss his great interest in the Andean cosmovision and mine in Māori economies of well-being. In June 2012 and September 2013, Mānuka invited me to attend Waitangi Tribunal[48] sessions in Kaitaia, a town in the Far North District of Aotearoa, where I observed how the Waitangi Tribunal operates. I also attended a hui (social gathering or assembly) in the Bay of Islands located in Northern Aotearoa with people involved in Māori land rights and food production, and with Māori entrepreneurs. I participated in various Māori hui (gathering), māra kai (food garden) community projects, and seminars on Māori land and sovereignty rights.

My active participation in academic and community-based projects sparked a series of both professional and personal relationships with Māori people. For example, in July 2012, I established a lifelong relationship with Uncle Percy Tipene, a treasured kaumātua leading a team developing a food sovereignty framework in support of Māori aspirations to be food secure. He was an organic farmer, founder and chair of Te Waka Kai Ora, the National Māori Organic Authority of Aotearoa that developed and runs the Hua Parakore system, an Indigenous Māori validation and verification system for pure foods. I visited Uncle Percy most often in the tribe of Ngāti Hine in the city of Whangārei and in his home of Kaitaia. The name of this town, which is in the far north of Aotearoa, translates to "food in abundance." I also visited him at the Papatūānuku Kōkiri Marae in the South of Auckland City when he would visit for community food events. We remained in touch until his death in January 2017. After Uncle Percy's death, I kept my promise to him, continuing to work on environmental sustainability, climate justice, and food sovereignty endeavors with Māori food gardeners and farmers in Aotearoa.

Connections Uncle Percy made for me continue to sustain my research, such as with Lionel Hotene and his wife Valerie Teraitua, who I met in 2012. They work at the Papatūānuku Kōkiri Marae, an urban organic community garden certified by the Te Waka Kai Ora (National Māori Organics Authority of Aotearoa). Since that first meeting with Lionel and

Valerie, I have worked closely with them and a team of volunteers, most of whom are Māori and Pacific Islanders, on the revitalization of Māori agricultural knowledge, including the planting of traditional foods and using the maramataka, the Māori lunar calendar. Through attending Waitangi Tribunal sessions, I also learned about the politics of Māori self-determination and gained further insights about the set of Māori cultural values, beliefs, and protocols that embody the concept of tikanga Māori. I attended conferences, workshops, and symposiums about Kaupapa Māori, Māori culture, environment, governance, and law organized by Māori-driven research centers such as the Ngā Pae o te Māramatanga, New Zealand's Māori Centre of Research Excellence, and the Mira Szászy Research Center. These cultural experiences enlightened my queries with regards to the relationships between Māori cultural identity, their connection with land, or whenua, and their food, or kai. I collaborated on an ongoing basis with senior researchers affiliated with the Mira Szászy Research Center and supported initiatives related to strengthening the socio-political and environmental systems of Māori, Peruvian, and Native American peoples as well as other Indigenous peoples around the world. Thus, implications of the connections between these two Indigenous communities, Quechua and Māori, which are geographically separate from each other, and reflections on particular issues from their different vantage points led to the formulation of my research topic and approach.

A Research Topic and Indigenous-based Research Framework Emerging from a "Relational Ethics" Approach

Through understanding Indigenous reality and forming long-lasting relationships with the Indigenous peoples of Peru and Aotearoa, I was able to validate findings from desktop research. In my visits and in reading over my fieldnotes I found that, indeed, Peru and Aotearoa share significant connections, namely through their Indigenous worldviews, agricultural prowess, and rich cultures, histories, and traditions. Moreover, these two countries are agricultural nations and are knowledgeable about agrobiodiversity conservation for food security. However, Indigeneity and the contributions of their Indigenous knowledge are often dismissed in the academy and in policymaking. To correct this deficiency in the academic literature, the Khipu Model addresses the central research question for this study: How can Indigenous peoples' philosophies—in this case, those of the Quechua and Māori—contribute to fostering a more inclusive, equitable, and healthy food system in their own communities and at a broader scale?

I have faced many challenges as an Indigenous scholar working within the confines of Western academia when trying to develop a research methodology that resonated with Indigenous ways of knowledge production and dissemination. However, through the development of the Khipu Model, I believe I have achieved what I set out to do: providing step-by-step guidance on developing respectful, ethical, empathetic, and useful research approaches, which benefit both the pursuit of knowledge and the people who hold it.

CONCLUSION

By creating the Khipu Model, I join in the voices involved in the democratization of knowledge in higher education to include Indigenous methodologies in research areas. The Khipu Model also joins global, decolonial, community-based research methodologies and epistemologies that contend that in order to conduct research on Indigenous peoples, accepted research methodologies first need to be decolonized across the globe.[49] The Khipu Model is an example of *transformative* research in that it provides an in-depth understanding of the theoretical and intellectual foundations of Indigenous methodologies from two continents—Oceania and Latin America. The Khipu Model demonstrates that it is essential that researchers pay greater attention to issues of power relations, positionality, reflexivity, participation, and accountability in studies involving Indigenous communities. Only in this way can we avoid the perpetuation of exploitative research that has repeatedly silenced, erased, and told the stories of instead of with and for the benefit of Indigenous communities and vulnerable societies. The Khipu Model supports *self-determination* of Indigenous peoples. Thus, it is a novel research model, one of a number Indigenous communities are heralding as part of a pathway to reclaiming their voice within research. It supports the well-being and sovereignty aspirations of these communities while broadening the insights of scholars. Finally, the Khipu Model is a tool for reclaiming *intellectual sovereignty*. It gives Quechua and Māori complete autonomy in the knowledge-production process, from the research design and implementation of data-collection methods to determining how data is analyzed and disseminated. Sociologists Maggie Walter and Chris Andersen point out several common deficiencies in the way statistics on Indigenous peoples are constructed, largely because these constructions are developed out of Western viewpoints and controlled by Western officials. The resulting data contributes further to existing pejorative judgmental perceptions of Indigenous realities and experiences. As they write, "For Indigenous peoples, especially in first world countries where population statistics powerfully influence government and social services, these numbers have become a foundational lens through which we, as Indigenous peoples, become known to our respective nation states and how we engage in many of our relationships with government actors."[50]

The Khipu Model underscores the significance of Indigenous autonomy over the validation of research findings, repositioning the power of data analysis and sovereignty over language translations and how knowledge is disseminated among Indigenous peoples. In placing control over data sovereignty in the hands of Quechua and Māori, the Khipu Model puts Quechua and Māori "voices, aspirations, and preferences" at the forefront of the project's research design. This approach infuses the three phases of the Khipu Model—knowing, being, and doing.

One of the contributions of the Khipu Model is that it provides a counter-story to mainstream research. It highlights the vital role of "accountability" in conducting research with Indigenous communities. It underscores our spiritual connection with the environment/land; how we feel, experience, and relate to the natural world; it influences our behavior; and it grounds our moral obligations and responsibilities within the ecosystems. In this context, Indigenous researchers' positionality and epistemologies provide the understanding that our lived experiences— particularly those centered on race, class, and gender—shape our worldviews and ultimately impact how we understand the nature of reality (ontology) and our responsibilities with entities and categories within reality (ethics), all of which Western academia has historically ignored. The other contribution is that the Khipu Model provides a platform for the co-creation of knowledge in a transformative and culturally sensitive manner for both Indigenous and non-Indigenous scholars and suggests how results can be used for the benefit of Indigenous communities. While key components of the Khipu Model framework, such as the Kaupapa Māori and TEK, may be familiar to Western researchers, this is the first time that they have been adopted in the design of an Indigenous-based research framework rooted in an Indigenous cosmovision. Establishing ethical protocols and cultural guidelines when interacting with Indigenous peoples may seem like an obvious measure to many researchers; however, as I observed, these protocols are often violated.

I hope the Khipu Model helps to build methodologies that resonate with the study communities' research needs, aspirations, and knowledge systems. In this way Indigenous peoples, minority groups, and other marginalized communities can reclaim intellectual sovereignty as academia begins to recognize and respect other ways of knowing and data sovereignty and focuses on aspirational rather than disparity data about and for Indigenous and local peoples. By sharing the development of the Khipu Model my overarching goal is to offer the lessons, challenges, and successes that I have experienced. I hope to inform the advancement of the contemporary food justice/sovereignty movement and to inspire the younger generation as we bring Indigenous methodologies into the research arena. In this way, I hope to contribute to enhancing social justice in research and practice and to forging futures that are of our own making.

3 Together, We Grow

QUECHUA AND MĀORI UNDERSTANDINGS
OF WELL-BEING AND SHARED SIMILARITIES
TO SUSTAINABLE FOOD SYSTEMS

"The land is our precious taonga [treasure]," Mate Heitia said.[1] She gestured to a vibrant, green field filled with kūmara (sweet potatoes), taewa[2] (Māori potatoes), kamokamo (marrow or squash), horopito (pepper tree), beetroot, carrots, peas, tomatoes, onions, cucumbers, and rongoā (Māori medicine): all traditional and staple food crops and plant life on the East Coast of Aotearoa. She had just finished describing how her ancestors had, through the centuries, linked soil health and human well-being by fostering good relationships with Papatūānuku (Earth Mother), atua (gods), tipuna (ancestors), and te taiao (environment).

Knowledge holder Amauta Condori demonstrated a similar ontology of land when he grabbed a handful of soil in the highlands of Peru and said, in his native language of Quechua, "Kaypa sutin: allpan, hallp'an! [The name of this is soil!]. But it is more than soil for us Runakuna."[3] Working the soil, both planting and cultivating, he told me, is where Runakuna maintains a deep connection with Pachamama (Mother Earth) and non-human beings, allowing a symbiotic nurturing state with her, the plants, ancestral spirits, and the entire web of non-living beings on Earth.

Both Quechua and Māori research collaborators' subjective ways of experiencing and making meaning of their environments provide them with first-hand experiences with food knowledge and traditions. I discovered that a fundamental commonality underlies their foodways, evident in the conception of an Indigenous holistic philosophy of well-being. Albeit distinct in Quechua and Māori communities, this philosophy is for both deep-rooted in an Indigenous worldview/cosmovision, a holistic understanding of the way we, as humans, relate to each other and with the "other-than-human" (all the creatures of this world, including the plants that convert solar radiation into food, water, forests, microorganisms, Earth itself, and spiritual beings). They are all key actors in a complex and holistic system of interdependent relationships that work together to steward the land. This relational understanding of life means that we are kin to each other and that our well-being as humans is inextricably tied to the well-being of the non-human. Holistic/collective philosophies of well-being urge humanity to question what thinking beyond the human can mean regarding spiritual, emotional, mental, and physical well-being, not only for people but the other non-human beings with whom we interact.

Interest in studying Indigenous philosophies of living well continues to grow in the humanities and social science disciplines, encouraging us to consider others' ways of knowing, voices, perspectives, and modes of experiencing the world. There is extensive literature on ideologies of well-being, mostly by non-Indigenous scholars, much of which draws on Indigenous thinking about the long-term sustainability of ecosystems. Examples of these include Serge de Latouche's décroissance or economy of degrowth, Ivan Illich's conviviality, and Arne Naess's deep ecology.[4] An examination of Indigenous philosophies for living well linked to decoloniality is also evident in the scholarship of decolonial and feminist thinkers in Latin America such as Aníbal Quijano of Peru, Silvia Rivera Cusicanqui of Bolivia, Boaventura de Souza of Brazil, Arturo Escobar of Colombia, and María Lugones of Argentina.[5] One common thread in these practical philosophies of "the good life" is that they highlight the importance of centering conviviality, solidarity, care, and well-being of both people and Nature as the basis for bringing back a human-Nature equilibrium. In this chapter, I explore the understanding of well-being philosophies within Quechua and Māori peoples' traditional settings. Then, I present epistemological and ontological commonalities emerging from this analysis, such as Indigenous ontologies of land, spirituality, and self-determination. Finally, I discuss the role of Indigenous holistic philosophies of life in driving a well-being agenda in the twenty-first century.

ALLIN KAWSAY WITHIN A PERUVIAN QUECHUA CONTEXT

The Quechua village of Chawaytire, located in the Andean mountain town of Pisac about twenty miles (thirty-two kilometers) northeast of Cusco City, was one of the first places I identified a collective expression of the traditional Quechua way of life. In my early research visits there in 2013, I saw that their ancestral language is alive and that locals live in ayllu, a Quechua concept that broadly translates to kinship, community, and self-governance. They work in a chakra—a Quechua term used in the Andean world to mean not only a farming land, but specifically the spiritual space of the nurturance and flourishing of all forms of life. This initial ethnographic work was where my understanding of allin kawsay—a holistic and relational philosophy of life practiced by this Indigenous Quechua community–began. Quechua Peruvian philosopher Javier Lajo writes in his 2006 book *Qhapaq Ñan: The Inka Route of Wisdom* that the Andean concept of allin kawsay emerges from the combination of allin/sumak (good, magnificent, and wonderful) and kawsay (life). Bringing them together, sumak/allin kawsay[6] encourages people to lead meaningful lives and seamlessly nourish others' lives, too.

In February 2014, I returned to Cusco City, where I spent several months strengthening relationships with the Quechua people living in the Sacred Valley of the Inkas, a region in Peru's Andean highlands nearby the town of Cusco and the historic sanctuary of Machu Picchu, such as Chawaytire and Sacaca. I also began establishing relationships with Quechua-speaking communities in the Lares Valley that still preserve their ancestral traditions in growing foods, herding llamas, and weaving textiles made of wool and traditional plants located in the department of Cusco. Three months later, I organized a community gathering (workshop) in the Quechua village of Choquecancha to explore the theoretical foundations of allin kawsay and food security in the Andes. Attendees included farmers, gardeners, seed keepers, Elders, and community leaders from the Quechua communities of Choquecancha, Rosaspata, Sacaca,

Pampacorral, and Ccachin, all of whom were knowledgeable about culture, soil health, and traditional food systems and practices.[7]

But before providing my analysis of allin kawsay, I want to mention that when exploring Indigenous philosophies of sustainable living within a Latin American discourse, academic literature often refers to the Kichwa idiom of *sumak kawsay* as "buen vivir" in Spanish. Buen vivir refers to several different Indigenous models of well-being: sumak kawsay in the Kichwa language of Ecuador, allin kawsay in the Quechua language of Peru, Opatsi in the Cofán language of Ecuador, and Suma Qamaña in the Aymara language of Bolivia and Peru among others. Each of these conceptions begins from within their respective Indigenous societies' cultural, historical, and political contexts. My studies with the Peruvian Quechua people taught me that variants of the Quechua language exist within the country and broader Andean region, denoting clear distinctions between Quechua-speaking people in the North, Central, and South Andes, and that these distinctions merit attention to avoid misleading generalizations.

Given these language nuances, it is not surprising that when I posed a question about the role of sumak kawsay in foodways, Quechua research collaborators in the highlands of Peru unanimously corrected me, saying that in runa simi, Peru's Quechua language, the correct term for living well is "allin kawsay." I highlight this distinction to underscore that Indigenous knowledge is place-based. There is no one Indigenous view of well-being or living well; nor is there a singular terminology within a Peruvian context and the broader Latin American "buen vivir" discourse.[8] Yet I found similarities between the Quechua and Māori that ultimately drove this study.

Gomercinda Sutta of the Quechua community of Pampacorral told me, "Allin kawsay is living well. That is, showing respect, love, and care with your community members, your family, and with apu [Andean deity] Ausangate, rivers, lakes, animals and plants. For me, every day is living in allin kawsay. It is part of my way of life. Allin kawsay guides how I think, feel, and act upon the land and everything that surrounds me."[9] Aniceto Ccoyo from the Quechua community of Sacaca explained that three tenets underpin the ethical and customary laws of Quechua people with Nature: allin ruay, allin munay, and allin yachay. Allin ruay means to do good deeds through ethical behavior at all times. Allin munay suggests that to

Figure 6. Quechua research partners sitting together, showing the wide varieties of potato, corn, and beans they grow collectively, embracing the allin kawsay philosophy. Photo: Mariaelena Huambachano

achieve a good life, humans ought to coexist in harmony with Pachamama by deeply loving and respecting the agency of non-human relatives (sea, mountains, and rivers). Allin yachay refers to thinking wisely or aspiring to be a wise person to ensure social equity and fairness within communities. Aniceto further explained that a person who does not achieve balance between these principles will not achieve allin kawsay.[10]

Sonia Ttito from the Quechua community of Choquecancha said that she learned about allin kawsay intergenerationally: "I simply grew up practicing this philosophy, and I learned it from my parents. I can't really say when and how I learned it because I grew up with it. I grew up practicing ayni [reciprocity] and seeing my mother and father together working in the chakra [agricultural field] from the moment the sun rises to when the sun goes to rest. Since I was a little girl, I recall helping my parents with the chakra and nurturing the plants and animals by talking to them and caring for them. You need to live in an ayllu [kinship, community] to experience allin kawsay."[11] Marisol Cruz of Ccachin agreed. "The philosophy of allin kawsay has been passed on from one generation to the next through oral history and through an active-learning approach in which close interaction with the chakra is integral to understanding it."[12]

Indeed, having lived and visited for extended periods various Quechua communities such as Choquecancha, Pampacorral, and Ccachin, I had the opportunity to immerse myself in Quechua ways of life, which I came to experience as holistic and ritualistic. Working with Quechua people in the chakra, attending communal events and celebrations, I witnessed how the community works together on seed preservation and pollination. I watched them share this knowledge with their children and observed how, through an experiential learning approach, Elders imparted astronomical wisdom about the Inti (sun) and Quilla (moon) agricultural calendars to the youth. I also learned through attending various agricultural celebrations how rituals and festivals express reverence, care, and respect to the land and to the spirits of the ancestors.

As I uncovered the philosophical foundations of allin kawsay, I realized that this ideology continues to reign in the agricultural and food systems of these four Quechua communities. For example, when I asked Crisostomo Quispe about key values informing allin kawsay in growing nutritious food, he said, "We have learned from our parents and grandparents to embrace our own traditions and values of, for example, ayni [reciprocity], ayllu [self-governance], chaninchay [solidarity] and yanantin-masintin [complementarity]. Without allin kawsay, we would not know about living in harmony, self-governance, resource management, and biodiversity protection, nor systems of natural law and order in our community."[13]

Coming back to the holistic framing of allin kawsay, these narratives bring attention to considering others' ways of experiencing the world, voices, and perspectives. It also encourages us to understand Quechua traditions, values, and beliefs and their application in achieving sustainable food systems and transmission of ancestral wisdom sustaining everyone from the Elder, to the community leader, to the children, as I explain in the next chapter.

UNDERSTANDING WELL-BEING THROUGH A MĀORI LENS

While well-being from a Māori perspective resembles the established allin kawsay philosophy in Peru, there is not, strictly speaking, a Māori term for well-being. From 2012, I began establishing trusting relationships with Māori engaged in the revitalization of traditional Māori food systems, rongoā Māori (traditional Māori plant healing knowledge), academics and business leaders. Percy Tipene, Lionel Hotene, Valerie Teraitua, Rob Whitbourne, Kiri Dell, Mānuka Hēnare (former Director of the Dame Mira Szászy Research Centre), Tūmanaku Wereta (Tuaripaki Trust), Che Wilson (Ātihau-Whanganui Incorporation), and Tom Walters (former trustee of the East Taupo Lands Trust) are some of them. I initiated these connections by contacting them directly, often visiting them in their tribal lands, like Ngāti Tūwharetoa, Ngāti Hine, and Ngāti Awa, all in the North Island of the Aotearoa. Additionally, I attended workshops on Māori maramataka—the Māori lunar calendar—led by kaumātua (respected Elder) Rereata Makiha and Māori scholars Pauline Harris and Rangi Mātāmua. I also joined food foraging exploration journeys in the Waitakere City, in the Auckland region, led by Mamakan.[14] I learned about traditional Māori food gathering traditions, astronomy, cultural protocols, and some tips on the ways to cook foraged Māori food.

Building from these relationships, I was able to conduct empirical research in Aotearoa between 2015 and 2016. I asked Māori collaborators from the tribes of Ngāti Porou, Ngāti Hine, and Ngāti Awa, and from the Papatūānuku Kōkiri Marae (urban organic community garden) and Wai A Ariki Onerahirahi (Food Forest) garden: "What would be the Māori concept for a living-well philosophy?" Across the upper North region of Aotearoa, in South Auckland, and on the East Coast, they all responded that fundamental to Māori well-being is upholding their cultural identity and the healthy state of the soil, whenua (land), the environment, individual health, and community wellness. They referenced the importance of speaking the language of their ancestors, that is, te reo Māori, and maintaining a close connection with their ancestral landscapes and extended kin. They also spoke about the imperative to restore cultural knowledge embedded in the teachings of their tupuna (ancestors) about methods for growing, harvesting, and processing foods—cooking, dehydrating, and storage—which they consider essential for the continuance of their foodways, food knowledge, and well-being.

Māori words such as hauora (health), whaiora (well-being), oranga (life, food, livelihood), and the most common, mauri ora (well-being), were embedded in our conversations about a Māori ideology of well-being. Every Māori tribe has its own interpretation of what well-being means and its application in food systems. For example, for Mate Heitia of the iwi (tribe) of Ngāti Awa, Ngāti Pukeku, and Ngai te Rangi on the East Coast of the North Island of Aotearoa, well-being is "taking care of the whenua [land] you live on, growing your traditional kai [food] according to your customary practices to ensure the hauora [health] and whaiora [well-being] of the land and people."[15] Hinetu Dell from the iwi of Ngāti Porou said that, for her, mauri ora came the closest to well-being; however, she said, "I am not sure if all we Māori would interpret it as a well-being." She added that, for her, "mauri ora is about nourishing your physical well-being and wairua [spirit] with good kai [food] from the whenua [land] and kaimoana [foods of the sea]."[16]

Mauri ora emerges from two Māori words literally translated to English as "life force" or "life spirit" (mauri) and "energy" (ora). Māori studies scholar Mason Durie highlights that mauri exists as part of the wider wairua (spirit) system and is what keeps people and things aligned with and within the flow of the wairua. Mauri occurs in different states, such as mauri moe, which is interpreted as a proactive but latent state of untapped potential; mauri oho, the awakening; mauri tū, a state of active engagement, rediscovery, and revitalization; and mauri ora, exhilaration and consciousness of being. Without juxtaposition to ora, mauri has no meaning.[17]

Although there is not an established well-being concept in Aotearoa, there are fundamental traditions and principles bolstering a Māori worldview of well-being linked to foodways. In reviewing the Māori literature on well-being, I found a growing number of studies in the health, education, and sustainability-related areas that acknowledged mauri ora as a critical concept in Māori philosophy. Many also recognized its utilization and created innovative models of well-being seeking to advance a holistic-oriented approach to healthy Māori selfhood and the natural environment.[18]

Figure 7. Māori food grower Mate Heitia explains what well-being means for her. Beside her is her husband, Sonny Heitia, checking the growth of the kūmara tipu (sweet potato seedlings). Photo: Mariaelena Huambachano.

In 1984, Mason Durie developed the "Te Whare Tapa Whā" (House of Four Sides) model based on the four walls of a house where all four corners had to stay aligned to ensure fulsome balance and well-being. These are taha tinana (physical well-being), taha hinengaroa (mental and emotional well-being), taha wairua (spiritual well-being), and taha whānau (family and social well-being).[19] Dr. Rangimārie Te Turuki Arikirangi Rose Pere put forward the Te Wheke: the eight-legged octopus model of health.[20]

The octopus was used as a symbol representing a Māori holistic view of health and well-being in which individual spiritual and physical wellness is intertwined with and inseparable from the health of the whānau, hapū (sub-tribe), and the iwi (tribe or nation).

The Te Wheke model extends the four dimensions of Te Whare Tapa Whā to eight by adding mauri (vitality, life principle), mana ake (appreciation of one's absolute uniqueness), hā ā koro mā ā kuia mā (breath of life from the ancestors), and whatumanawa (healthy expressions of emotions and feelings). The model proposes that sustenance is required for each tentacle or dimension of the octopus to attain waiora or total well-being, and that sustenance consists of adequate nutrition, shelter, clothing, exercise, and positive feelings, among other things. The Mauri Model is another innovative well-being model created by Dr. Te Kīpa Kēpa Morgan based on the concept of mauri (life essence).[21] It is a Māori assessment and decision-making tool to integrate economic, social, and cultural dimensions in a measurement of sustainability, human well-being, and the interconnectedness of all human and non-humans. A common thread in these Māori models for health and well-being is their whole-systems approach.

QUECHUA AND MĀORI COMMONALITIES IN FOOD SYSTEMS WELL-BEING

In my work spanning over a decade of close-knit relationships with Quechua and Māori research partners and using the Khipu Model, I was able to unearth their distinct and millennia-old foodways and traditions, which I validated with them. I identified six similarities imbuing their lifeways and food systems. In identifying commonalities between them, I do not mean to ignore important cultural or knowledge distinctions between my Quechua and Māori research collaborators. They exhibit distinctive, localized values and principles in environmental stewardship, food traditions, and land governance. Yet, I found that they share a fundamental epistemological and ontological similarities, which I theorize as a holistic/collective well-being philosophy. Additionally, Indigenous TEK, ontologies of land, understandings of spiritual well-being, self-determination, and intergenerational equity and justice appear similar.

Holistic/Collective Well-Being Philosophy

The first shared similarity is a "holistic/collective well-being." This philosophy is informed by Quechua and Māori research partners' cosmovision, which forgoes notions of human superiority in favor of establishing reciprocal relationships to the land and all living beings, treating them as living entities with agency. This philosophy does not only concern individual well-being; it pertains to holistic/collective well-being, including non-human relatives. In this context, I learned that food encompasses all facets of being for Quechua and Māori: the physical, the emotional, and the spiritual. I purposely include "holistic/collective" to highlight the intangible factor of spirituality, infusing alchemy of energy in all aspects of their food systems and strengthening socio-ecological links through rituals and ceremonies exuding gratitude to the forces making it possible to obtain food: the spirits of the food, seed plant relatives, and the nurturing hands of humans. It was through understanding this holistic/collective well-being ideology that I realized that the values of Indigenous foodways and food sovereignty for Quechua and Māori collaborators are cultural, ceremonial, political, and sustaining. This ideology nurtures the multiple life worlds of Quechua and Māori research partners who depend on these foodways for their physical and spiritual well-being.

Self-Determination

The second shared similarity is their belief in their right to self-determination. Quechua and Māori research partners pointed to the need for greater recognition and strengthening of their right to self-determination to govern social-political and economic institutions within their territories, including, where applicable, families, clans, homelands, communities, and the natural world. Research partners in both countries emphasized that the well-being of the collective is inextricably linked to self-determination, which has been diminished in Peru and Aotearoa since the colonization that continues to ravage Indigenous lands and sever their spiritual-cultural-land relations. This is an ongoing process in both countries—for example, in the systems of occupation, control, and exploitation that define gastrocolonialism,[22] mining, and other extractive industries.[23]

Article 3 of the United Nations Declaration on the Rights of Indigenous Peoples (UNDRIP) declares that "Indigenous peoples have the right to self-determination. By virtue of that right they freely determine their political status and freely pursue their economic, social and cultural development."[24] Despite the recognition of Indigenous self-determination at the international level and in some states, Māori and Quechua peoples face challenges in being able to exercise it in practice. Peru is a signatory to a series of international law instruments that includes UNDRIP. The UNDRIP sets the international standards for the recognition of Indigenous peoples as a stand-alone group within a nation. It is considered one of the most significant milestones achieved by Indigenous peoples. However, in Peru it only applies to Native communities legally recognized in the Peruvian constitution under the law decree 89.[25] Those without such recognition face challenges gaining access to land for food production. Highlighting the vulnerability of Indigenous Peruvians in asserting their rights to self-determination are the Yanacocha and Conga mines causing negative environmental and social impacts, such as water and air pollution and displacement or forced migration for the people of Cajamarca in Peru's northern highlands.[26] The emblematic case of Máxima Acuña-Atalaya v. Newmont Mining Corp exposes the difficulty and danger of Indigenous peoples of winning those rights.[27] Another example is the 2009 Baguazo. Indigenous Peruvians of the Amazon region blocked a highway near the town of Bagua for months, demanding the annulment of economic laws approved by the former Peruvian president Alberto Fujimori (1990–2000) and carried out by the administration of Alan García (2006–2011) that threatened the safety of their natural resources. Specifically, they were protesting the Law on Sustainable Investment in the Amazon: Decree 27037, which opened Native territories in the rainforest to oil, mining, and logging companies, violating rights guaranteed in the Peruvian constitution. The Peruvian government was forced to re-evaluate its legislation concerning Indigenous peoples' rights, but deadly clashes between Indigenous protesters and police officers left thirty-three people dead, including twenty-three policemen, five Bagua community members, and five Indigenous Amazonians. Around two hundred were injured.[28]

In 2011, the Peruvian Congress granted Indigenous people the right to free, prior, and informed consent (FPIC) on laws or infrastructure projects that would affect them or their territories. Nonetheless, my empirical investigation regarding the environmental impacts of the Camisea Natural Gas Project in the highlands of Peru confirmed that in 2014 the concession license to exploit natural gas in Block 88, commonly known as Gas de Camisea, where the country's largest natural gas reserves are located, posed serious social, economic and environmental threats to the Quechua communities of Shivancoreni and Shimmaa.[29] As the rivers of the Shivancoreni and Shimmaa peoples were populated with oil spills, so was the decline of access to fish vital for their food security. Indigenous peoples' agency and right to FPIC had been disregarded. Clearly the government of Peru has ignored many of the provisions of the legal instruments to which it is a party.

In Aotearoa, by contrast, Māori people won several battles in asserting their sovereignty rights, cultural customs, and traditions as tangata whenua (people of the land) in the final two decades of the twentieth century. In spite of subterfuge by the British Crown in the Te Tiriti o Waitangi (Treaty of Waitangi) of 1840, it has been the basis of these victories. In the Māori language version signed by rangatira (chief) Māori, the Treaty acknowledges Crown governorship of lands, but Māori retain sovereignty. Discrepancies in the English and Māori versions over the notion of sovereignty have long been the subject of debate, and as soon as the Treaty of Waitangi was signed, a slow and ongoing process of settler colonialism based on segregating Indigenous people from the land and, hence, from their access to traditional foods began in Māori lands. There has been some reversal since 1980, however.[30]

For Māori and Quechua alike, the land is part of cultural identity. Therefore, it is central to movements that ground calls for self-determination, such as political protest movements responding to major land confiscations and demanding the restoration of Indigenous food systems. In the context of Peru, the Quechua term Pachamama is the name for Mother Earth and honoring relationships with Nature is central to the Indigenous-led agricultural and food activist traditions of the country. In Aotearoa's tribal traditions, female deities Papatūānuku (Mother Earth) and Hine-ahu-one (Earth-formed woman in the Māori language) play important roles in Māori food growing, soil health, and food sovereignty practices. For both the Quechua and Māori, strong cultural identities, collectivistic capabilities, and knowledge embedded in their holistic/collective well-being philosophies provide them with the basis to claim their rights to land and its resources, especially when other entities infringe upon those rights and resources in the name of capitalism and colonialism.

Beyond Peru and Aotearoa, other similar examples are found in India. For example, Navdanya International, led by Vandana Shiva, champions sustainable agriculture, biodiversity, food sovereignty and the rights of small farmers.[31] Slow Food Peru, which is part of the global Slow Food grassroots organization founded in 1989, is led by Indigenous farmers and seed keepers to prevent the disappearance of Indigenous and local food cultures, traditions, and seeds.[32] In Turtle Island, many Native nations are part of women-led "seed rematriation" movements that reclaim maternal powers for restoring sacred understandings of ecosystems and culture through food growing and seed-sharing practices. These Indigenous-led food sovereignty initiatives enact the self-determination of Indigenous peoples over their food futures and provide beacons of hope and roadmaps for humanity to pursue sustainability in food systems for all.

Quechua and Māori Ontologies of Land

The third similarity is that Indigenous ontologies of land are anchored on relationality and reciprocal obligations among humans and non-humans. I witnessed distinct ontologies of land from societies resisting settler colonialism and their ongoing resilience and resurgence in relation to ancestral foodways and food traditions and practices. The narratives that I present in this chapter helped me recognize two things. On the one hand, I saw ontologies of land from two Indigenous societies living in settler-colonial countries seeking to revitalize their ancestral lands and food systems through their own traditions and practices. On the other, I saw how they differ from a settler ontology. As discussed in chapter 1, colonization works to commodify, dispose of, and extract economic value from land, unwrapping the diverse ways the land is constituted and contested for food security and food sovereignty objectives. For some Indigenous peoples, as well as peasants and other agriculturists, settler colonialism and its tactics of land dispossession are imbued with relations of power and domination.

An example is the Doctrine of Discovery that has been deployed in extant struggles for land-grabbing. Environmental injustice is experienced as more than alienation from a means of subsistence production. If the land—Pachamama/Papatūānuku—is taken away from Quechua and Māori, if the lakes or the rivers are polluted, if the mountains are exploited, if the valleys are fragmented, land-people links will be disrupted.

Thus, depriving Indigenous peoples of their ancestral lands represents the disruption of "collective food relations," which underscores how the value of food relates to the self-determination and well-being of human groups such as urban communities of color and Indigenous peoples, among many other groups, to govern their political, cultural, and legal food systems.[33] Adrienne Puckey explains how the process of settler colonialism in Aotearoa began as soon as the Treaty of Waitangi was signed in 1841. In less than ten years, in the 1850s, Māori of the North Island of Aotearoa were subjected to the disruption of their cultural-land/resource connections with Papatūānuku. Puckey notes that the spread of the capitalist ideology largely triggered the decline of Māori traditional agriculture practices in the North Island of the country. Under this ideology land British settlers claimed to own Māori land and used it for commercial products such as tobacco and kauri gum.[34] Māori food studies scholars argue that dispossession of Māori from their land is a breach of the Treaty of Waitangi and contributed to the decline of flourishing Māori food communities and with that the disintegration of cultural-land based knowledge.[35]

Thinking through the different ways land is understood and experienced provides a window into the role of land ontology in movements for social and environmental justice for Indigenous peoples. The goal of these social and political Indigenous movements is to preserve the integrity of Mother Earth and Indigenous identity, culture, languages, heritage, livelihoods, and transmission of TEK from one generation to the next. It is unsurprising that "Pachamama is my mother" and "I am tangata whenua" are the phrases that stood out to me when I asked Quechua and Māori research collaborators for their thoughts on improving food security and soil health. Indigenous leader Dionisio Foco from the Quechua community of Ccachin explained this concept: "To me, Pachamama is my mother! A mother express love and cares for her children through multiple nourishing gestures, and so does Pachamama by gifting us many things. If you look around, we have plenty of gifts from her—potatoes, corn, beans, muña [plant medicines], llamas and cuys [Andean animals]."[36] In a similar vein, in Aotearoa Fred Tito of the Wai A Ariki Onerahirahi [Food Forest] garden said: "Papatūānuku for me: well ... it's everything. It is a bond we Māori have with her since we are born. Whenua is our Māori word for land, which also means placenta. Yes, I am referring to the placenta that nourishes a baby in the womb. Knowing that I am the offspring of Papatūānuku [Mother Earth] and Rangi [Father Sky] influences how I think and behave toward others and with the whenua [land]; it just plays such an important part of who I am as tangata whenua."[37]

Tenaiti Tereo of Ngāti Porou explained his intrinsic bond with the land by speaking metaphorically about the whenua, as in the land and as the placenta or afterbirth. He said, "As tangata whenua, you are born from the land where you live, and so you have authority in a particular place. The pito [umbilical cord] and whenua [placenta] of newborn babies are buried in a place that holds significance for you and your whānau [family]. You know where your roots come from. Like the whenua of my mokopuna [grandchild], was buried up here with mine so he can whakapapa [trace his genealogy] to here. I actually found my one, where it was buried. It was where I was told it would be when I was a kid. So, I went to this place, and I dug down about one meter (three feet), and there it was; I knew it would be there."[38] Study partners across both Māori tribes mentioned that after a Māori woman gives birth, the placenta and umbilical cord of the baby is buried in a special place, usually at the whānau's tipuna (sacred mountain), where no one can walk over it. In the Māori worldview, they descend from and return to Papatūānuku. Such understandings elicit traditional Quechua and Māori ontologies of the land, personified in Pachamama/Papatūānuku or Mother Earth. In this study, the land is more than an agricultural space. The land is the sacred space. In it all forms of life flourish through the nurturance of Pachamama/Papatūānuku, and this is vital to the well-being and sustenance of humanity.

Quechua and Māori understandings of land reflect a distinctive Indigenous way of being in the world and ways of knowing oriented by their laws of origin and creation stories. These stories give sense to their existence as one of many components in the complexity and diversity of the web of life, none of which are arranged in a hierarchical way. Mason Durie explains that Papatūānuku provides "a symbol of continuity with those who have passed on, and respect for land augments one's strength.... [T]he health history of Māori people would confirm the central importance of land to health."[39] This study resonates with Durie's reasoning and shows evidence that Māori perspectives of being and belonging to Papatūānuku establish a spiritual, cognitive, emotional, and physical connection with it and others who emanate from Papatūānuku. A clear example is the Māori customary practice of burying the placenta within the whenua to which the child belongs as a symbolical of cultural identity affirmation, forming the basis of the concept of tūrangawaewae (a place to stand), as I will discuss in chapter 5. Tūrangawaewae asserts Māori identity as inextricably linked with their ancestral lands. On death, the relationship is once again affirmed through the return of the tūpāpaku (body) to Papatūānuku.

In many Indigenous contexts, the land is not an object of management but a cultural-spiritual relationship between all living and non-living elements. As food sovereignty scholar-activist Dawn Morrison (Secwepemc) states, Indigenous eco-philosophies reinforce the belief that "humans do not manage the land, but instead can only manage our behaviors in relation to it."[40] Therefore, Indigenous ontologies reject the belief that humans are separate from and superior to Nature. Quechua and Māori research partners expressed that the dominant Western paradigm of Nature hinders their food systems. This Western perspective is exemplified in monoculture agriculture wherein seeds are reduced to a raw input for agribusiness. It reflects a rational and controlling approach of Nature for economic exploitation only. In this sense, the capitalist ideology of land, which sees the environment as existing independently from humans and as the principal (if not sole) end of concern, undermines Indigenous peoples' ontologies of land and their capacity for autonomy and self-determination.

Indigenous TEK: Mātauranga Māori and Yachay Quechua

The fourth similarity between Quechua and Māori is traditional ecological knowledge (TEK), which as I explained earlier, is a reservoir of Indigenous science and agroecological methods and skills that are richly embedded in spiritual practices and traditional agricultural and technological innovations. In this study, I found core similarities of the TEKs in the sustainable food systems of Quechua and Māori, which are evident in their cultural foodways and environmental stewardship. The TEK of Māori—mātauranga,[41] or "Māori knowledge"—encompasses Māori worldviews, traditions, values, ethics, concepts, and philosophies. Similarly, the Quechua TEK, known as yachay,[42] reflects the unique ways of knowing and being of the Quechua people.

In precolonial Aotearoa, Māori traditionally organized their food production into gardening and fishing circuits dictated by soils, fish stocks, and the Māori maramataka.[43] Oral traditions about Māori traditional food systems have played a key role in transmitting mātauranga and food ethics, and such traditions have been passed down through generations in the form of rituals and ceremonies as well as written sayings and proverbs.[44] Aotearoa's climate is complex thanks to a temperate zone influenced by oceanic climates that covers diverse areas from the subtropical to alpine due to elevation and proximity to the Ocean. Traditional Māori[45] adapted tropical imported foods that arrived either with the first Polynesians or later colonial contacts such as the kūmara (sweet potato), taewa (Māori potato), taro, and gourd to their new environments and tested new food storage systems such as the pātaka kai, a communal store house or pantry.

The horticultural skills of Māori are attributed to the mātauranga, teaching them that yams and taro survived only in warm regions while the kūmara only survived in winter periods if stored underground.[46] Another key mātauranga technological innovation shaping traditional Māori food systems is the maramataka, the Māori lunar/moon calendar. It has proven invaluable in the face of threats that climate change can disrupt food availability and affect food quality. Specialists in Māori astronomy such as the maramataka were known as tohunga kokorangi (astronomer) and tohunga tātai arorangi (knower of celestial bodies). Traditionally only a select few Māori had in-depth understanding of this knowledge and it was their role to guide their community in using it. One of them is Rereata Makiha, who has tribal affiliations to Te Mahurehure, Ngāti Pakau, and Tuhourangi/Ngāti Wahiao in the North Island of Aotearoa. He told me: "We are reviving the mātauranga Māori of our tupuna [ancestors]." He went on to explain that he is experiencing a revival of the use of the maramataka in both rural and urban areas. He said "Thanks to this

Figure 8. A pātaka kai, a communal food store house in the Hamilton Gardens, in the Waikato Region of the North Island of Aotearoa. Photo: Mariaelena Huambachano.

mātauranga of the maramataka, Māori can foretell suitable times for fishing and harvesting crops, enabling them to adapt to changes in the climate to produce adequate amounts of foods for the community."[47] Rangi Mātāmua, another respected Māori maramataka knowledge holder, explained that the maramataka is based on the phases of the moon, the timing of the solstices, and the movements of heavenly bodies across the night sky, all of which provide indications of optimal times for the growing of food.[48] Following the European settlement in Aotearoa, timekeepers such as clocks and the Gregorian or monthly calendar system progressively replaced the use of the maramataka. Also, the value of mātauranga Māori as a valid body of Indigenous science remains contested in modern Aotearoa.[49] However, Māori research collaborators continue to acknowledge mātauranga as a unique body of Māori knowledge. They also attested to the prevalence of the maramataka in Aotearoa today and of its value in informing them of the actual days on which particular food and its related activities are or are not advised to harvest. Rereata explained that Matariki (the constellation known in English as the Pleiades) plays a vital role in informing the Māori maramataka. Matariki is an abbreviation of 'Ngā Mata o te Ariki Tāwhirimātea' (The eyes of the god Tāwhirimātea). As Rereata explained, "if Matariki is seen to twinkle in brightly, it is a sign that the year will be a good one for growing kai and the fruits and vegetables will be vast and plentiful." One of the key features of the maramataka is observing the Matariki stars that signal the Māori New Year. The Matariki celebrations commence with Hinamarama, the new moon following the heliacal (dawn) rising of Matariki. The Matariki festival represents the completion of one year and the approach of another in the Māori calendar. A lunar cycle consists of 30 moon nights or 29.5 days. In June, Matariki occurs at the end of the harvest season, and pātaka kai (storage houses) were filled with food, especially kūmara. Also, the sea's bounties were present with an abundance of fish like moki and korokoro. Before the new moon in Pipiri (June-July) of the Matariki year, a karakia (prayer) can be done to end the year and acknowledge all the work that has been accomplished during this time. Some use this time for reflection, and to discuss goals and aspirations and plan for the year to come.

Similarly, yachay[50] imbues Quechua cosmovision, Indigenous science, customary laws, and practices. At various times, I learned that this body of Indigenous TEK is vital in preserving local agroecological practices and soil health management for safeguarding the biodiversity and food sustenance of Quechua communities and all Andean people. One such time was when I observed how Quechua farmers use their yachay on astronomy to forecast suitable weather seasons for agricultural production. At a talking circle on the Inka calendar, my Quechua research partners were discussing their observations of the Pleiades star cluster. The Inka calendar[51] is based on a solar year of 365 days. It consists of 12 lunar months of 30 days each, with each month having its own festival, and an additional 5 days. My Quechua research collaborators use the Inka calendar for agricultural purposes, religious ceremonies, and other important events.

Valentina Avilés of Pampacorral explained, "My taita [grandfather] is the one who has a vast knowledge of the Inka calendar. Every year on June 24 at 3:00 a.m. or 4:00 a.m., our paqos (Elders) gather around the high mountains to observe the Qollqa (a set of dark or black constellations) that is very important for guiding our agricultural system and food security. If the stars are opaque, it will be a dry year, so we are alerted about water shortages to irrigate our crops and begin finding solutions to mitigate them. But if the stars are bright, it will be a wet year, and our crops will grow healthy."[52] Delia Qocha of Ccachin said: "We listen to our environment and follow local environmental indicators such as animals and wild plants. When the atoq [fox] cries or sings, he transmits a special squeal that goes like this: 'Wuaccaccaccacc'— and so it is a long squeal and gives the impression of laughter or happiness, and therefore the year will be a rainy season. But when the atoq is crying or making a small and unique sound that goes like this: 'waccaccc'—then the year will be a bad one."[53]

Crisostomo Quispe of Choquecancha explained that members of his community also listen to the sound of the air and look at wild plants such as añapanco (cactus) or turnip to predict agricultural seasons and prepare a contingency plan. He said, "The añapanco is a wild plant that is hardly noticeable, but when you see it growing in our ayllu [community], there will be food scarcity. So we all discuss potential traditional methods to counteract water scarcity, plant diseases, and plagues."[54] These narratives refer to the comprehensive astronomical knowledge of the Quechua people and its role in guiding the efficiency of their agricultural system inherited from their Andean ancestors, who were master agriculturalists and experts in the domestication of crop species that created the biodiversity and identified genetic strains that can resist climate change.

In October 2018, I visited Moray, one of the largest agricultural terraces of the Inkas, located at an altitude of approximately 3500 meters above sea level (11,500 feet). During this visit, I learned that before the arrival of the Spaniards in 1532, Moray was a strategic agricultural research station. Here the Inkas domesticated approximately seventy crop species, including potatoes, corn, and chili.[55] In precolonial times, Andean food scientists experimented with seeds to determine which plants were more resilient to extreme weather conditions of the highlands to ensure biological agricultural preservation. They then purposefully spread the biological species and the knowledge of how to cultivate these new varieties of seed throughout their empire. Inkas imparted agricultural wisdom and seed varieties to all community members, underscoring the

Figure 9. Quechua collaborator Marisol Quispe holding seeds of paracay, a native yellow corn, as she explains the seed-saving process of drying seeds and selecting them for their flavor, beauty, resilience, and abundance. Photo: Mariaelena Huambachano.

value of Indigenous TEK and seed sovereignty to preserve the continuity of their food self-sufficiency and to ensure that everybody had access to these seeds for the greater common good of society. Also, in conversations with Quechua research collaborators I learned of the importance of having an ecologically sustainable and resilient seed system, which has been and continues to be vital to the efficacy of safeguarding the Quechua peoples' food security.[56]

Drawing from their cultural and intergenerational TEK, Quechua research collaborators remain consistent with carefully selecting seeds to save, cross-pollinate, and exchange with other nearby communities to bolster the resilience of their seed systems and agrobiodiversity. Seed keepers Sonia Quispe and Maria Titto of Choquecancha enthusiastically acknowledged Andean agrobiodiversity in the abundance of their crop varieties: "We grow more than fifty varieties of corn here in Choquecancha."

Figure 10. Quechua seed keeper Maria Titto enthusiastically explains Andean agrobiodiversity while holding a basket of coca leaves and one of the vast varieties of native corn grown in the Lares Valley. She wears the traditional clothes of Choquecancha: a black skirt, a colorful shawl, and hat that are all hand-knitted. Photo: Mariaelena Huambachano.

Indeed, Peru has one of the highest levels of agricultural biodiversity/ agrobiodiversity in the world. For example, Peru is home to over 4200 varieties of potatoes,[57] as well as other valuable Andean food crops such as corn, tubers such as uqa,[58] plants like quinoa,[59] and root crops like maca.[60] However, despite evidence of Indigenous TEKs, as in the case of mātauranga Māori and yachay Quechua, contributing to realizing sustainable food systems, my Quechua and Māori research partners discussed their struggles over recognizing and preserving Indigenous TEK, the sustainability of their lands, foods, and seed sovereignty.

Indigenous peoples in both countries and around the globe are grappling with issues of toxic organochlorine pesticides, herbicides, chemical fertilizers, and genetically modified (GM) crops.[61] Since the early 1980s, GM crops, a term that refers to plants with genetic information that has been altered by introducing genes from another species, have been developed in laboratory settings to increase agricultural production. Since 2018, the intensification of investment in GM crops, including traditional Indigenous food crops such as maize, has been led by what food systems scholar Philip Howard described as the "big four" agrochemical firms: Bayer, Baden Aniline and Soda Factory, Corteva, and Sinochem.[62] GM crops have been highly controversial since their introduction. On the one hand, proponents assert the use of GM crops are necessary to produce sufficient food to feed a world population expected to reach 9.7 million by 2050, reduce the application of pesticides, and adapt agricultural systems to the ever-increasing challenges of climate change. On the other, opponents cite their potential to harm human health, the decline of biodiversity, and the displacement of small-scale and Indigenous farmers by multinational agri-business firms.

Quechua and Māori have long resisted GM crops as incompatible with protecting their Indigenous science, traditions, and ethics and endangering their sovereignty capacities over their traditional foodways and their ability to produce, distribute, and consume food. In solid opposition to the use of chemical pesticides, herbicides, and genetic engineering of plants and animals on Māori soils, in 2022 Te Waka Kai Ora (the National Māori Organics Authority of Aotearoa) produced the report "He kai te rongoā he rongoā te kai (food is medicine, medicine is food)," conveying their struggles to preserve Māori foods systems. An understanding of political and environmental instruments such as the Waitangi Tribunal and Wai 262 claim is essential to explain the significance of this report in defending Māori traditions, moral principles, and mātauranga of sustainable food systems. In 1975, the New Zealand government established the Waitangi Tribunal. This permanent commission of inquiry considers and makes recommendations on claims brought by Māori about Crown acts or omissions that breach the promises made in the Te Tiriti o Waitangi 1840 (Treaty of Waitangi). Examples of such breaches include the loss of Māori tribal land and Crown suppression of the Māori language and culture through the education system and laws such as the Tohunga Suppression Act 1907, which was intended to stop the use of traditional Māori healing practices.[63]

The Wai 262 claim, otherwise known as the "flora and fauna" claim, is about restoring and enhancing the mauri (life essence, well-being) of tangata whenua (Māori) and of all native species of flora and fauna. It seeks to establish the ownership and use of Māori knowledge, cultural expressions, and Indigenous species of flora and fauna, all of which are known as taonga (treasures), and inventions and products derived from Indigenous flora and fauna and/or utilizing Māori knowledge. The Wai 262 claim was first lodged with the Waitangi Tribunal in 1991 by six claimants on behalf of themselves and their six different iwi (tribes): Haana Murray (Ngāti Kurī), Hema Nui a Tawhaki Witana (Te Rarawa), Te Witi McMath (Ngāti Wai), Tama Poata (Ngāti Porou), Kataraina Rimene (Ngāti Kahungunu), and John Hippolite (Ngāti Koata). The claimants map out how the denial and deprivation of tino rangatiratanga, a Māori term that broadly translates to sovereignty and self-determination guaranteed in Te Tiriti o Waitangi, have led to breaches of the Treaty.

Drawing from the importance of tino rangatiratanga in Māori political and cultural affairs, the claimants asserted that, consistent with tino rangatiratanga recognized in Article 2 of Te Tiriti o Waitangi 1840: "Iwi hold all rights relating to the protection, control, conservation, management, treatment, propagation, sale, dispersal, utilization and restrictions on the use of Indigenous flora and fauna and the genetic resources contained therein."[64] The He kai te rongoā he rongoā te kai report provides evidence that modifying genes within an organism and across species profoundly disrupts the organism's well-being, spirit or soul, and cosmogenealogy that Māori consider sacred. In Indigenous cosmogenealogical terms, food helps communicate intergenerational knowledge. It is part of the whakapapa (genealogical) relationships between people and all aspects of the natural world, including lands, waters, animals, insects, stars, and soil microbes. Because of this, GM crops pose threats to Indigenous flora and fauna and thus to food systems, the environment, and the continuance of traditional Māori knowledge.

In April 2011, Peru experienced widespread protests, especially in the capital city of Lima, in response to the potential approval of the cultivation and breeding of Genetically Modified Organisms (GMOs) and other transgenic products in Peru.[65] The widespread support for a GMO-free Peru was ignited by Indigenous and local farmers, intellectuals, scientists, chefs, restaurant owners, non-governmental organizations, politicians, and other civil society members from around the country. They came together to preserve Peru's biodiversity and agrobiodiversity through the conservation of traditional varieties of native seeds and farming methods. The protests to reject the cultivation and trade of GM crops in Peru's soil reflect the grit and determination of Indigenous Peruvian farmers and allies to protect ancestral knowledge, biodiversity, family farming, and culture-related food practices. As result, in December 2011, Peru's newly appointed Peruvian President Humala signed a ten-year moratorium imposing restrictions on the trade and usage of GM crops in Peruvian agriculture.[66] Following an extensive campaign led by more than thirty organizations, under the banner "Biodiversity Is Our Identity: United for a GMO-free Peru," a second moratorium was passed in January 2021 prohibiting the production of GM crops until December 21, 2035.[67] However positive this result, these events illustrate the threat that Indigenous peoples continue to endure in the twenty-first century under a capitalist food system. They reaffirmed my determination to support the Indigenous peoples of Peru, Aotearoa, and globally in conserving the knowledge and practices of their biological resources, such as native seeds, against large food corporations and governments' economic interests.

Although the TEK of these two Indigenous groups is place-based, they provide evidence of the similarities of their bodies of science and resilience in relation to sustainable food systems that could yield valuable information and knowledge for other Indigenous peoples in different contexts, enabling the scaling up of Indigenous TEK in sustainable agriculture and food sovereignty. (I discuss this in greater detail in chapter 6.)

Spiritual Well-Being

The fifth shared commonality is spiritual well-being. In understanding Quechua and Māori conceptions of well-being linked to foodways, there emerges, in distinctive ways, a relational, fundamental thinking and living grounded in spirituality that alchemically infuses energy in the balance between humans, non-human species, and Earth herself. In this study, food traditions such as feasting, ritual, and ceremonies pay tribute to the spirits of the Quechua and Māori ancestors and are used to connect and maintain the human and other-than-human worlds in equilibrium. The ultimate goal is to realize a "holistic balance," that is, to preserve Indigenous cultural and spiritual knowledge through maintaining a balance between one another and with the natural and spiritual worlds. Spiritual energy is ever-present in the Andean highlands of Peru. The month of August is of great significance for the Runakuna of Ccachin, Sacaca, Pampacorral, and Choquecancha because it is the month when Pachamama, the feminine representation of the natural world and force on Earth, is the most fertile. In this month, the Andean world celebrates with a Ch'alla (Andean ritual) to Pachamama.[68] Offerings are brought to Pachamama and other deities—or wakas, in Quechua—such as the mayu (rivers), for enabling them to get fish, and qochas (lakes), as thanks for providing water to their animals and food crops. "In August, we all decorate our houses, cook traditional dishes, and perform many offerings to Pachamama to express our gratitude for all her gifts given to us: food, water, shelter," Valentina Pillco of Rosaspata explained.[69]

In traditional Māori spiritual beliefs and practices, everything has mauri—birds, trees, rivers, stones, people—individually and collectively. Mauri is translated as the "life force, energy, and essence of life." Reverend Māori Marsden describes "a clear distinction between the essence (mauri) of a person or object and the distinct realm of the spirit which stood over the realm of the natural order and was indwelt by spiritual beings" among Māori. Mauri, he notes, is the life force that generates and regenerates and upholds creation, and it is the bonding element that gives creation its unity in diversity.[70] Thus shifts in mauri of any part of the environment—for example, through use—would cause changes in the mauri of other components of the ecosystems. Ultimately the whole system shifts. For example, through karakia (prayer) Māori preserve the mauri of food and rejoice when the life essence or mauri of the food is preserved. Through karakia, they access a spiritual human-nature connection. During my time working with Māori in the revitalization of their foodways, I learned that Māori food-growers, gardeners, and cooks prioritize enhancing the mauri of food crops because to diminish mauri is to decrease the capacity to support other life: without mauri, all things cease to exist. The value of preserving and supporting the mauri in Māori lifeways and foodways is of utmost concern for Māori, as Uncle Percy Tipene of Ngāti Hine said: "It is important to protect the mauri and, thus, the health of the various elements of your māra kai (food garden) to ensure the quality and integrity of the food it produces is high and that the people who consume it are healthy."[71]

Intergenerational Equity and Justice

The sixth shared philosophy is intergenerational equity and justice. Both Quechua and Māori emphasize promoting egalitarian relationships between members of society (without class, gender, and generational hierarchies) when producing foods. After colonization these practices continue to play an important role not only in identifying self-representations but also (and, perhaps, more importantly) in safeguarding healthy food systems. In both the Quechua and Māori cases, their love of and respect for Pachamama/Papatūānuku, as well as their values and ethics, are drivers of unity and solidarity in developing tribal policies about the preservation of biodiversity and the revitalization of food sovereignty to guarantee living well for all. These two Indigenous groups are reconfiguring what well-being means to them by resisting capitalism and the dominant intensive, industrial approach to farming, both of which disrupt their spiritual and cultural relationship to food systems. By adhering to cultural practices, such as working as a collective in the chakra and māra kai, and by embracing traditions such as food rituals, these communities reestablish relationships with their human and non-human kin and pass on this knowledge to the younger generation through experiential learning.

The philosophy of equity and justice is paired with the concept of accountability. As caretakers of the land, Quechua and Māori express respect for Nature through the practice of ceremonies and rituals. Through these they renew their gratitude and deep respect for terrestrial and marine landscapes. They also demonstrate a profound responsibility to care for the integrity of ancestral territories by acting as their guardians, caring for Pachamama/Papatūānuku and all life forms through a nurturing approach that minimizes or prohibits exploitative actions such as hydraulic fracturing ("fracking") and over-exploitation of food resources. A kinship-centric approach that links the human and non-human world is acknowledged in the equitable sharing of seasonal resources between men, women, and children and in the teachings imparted by the collective to live sustainably with all elements of Nature. An example of this shared commonality is the practice of reciprocity, which articulates the moral obligation and spiritual practice to only take what you need from the land without depleting the environment for the next generation. Another practice that elicits reciprocity is the sharing of communal work in farming and equitable trade of goods or services between individuals and with broader communities, forming the basis of a just society. Practices of respect, love, care, and reciprocity encapsulate accountability, and from this basis comes the understanding that this thinking can enrich or diminish our lives. It is vital to pay attention to how Indigenous communities understand accountability because, by mapping the relationships within which we stand, we also map a system of accountability entailing respect, care, and responsibility to protect Nature and our extended kinship-centric communities.

The development of the Khipu Model, a knowledge-based research framework that is transparent and attuned to Indigenous ways of acquiring knowledge, is based on the two communities' understanding of accountability. As I explained in detail earlier, the Khipu Model focuses on research with and for the benefit of Indigenous communities, highlighting the ethical considerations and mutual responsibilities between the researcher and study communities in knowledge production. The Khipu Model includes a community-based participatory research approach, ethical protocols, and cultural guidelines emerging from Quechua and Māori traditions. The way I framed the Khipu Model in collaboration with Quechua and Māori enabled me to form substantial, trusting, reciprocal, and respectful relationships with Quechua and Māori communities, which I consider indicators of accountability as a researcher working with Indigenous communities.

ONE BREATH: INDIGENOUS PEOPLES LEADING A WELL-BEING AGENDA

Across the world, Indigenous peoples are making decisions to bring their peoples into the future while retaining their traditions, knowledge, values, and principles. Indeed, Indigenous peoples and their allies are driving a meaningful dialogue on alternative understandings of living well. At the international level, in the early 2000s, a joint effort between the United Nations Permanent Forum on Indigenous Issues and the International Indigenous Forum on Biodiversity mobilized a coalition proposing indicators of well-being relevant to the living conditions and ways of knowing of Indigenous peoples. Through a series of regional and international workshops in 2006 and 2007, the coalition developed Indigenous indicators aimed at achieving the Millennium Development Goals and the work of the Convention on Biological Diversity.[72] The goal was to include and recognize Indigenous peoples' cultural, social, and economic nuances to develop better-informed sustainable development policies, programs, and research and to aid policymakers in decision-making about well-being. In South America, the recognition of Indigenous peoples' philosophies of living well was achieved in 2008 and 2009, when Ecuador and Bolivia amended their national constitutions to recognize the rights of Pachamama.[73]

Other proposals for designing and operationalizing indicators of well-being that are relevant to Indigenous peoples include the "Towards a Māori Statistics Framework" initiative in Aotearoa, which follows earlier innovations and transformations in Māori health policy.[74] In North America, Thomas Andersen and Birger Poppel,[75] academic allies to Indigenous peoples, developed a system for collecting data on the living conditions of the Inuit, Saami, and Chukotka people that emerged from those communities' ways of knowing and understandings of good living. This system urged the revision of previous models of measuring well-being that did not capture the effects of social, cultural, political, and economic changes impacting Indigenous peoples' living conditions in the Arctic. These examples are evidence of a paradigm shift from Western measurements of well-being to center Indigenous good living frameworks and policies to achieve a holistic understanding of health and well-being and develop better-informed policies and methods for measuring them.

Recently, Steve Gliessman, Harriet Friedman, and Philip Howard, renowned scholars in agriculture and food studies, asked, "What would societies and landscapes look like if food systems were designed to promote the good life?"[76] I expand this point of inquiry to ask how Indigenous peoples' philosophies—in this case, those of the Quechua and Māori—can contribute to fostering a more inclusive, equitable, and healthy food system in their own communities and at a broader scale. Chapters 4 and 5 address this question by focusing on allin kawsay and mauri ora's traditions, values, ethics, and their contributions to the discourse of sustainable food systems.

4 Allin Kawsay and Values and Principles for Sustainable Food Systems

> Quechua is more expressive than Spanish in conveying feelings that are characteristic of the Quechua soul: tenderness, affection, and love for Nature.
>
> —José María Arguedas, Canto Kechwa

On April 12, 2014, at 4:30 a.m., I departed from the Avenida Puputi, the local transportation hub in Cusco City. Forty-five minutes later, I was in the picturesque town of Pisac, in the Sacred Valley of the Inkas northeast of Cusco. In Pisac, you will find buses to other agricultural centers such as Ollantaytambo and Chinchero, which I had visited before. However, this time, I was interested in making the 2.5-hour bus ride from Pisac to the Calca market to catch the bus to the valley of Lares.

Lares is one of the eight districts that make up the province of Calca in the department of Cusco in Peru. It has an Andean geography with beautiful landscapes and is close to lagoons and snow-capped mountains. One of the main productive activities that provides food security for families in Lares is agriculture. The district of Lares presents a diversity of ecological zones, with many geographical contrasts that determine a great variety of genetic resources and a high level of biodiversity.

I lived with the local Quechua communities of Choquecancha, Ccachin, and Pampacorral in Lares for a year, from April 2014 to March 2015. During that year I traveled frequently to and from the Quechua community of Sacaca located in Sacred Valley of the Inkas to visit with various Elders, food growers, and seed keepers. I had visited them once before in 2013

Figure 11. View of the main entrance to the Valley of Lares located at 3200m (10,498 feet). Photo: Mariaelena Huambachano.

and would make annual visits (except in 2020 and 2021) thereafter. The Runakuna of these four Quechua communities always welcomed me, allowed me to work alongside them on their land, fed me delicious and nutritious foods, and nurtured me with affection as a family member. In the memory work that follows from fieldwork, I have explored the value of ancestral foodways of the Runakuna of Choquecancha, Sacaca, Pampacorral, and Ccachin through a land-based experiential learning approach. This has taken place while breeding and cultivating potatoes and corn, foraging, engaging in food exchange in bartering markets, and taking part in food rituals.

These actions helped me to understand that being able to grow, gather, cook, consume, and recirculate their ancestral traditional foods is a marker of Indigenous Food Sovereignty, which includes self-sufficiency, agency, food accessibility, health, and well-being. Indeed, my research collaborators in Choquecancha, Ccachin, Pampacorral, and Sacaca draw on ancestral traditions, values, and innovation embedded in a holistic Andean cosmovision to ensure the sustainability of their food systems and that food in their community is accessible to everyone. Granted, interpretations of these traditions vary even within those Quechua communities. In this chapter, I detail the interplay in their foodways of the Quechua tradition of ayllu (self-governance), values of ayni and mink'a (reciprocal work), cchaninchay (solution) and principles of yanantin-masintin (complementarity). I show how they foreground cultural, political, and ecological institutions, underpinning an ideology of well-being, or allin kawsay.

IN AYLLU, WE BREATHE, EAT, AND DANCE TOGETHER

I begin this memory work by describing the Andean tradition of ayllu. When the bus from Pisac, a village north of the Inka capital of Cusco, arrived at the main square of the town of Lares, it was approximately 10:00 a.m. After I bought some water and fruit, I hiked for about 2.5 hours to the home of Sonia Quispe, a resident of Choquecancha I had met on my preliminary field trip in 2013. She had invited me to stay with her and her family when I returned for field work. I would stay in Choquecancha for four months, then go on to Ccachin and Pampacorral for approximately similar periods. I got around by hiking or riding a bus. Another feature of my stay in the valley of Lares was the opportunity to visit with members of the Quechua community of Sacaca located in Pisaq.

One of the findings of this study is that the Quechua people's determination to safeguard traditional food systems and food security is anchored on the tradition of "ayllu," which I came to understand as a communal governance land system with social and political units bound together by rules of kinship affiliation. Petronila Quispe of Choquecancha told me: "Ayllu is our communal way of life. We all share the same understanding that our connection with Pachamama [Mother Earth], spiritual deities, animals, mountains, lakes, rivers, pastures, food crops, and wildlife is intimate and symbiotic—we are all interconnected. So in ayllu we all [meaning humans and non-humans] live together, respecting and caring for one another."[1] Perhaps one of the best ways to understand

Figure 12. While holding native potatoes, Crisostomo Quispe explains that in the ayllu of Choquecancha, they collectively decide how much food to cultivate, how many seeds to keep for the next season, and barter with nearby ayllus. Photo: Mariaelena Huambachano.

how the ayllu system works is through Quechua traditional food systems. In addition to producing a vital food resource, the cultivation of these traditional foods reveals the social, economic, and political fabric of the four Quechua communities transmitted from generation to generation and made possible through the tradition of ayllu. Research collaborators in all four communities described the composition of the ayllu in their communities as a sovereign system with three levels of administration:

the nuclear family level, the group of kinship families that share the same territory, and a larger organizing unit mobilized by all groups in the Lares Valley known as "ayllu Lares." The structure of the ayllu tradition highlights its effectiveness in the flourishing of the rich variety of all life on Earth known as biodiversity and by extension, sustainable food systems in these four Quechua communities.

Carmen Sicos of Pampacorral explained, "In ayllu, we decide who will cultivate specific seasonal food crops, how many seed varieties we keep for the next season, and how much food we exchange with a nearby ayllu. In this way, we don't exploit Pachamama [Mother Earth], and we don't waste food by growing what is needed only. This is how we preserve the well-being of Pachamama."[2] In line with this, I observed that the four Quechua communities deploy a "mutual nurturing" approach in cultivating wide varieties of potato, corn, plant medicines, and animal husbandry as sustainable approaches to biodiversity preservation, soil resiliency, and sustainability fundamental for sustainable food systems. Tubers such as potatoes and mashua, corn, and food plants like quinoa and amaranth[3] result from the caring, loving, and respectful relationship between the Runakuna of Ccachin, Pampacorral, Sacaca, and Choquecancha and Pachamama.

In a similar vein, Juana Suñiga, a resident of Ccachin, told me about the importance of each ayllu as a separate keeper of traditional ecological knowledge (TEK) in preserving sustainable livelihoods and biodiversity. She added,

> In Lares, we have three agroecological zones. The Quechua zone [is] characterized by a temperate climate, between 2300 (7,550 feet) and 3500 (11,500 feet) meters above sea level. The Suni zone has a temperate cold climate with a very dry environment and seasonal rainfall between 3500 (11,500 feet) and 4100 (13,500 feet) meters above sea level. And the Puna zone is characterized by its cold weather and is located between 4100 (13,500 feet) and 4800 (15,800 feet) meters above sea level.[4]

Each agroecological zone requires in-depth TEK and practices to predict what kind of crops, vegetables, and fruits can grow there. Indeed, I learned that each community has a unique TEK about what kind of potatoes can be grown at 4500 meters [14,700 feet], while citrus fruits will only survive up to 1800 meters (5,900 feet). To illustrate, the Runakuna of Sacaca located in the lower part of the highlands at approximately 2400 meters (8,000 feet) above sea level know that the temperate climate of this community is optimal to grow a wide variety of beans, vegetables, and native corn such as parakay, which is a long white corn widely consumed in Cusco. The Quechua community of Pampacorral, located at 3,200 meters (10,500 feet) is known for growing a rich variety of native potatoes and other varieties of tuber species like uqa, ulluco,[5] and mashua. Choquecancha is at approximately 3,850 meters (12,600 feet), and its farmers grow over fifty varieties of native corn seeds such as paraq'ay, waq'ankillay, and q'ello owina. They also cultivate edible plants such as kañihua[6] and raise livestock such as llamas, alpaca, sheep, and cattle.

Understanding these agroecological zones is crucial to preserve agricultural agrobiodiversity, such as native food crops and medicinal plants, within each and across all ayllus, especially amid the challenges of climate change. All community members across the four Quechua communities referenced issues they had experienced in the past five years with drought and increase in both fungal diseases and pests in the production of native potatoes. As Julio Sunco of Pampacorral told me, "The ranch (late blight) poses a big risk in growing our native potatoes here in Lares. We don't want to add fungicides to our crops that damage the health of the soil. This is why we need to work concertedly in ayllu to know about these diseases and use our knowledge about growing potatoes resistant to late blight to help maintain the genetic diversity of staple crops like potatoes."[7]

Lino Mamani from the Quechua community of Sacaca reinforced the fundamental role that the ayllu plays in biodiversity preservation and underscored the need to preserve Quechua traditions in light of outside threats to their ways of life and knowledge. He explained, "Living in ayllu, being respectful and kind to Pachamama and the living and non-living, influences greatly the health of our traditional foods systems now and [in] futures to come. Sadly, I learned the hard way that not everybody shares our ideology of allin kawsay." When I asked why this was the case, he explained that "beginning in [the] 1990s, people from the [Peruvian] Ministry of Agriculture came to the highlands bringing a new variety of potatoes seeds for us to grow in the chakra, which they called [improved] seeds. I remember we [Indigenous agriculturists] had to line up to receive a sack of these improved native potato seeds, two plastic bottles of pesticides, a pair of latex gloves, and some pamphlets written in Spanish about the benefits of these new seeds."8

In researching why the Peruvian government began supplying these new improved seeds to Quechua farmers in the highlands of Peru, I found that Peru's economic models of capitalism, neoliberalism, and globalization were at the heart of these efforts. Peru is an agrarian nation, a source of agricultural and biodiversity knowledge, and its lands gave birth to one of the major food crops worldwide—the potato. The country embraced neoliberalism progressively over the course of the 1980s to the 1990s. This suite of economic policies such as the lowering of taxes on corporations and the wealthy, liberalization of trade, and privatization of public goods is threatening the well-being of many. Neoliberal agrarian legislation in favor of farming based on growing one type of a crop at one time on a specific field destined for overseas markets provoked the efforts to dismantle the polyculture system formerly in place in which a field is sown with two or more crops at a time. Thus, Lino Mamani's experience with actions to undermine Indigenous ways of growing sustainable foods is not surprising. Yet his narrative underscores the agency, resilience, and determination of Quechua research partners to preserve their foodways. As he explained, "because we did not know the genetic makeup of these improved seeds and to get them [meaning the emissaries from the Ministry] off our backs, we came together and in ayllu agreed to grow these improved potatoes separate from where we grow our native potatoes. I am glad we talked over this matter because decades later we are finding more and more that the health of the soil where we grow those potatoes [from the improved seeds] is deteriorating and they do not grow as health-giving as our native potatoes. We know it is an indicator that our mother—Pachamama—is unwell." The communal decision to segregate the seeds from the government reflected a resilience that the Runakuna have long displayed.

Another example appeared in their response to the Peruvian government's elimination of the term "ayllu" in favor of the Spanish "Comunidad de campesinos" (Andean peasant community) in the twentieth century. As Rosita Huilca of Ccachin told me, "the politicians in the capital, those men in power since the 1930s and, worse, in the 1950s, came up with the idea of changing the Quechua name of ayllu to the

Spanish version of comunidades de campesinos. The intention was to disenfranchise us from our ayllu tradition by no allowing us to call it in our native language. So that they would leave us alone and not come up here, we all agreed to call it comunidades, but around here, we still call it ayllu."[9] Similarly Carmen Sicos of Pampacorral added, "in despite of the many struggles we face to preserve our traditions and language, we continue living in ayllu. We have full governance of our ancestral lands. This is how it has been done for centuries, and we continue practicing it and teaching it to our children to live in ayllu."[10] This narrative describes the agency of research collaborators to push back against laws and regulations imposed on to them that focus on profit maximization only and disregard the cultural and ecological landscapes of the Runakuna.

Since precolonial times, the Quechua communities where I visited have been embracing the ayllu tradition conveyed in their communal governance, agency, and autonomy over what, where, and by whom food is to be produced. These four Quechua communities prioritize local agricultural economies by producing food for their own families and then for community consumption, and they exchange any surplus through ch'alay (bartering) with other nearby ayllu. The ayllu is just as much a cultural characteristic of these highland communities as it is an agricultural strategy to ensure no one lacks food. It is an egalitarian society in its purest form, without established political or religious positions. It is historically and conceptually associated with a Quechua cosmovision grounded in a kinship-centered social unit in terms of ascribed human and non-human kinship groups.

Community members explained that living in ayllu means being part of a collective in which share the same interests and aims of building positive relationships between one another and their social and natural environments. Upholding the practice of communal ownership of all of the land's production, no private ownership of land exists. The Runakuna's continued use of the term ayllu is an expression of their resilience in maintaining their social fabric and assertion of their self-governance. The continued existence of the ayllu system relies heavily on the bonds built through the give-and-take of mutual relationships that constitute a concept I will explore next: the tight web of *ayni*.

WEBS OF RECIPROCITY FOR THE GREATER COMMON GOOD: AYNI AND MINK'A

Life in the four communities I visited revolves around "ayni," which is the abbreviation of the Quechua word ayninakuy, broadly interpreted as "reciprocity" or common good. Peruvian ethnohistorian Waldemar Espinoza explains that ayni originated in the Andean peoples' worldview of maintaining and reciprocating their intimate and sacred relationships with their gods, the earth, the sky, and the sea, and I observed this in the four Quechua communities I visited.[11] This study extends knowledge about the role of ayni in food systems by providing evidence that the ayni goes beyond trades between families. Rather, the ayni is a key ethical principle. As Bernardina Ttito of Choquecancha defines it, "ayni is a cooperation system transmitting principles of, for example, reciprocity, caring, and kindness."[12] Dionisio Quispe of Ccachin said, "Our ancestors have practiced ayni, and we practice it with our children, because without it we would not be able to cope with producing the food for ourselves and so we need the help and support of other families. And so with ayni, we can work our land and feed ourselves."[13] Ayni is widely understood by all Quechua collaborators to mean that people should only take that which can be taken from the land without depleting ecological systems, but its meaning goes beyond this.

In this study, ayni is a coherent food sovereignty strategy. It functions as the link within a community's cooperation system that ensures the social inclusion of community members, focusing on embracing equality and social fairness. Ayni is a humanistic and spiritual expression of "collective common good" achieved by working collectively in order to maintain an equilibrium with Pachamama, runas (humans), and the spiritual world to achieve allin kawsay. To illustrate this point, I observed that Quechua research partners embraced the belief that "all you give must be returned to you in its pure form," thus encapsulating the principle of reciprocity. They did this by graciously receiving the gifts in the form of foods of the land and sea from Pachamama, in return for which they safeguard her well-being. Expressing gratitude to her and extended non-human kin through rituals and ceremonies to honor the spirits of the ancestors is a way of maintaining that tradition. The success of ayni depends on each community's knowledge cooperation system or mutual aid. This system encompasses values of trust, solidarity, reciprocity, and work ethics of community members. The colloquial Spanish phrase "un dame y toma sin fín," or "give and take without end," which in Indigenous philosophy translates to "indefinite reciprocity," was widely recognized as the core value of ayni within the four Quechua communities.

Andean networks of reciprocal practices and exchanges form a historical, socio-cultural, and economic system that continues to evolve, and there are variations in its practices and the names by which it is known. For example, ayni connotes aid generally, whereas mink'a refers to aid in the form of work or labor exchange; generally, a mink'a involves two or more families working together who apportion their shared harvest. In both ayni and mink'a, there is an expectation that any assistance received should be repaid in kind. The distinction between mink'a and ayni is rooted in asymmetrical, reciprocal relations in which one party owes services to the other. Thus, the variations of ayni and mink'a modalities depend on the mechanisms in which a reciprocal kinship system takes place. These practices of reciprocity do not apply only to agriculture. Families build a number of work relationships to reciprocate, barter, and/or exchange goods and services, including such services as the erection of a dwelling.

Gomercinda Sutta of Pampacorral explained how broad the system is thus: "Earlier in the year, my family needed help in the chakra to grow our traditional food crops because my daughter was getting married at the end of the year. We used mink'a, and five families came to help us to grow enough food to serve to guests at my daughter's wedding without overproducing the land, and in reciprocity, we helped them, too. Also, in gratitude, once the mink'a [was] completed, we cooked a special dish called chiri uchu."[14] Chiri uchu is an Andean traditional dish made of cold meats, seafood, and Indigenous crops and vegetables. It is a symbol of chanikuy waqekuy. The term translates to "hospitality," but it actually encompasses reciprocity and gratitude through the act of growing, sharing, and enjoying food as a collective.

While the general meaning of the chiri uchu is uniform across the four communities, as a dish designed to boost collective well-being its composition differs because each ayllu grows specific food crops and animals and has distinctive knowledge and culinary techniques. For example, Petronila Quispe described her family's version of the dish: "Our chiri uchu dish has meats such as kuy [guinea pig], river fish, chicken, charqui [dry llama or alpaca meat], and chalona [dehydrated lamb meat]." The one I had in Sacaca included roasted corn, torreja (which has a texture similar to an omelet and is made of corn and pumpkin), cochallullo (algaes from the river or sea that are rich in proteins), and other traditional crops. Ayni and mink'a are not simply acts of trade-off between families. Rather, they represent Quechua research collaborators' values of generosity, gratitude, and respect toward Pachamama and with the web of life to ensure the collective common good. Through food rituals such as the chiri uchu, Runakuna try to keep a permanent equilibrium through ayni and mink'a with their community, their habitat, and their deities.

CCHANINCHAY: EMPOWERMENT THROUGH BUILDING FOOD SYSTEMS

In 2015, I held a talking circle in the Quechua community of Chawaytire on food security and climate change in collaboration with community members and main leaders of the communities of Choquecancha (Petronila Quispe), Rosaspata (Valeria Aviles), Sacaca (Lino Mamani), and Ccachin (Marisol Quispe). The Quechua word cchaninchay, which translates to "solution," emerged as a critical concept to understand in solving a problem with their household, communal, and regional food systems. As Lino Mamani explained, "Cchaninchay represents the solution to a food security problem. We help one another, especially the elderly, pregnant women, and the widows. We go and gather food on their behalf or with any household work they may need. In doing so, we all have a sense of responsibility to care for one another. We make sure all members of our ayllu are looked after."[15] Marisol Quispe added, "Cchaninchay for me means solution. Saving healthy seeds is an essential piece of our food security. But climate change threatens it. We have been facing droughts, so our food crops grew tiny, and others deformed. So, we collectivized to find a solution by selecting the most knowledgeable about seed saving. I helped because I know how to choose the best seeds even if deformed. If the kernels of the corn don't have hair, it means the corn will not grow. But if it has hair, that's a good seed to save. So, we found a solution together. That's cchaninchay." Thus, cchaninchay is understood as solutions to safeguard the well-being of community members. Cchaninchay is the least known of the four Quechua fundamentals; indeed, there is almost no mention of it in contemporary research. But, like the other fundamental values, it helps individuals and community members to strive for collective unity to maintain an equilibrium with the human, natural, and spiritual world for the attainment of allin kawsay.

YANANTIN-MASINTIN: COMPLEMENTARITY AND EQUALITY

The traditions of ayllu, ayni, mink'a, and yanantin-masintin are defining features of allin kawsay. Exploring yanantin-masintin as linked to allin kawsay emphasizes the importance of complementarity and equity in ensuring food-secured communities. Yanantin-masintin is rooted in the thinking that the polarities of existence such as male and female, dark and light, inner and outer are interdependent and essential, equitable parts of a harmonious whole. The term yanantin comes from the Quechua root yana, which in Spanish means "couple," two people who are romantically attached. The suffix -ntin pluralizes it, indicating that the action of the verb is performed in society or in the company of people, animals, or things.[16] Yanantin is the result of the application of a complementarian, hierarchical, interdependent opposition principle associated with the notions of masculine and feminine. Masintin is broadly translated to equality, identity, analogy, and correspondence. The Runakuna establish these norms between the components of two or more pairs of complementary opposites based on qualities or circumstances common to them. As Quechua collaborators told me, everyone and everything is connected to someone else, and together they form a complementary whole; therefore, equivalence is fundamental to harmonious living. Yanantin-masintin implies symmetric exchanges of balanced reciprocity, complementation, and with that, rights and obligations. When I asked about the meaning of yanantin-masintin, Runakuna quickly responded with the terms "warmi-qhari" (woman-man) and "inti and killa" (sun and moon). These words alluded to the complementarity and equality that they understand as important for preserving reciprocal and good relationships with one another and with non-human kin. I learned that in farming, male and female activities are conceptually distinct and complementary. For example, men and women help each other in agriculture by playing supplementary roles in the planting of seeds. Men plow the earth using the chakitaklla (Andean foot plow) and open the furrow, and women place the seeds.

The spring equinox marks the beginning of warmi pacha (fertility of women and of Pachamama) and the rainy season, which lasts until the end of March. In 2019, I attended another customary celebration during the spring equinox: the farming ritual of sata qallta (sowing time). During it I observed Runakuna of all ages cross the mountains, dancing and singing joyfully to revere their cosmic brothers and sisters—the sun, rain, air, and earth—and to ask for their consent to begin the sowing of the land. Once the cosmic brothers and sisters have granted permission for the beginning of the planting season, the ayllu leader proclaims that plowing season has begun by digging a hole into the ground with a chakitaklla (Andean foot-plow). Four women representing the sun, rain, earth, and air wear brightly colored polleras, a traditional large one-piece skirt made of cotton or wool decorated with colorful embroidery, embodying the vibrant soul of the Andean woman. Then comes the plowing, during which men and women plant male and female seeds so they can germinate and produce nutritious food. Afterward, the women greet their four cosmic brothers with joyful dances and chants and swing their colorful polleras around, creating the illusion of a bright rainbow. Then it is the men's turn to form four groups, representing the four basic principles of life: space, time, matter, and energy. Dancing together and digging the chakitaklla into the soil, they welcome the sowing season. The complementary roles of men and women to achieve food security are thus sanctified in this ritual. This Indigenous way of thinking, rooted in the importance of bringing the seemingly conflicting opposites into harmony without destroying or altering either one, is in stark contrast to patriarchy, a system of society or government in which men hold the power and women are largely excluded from it.

The narratives presented in this chapter provide insights of the Runakuna of the four Quechua communities' foodways, traditions, and cultural-spiritual food practices, which are the soul of Andean agriculture. The traditions and social, political, and ecological values and principles discussed above—ayllu (self-governance), ayni and mink'a (reciprocal work), cchaninchay (solution), and yanantin-mansitin (complementarity)—are not an exhaustive list. However, I chose them because they resonate with the essential traditions of Māori research collaborators, giving a strong sense of the meaning of Indigenous principles and values in achieving sustainable food systems, which I will explain in the next chapter.

5 Well-Being through a Māori Lens: Māori Principles and Values Linked to Sustainable Food Systems

Nāku te rourou nāu te rourou ka ora ai te iwi:
With your basket and my basket, we will sustain everyone

—Māori whakataukī (proverb)

I met Lionel Hotene in 2012. In July 2013, we worked alongside each other in the māra kai (food garden) at the Papatūānuku Kōkiri Marae in the south of Auckland City. While weeding and planting some kamokamo (Māori squash), Lionel asked me: "Have you heard about peruperu potatoes?" When I told him I had not, he said, "Oh! You should visit the East Coast and talk with the people there because they know more about the whakapapa (genealogy) of the peruperu potatoes, which I believe come from your country of Peru." Intrigued by this description, I sought out Māori farmers on the East Coast with whom I could begin to establish relationships. Yet, it was not until a conversation with Kiri Dell, a Māori scholar, friend, and colleague, that I was able to accompany her on a visit to her tribe of Ngāti Porou in April 2015. It was at this visit that I discovered shared commonalities between Quechua and Māori, as outlined in chapter 3. It was also during this time that the deep relationships I had formed with Māori food growers, kuia (female Elders), kaumātua (male Elders), Māori food sovereignty advocates, and scholars in both rural and urban settings who took part in this study were reaffirmed. All this helped me to understand some of the core cultural, ecological, and spiritual values that run deep in many aspects of the daily lives of Māori research partners.

CHAPTER 5

In this chapter, I explore the values and concepts of whakapapa (genealogical connections), mana whenua and mana moana (authority over lands and resources), kaitiakitanga (trusteeship, guardianship of the land), tikanga (ethical values and practices), and manaakitanga (hospitality) in relation to food systems. Yet I ask the reader to bear in mind that knowledge is not static, and ethical values and practices, which are numerous, diverse, and highly localized because each tribe has its own histories and customs, are always evolving.

WHAKAPAPA: I KNOW MY KIN AND WHERE I BELONG

It was a frosty morning, though bright and sunny, when I arrived on the East Coast of Aotearoa at the Gisborne Airport on April 8, 2015. I was reminded of the highlands of Peru, where spectacular misty mountains make everything feel dreamlike and pulsing with life. Kiri was already waiting for me at the baggage claim, just meters away from the landing area. "Kia ora! Welcome to Ngāti Porou," she said. Ngāti Porou is a Māori iwi (tribe) located on the East Cape of the North Island of Aotearoa. Kiri is of the hapū (sub-tribes) of Te Aitanga a Mate, Te Aowera, and Te Awe Mapara, situated near Ruatoria in the iwi of Ngāti Porou. With my fieldwork equipment placed in the trunk of her car, we embarked on a road trip to Whareponga, a rural Māori community of Ngāti Porou located close to the Waiapu Valley. Kiri drove along the East Coast scenic route, which offers views of high peak mountains, a distinct fauna with native trees such as mānuka and kānuka, native birds such as kereru, and endless beaches.[1] As we drove, Kiri told me about the rich history and culture of Ngāti Porou, in particular of her hometown of Whareponga. She explained that the Waiapu River is of immense cultural, spiritual, and economic value to local Māori and that she is known as Waiapu Koka huhua—the mother of many and abundance. After driving for two hours and veering east to the town of Ruatoria, which is situated four and a half miles north of Whareponga, we encountered a gravel road of roughly nine miles that leads to the end of the valley where the Whareponga marae (sacred meeting place) is located. The marae is nestled in beautiful hills clad in green bush, next to the moana (sea), and with an exposed cliff vista.[2]

Figure 13. The Whareponga marae is the meeting place of Māori with affiliations to the tribe of Ngāti Porou. Photo: Mariaelena Huambachano.

From Whareponga, I traveled to Tititiki, a small town in the Waiapu Valley near the mouth of the Waiapu River on the east coast of Tūranga-nui-a-Kiwa (Gisborne). There I visited with Keri Kaa. Over tea, I asked her to tell me about herself. She answered, "My name is Keri Kaa. My tribal affiliation is of Ngāti Porou. I am of descent of Porourangi, although my original ancestor is Māui. Then there is also Rangi and Papa, the parents of all the little gods that control Nature and are role models to everything else." She went on to list some of these gods, which she called atuas: Tangaroa, Tāne, Tāwhirimātea—the gods of the oceans, forest, and agriculture, who are all considered siblings. "If you think about it, we are all interconnected, and you give thanks to the atuas for everything you obtain from them," she said.[3] I thought of Lionel Hotene then, because when I asked him the same question he said, "My name is Lionel Hotene. I whakapapa to Ngāti Awa and Tainui. We all connect to the same ancestor. There's one ancestor who came on the waka (canoe): he is Chief Hoturoa, and everybody traces their ancestry back to him."[4] These similar Māori introductions reveal a central concept in Māori culture: whakapapa. Whakapapa mostly translates in English as "genealogy." However, its full, broad spectrum of meanings, such as "ancestral lineage," "relationships," and "links to ecosystems," extends far beyond the everyday understanding of genealogy as a family tree.

Whakapapa is a reservoir of knowledge of the Māori worldview. It is key to understanding Indigenous Māori views and the ethos of relating to the natural and social worlds. Thus, considering the integral role of whakapapa as the basis of Māori knowledge to which all other Māori concepts and values discussed in this chapter are attached, I seek to establish it early on as a fundamental element. The term consists of the prefix whaka, "causing something to happen," and the stem word "papa," which references the role of Papatūānuku (the land) that is entrenched in Māori worldviews. Whakapapa means, then, something like "to create a base or foundation" or "to make layers." "Genealogy" is another word that aims to capture the relationality aspect of whakapapa, in the sense that it helps to trace back genealogies of ancestors, family, and kin.[5] As Āpirana Turupa Ngāta explains, "Whakapapa is the process of laying one thing upon another. If you visualize the foundation ancestors as the first generation, the next and succeeding ancestors are placed on them in ordered layers."[6]

Thus, it is unsurprising that when I asked Keri and Lionel to tell me about themselves, they immediately recited their whakapapa, reflecting a philosophy of kinship and respect between human beings and all the rest of the elements of the natural world in which we live. Māori scholar Ngahuia Murphy argues that "our sacred stories carry the instruction of our tīpuna [ancestor] about proper conduct to maintain the balance."[7] This holds true in whakapapa cultural narratives of Māori research partners. They highlighted the Māori way of thinking, knowledge, and ethos that pertain to the health of the soil, water, living organisms, and everything else sustaining life on Earth to maintain a harmonious human-Nature balance. To illustrate, at the heart of a te ao Māori (the Māori world) are their primordial parents: Ranginui (Sky Father) and Papatūānuku (Earth Mother). Their children are the guardians of the natural world and its resources as articulated in Māori narrative of creation stories. In this narrative, the children of Ranginui and

Papatūānuku—from which emerged ecosystems, soils, fauna, and flora—sought ways of separating their parents because they were not content with existing in darkness (Te Po). Through the act of separating their parents and coming into the world of light (Te Ao Marama), the children themselves became tutelary gods of the divisions of Nature and the environment. Human beings emerge from this complex whakapapa assemblage (ancestral lineage) and continue to evolve with ecosystems.[8]

Whakapapa is vital in providing context for understanding Indigenous Māori ethical relationships between te taiao (the natural environment), Māori as tangata whenua, and atua (spiritual ancestor) for their food sustenance and livelihood. From this relational basis, all human and non-human beings—such as the land, rivers, plants, animals, and deities—have a mauri, an essence of life or life working capacities, and a wairua (spirit).[9] The traditional Māori food system originates within these creation stories. For example, Tangaroa became god of the oceans; Rongomātāne, god of the kūmara; Haumia, god of fern root, wild herbs, and berries; Tūmatauenga, god of war; and Rūamoko, god of earthquakes and volcanoes. In essence, the Māori believe that the environment shaped the traditional foods available for their consumption, which have a shared whakapapa, or a lineage and connection to the various offspring of Ranginui and Papatūānuku. In Māori traditions, kai (food) like the kūmara (sweet potato) have the power to carry the energy or essence of these gods to feed their bodies, intellect, spirit, and family. Whakapapa illuminates the layering of relationships between Māori and the wider community in which mountains and rivers are regarded as sacred, living entities. Knowing one's whakapapa is imperative for Māori cultural identity.[10]

While there is no single, exact measure of what constitutes Māori identity, determining a person's genealogical connection (whakapapa) to particular marae, hapū, and iwi is necessary for enjoying the many benefits of belonging to them.[11] But whakapapa plays a central role in relation to food systems too. This is because whakapapa is about understanding the ancestral connections not just with people, but with whenua tipu (traditional lands), mahinga kai (Māori customary food-gathering sites and practices), and māra kai (food gardens). This is particularly important for asserting a community's role as guardians or caretakers of the land.

Intimate understanding of food crops, seeds, and culinary knowledge extends whakapapa and strengthens connection with the land.

TIKANGA: ETHICAL VALUES AND PRACTICES

If whakapapa is key to understanding Indigenous Māori views of the natural and social worlds, tikanga is the set of beliefs guiding human behavior and ethical relationships between humans and non-living things that embodies the essence of being Māori.[12] Tikanga has been defined in many ways. Joan Metge describes it as "the right Māori ways."[13] Edward Taihakurei Durie defines it as the "values, standards, principles or norms to which the Māori community generally subscribed for the determination of appropriate conduct."[14] In *Tikanga Māori, Living by Māori Values*, Hirini Moko Mead states that all "tikanga Māori are firmly embedded in Mātauranga Māori."[15] Moko Mead argues that "tikanga, at one level, is conceptual and represents a set of ideas, beliefs and practices. At another level, it has to do with practice. Tikanga may be translated as customs (which applies especially to the practice of tikanga), or it might be referred to as a customary concept (which focuses on the set of ideas)."[16] This holds true in this study: research participants acknowledged tikanga as a diverse corpus of beliefs and practices shaping their lives and behavior and, ultimately, informing their attitude to harmonize relationships with all living and non-living kin for healthy food and well-being.

Tikanga is a very complex and dynamic concept. To understand it, I sat down with Rereata Makiha, a kaumātua raised in Hokianga in the North Island of Aotearoa, to discuss the role of tikanga in Māori food systems. He explained:

> The old people devised what we call tikanga for the different things that you do. One of them is karakia (prayer), rooted in tikanga. When you go and get medicine plants, the first thing you do in tikanga is asking permission from Tāne [god of the forest]. Showing [respect] and obtaining consent is important. Since you are going into Tāne's realm to collect your kai, you need to ask for his permission. And then you go and get your medicine, and then you say thank you. That's the basics of tikanga. And then you plant your crops; you go and do a karakia to Rongomātāne or Haumia-tiketike, to the

Figure 14. Tikanga practices have played, and continue to play, a vital role in Māori food traditions. This photograph of "splitting, boning and drying eels at Lake Forsyth, Canterbury" was taken in May 1948. Photo: K. V. Bigwood, Photographic Collection Ref: 1/2-040044-F, Alexander Turnbull Library, Wellington, New Zealand.

cultivator of plants. This is the tikanga I grew up with and one I still put into practice. I think it's like other Indigenous cultures around the world where you go and get permission to plant kai and ask all the gods to look after your kai.[17]

Here, Rereata explains that the ritualistic nature of tikanga influences the moral judgments of Māori about appropriate ways of behaving when growing food. A karakia is a vehicle for recognizing the duty to follow a morally correct path—to ask for consent from the plant, animal, or fish community to grow or gather food. The continuation of this practice within a māra kai context ensures intergenerational knowledge. Rereata names the ethical principle of "respect" as an additional tikanga practice of food production. "When I go to harvest things, I talk to the plants before I cut them. I ask for permission to pull them out from the soil. So even if people are growing food to sell, there still needs to be a process of [respect] in place. And you only take enough for you and leave the rest. You are not greedy, and this is what I grew up with—hard tikanga rules." Rereata's narrative conveys humans' moral obligation to their extended non-human kin, centered on the principle of respect, which permeates everyday interactions with the ecosystems and the services they provide to us. This moral responsibility is captured in narratives chronicled in many forms of oral and written tradition throughout Aotearoa, from the pātere (chant) Te Koko ki Ohiwa from the Bay of Plenty to the diaries of customary harvesters who have spent many decades harvesting muttonbirds as food.[18] Good tikanga practices through karakia energize the mauri (vital essence) of humans and the natural world; each has a mauri within them. Because of this, applying good tikanga practices strengthens a spiritual connection between humans and Nature.[19]

The application of tikanga within traditional Māori food systems ensures that all participants in the growing, harvesting, sharing, and continually growing food follow appropriate behavior to nurture the mauri of all human and non-human kin, who are vital actors in the production of kai. Tikanga Māori still reverberates in Māori culture; however, it was not easy for Māori to continue embracing and practicing this Indigenous concept in both their daily lives and in the growing of food. When the Europeans arrived in Aotearoa, they set about establishing their own socio-political institutions and religious beliefs.[20] The suppression of Māori knowledge since at least the 1860s, much of it instigated by government legislation, caused trauma and a rupture in their knowledge and value systems.[21] Two of the core Māori cultural concepts of tikanga and mātauranga (knowledge) were absent from school curricula for over a century; only the Māori arts, crafts, and dance were allowed by the government at schools in the 1930s.[22] However, the revival of Māori culture, language, customs, and traditions began in the final two decades of the twentieth century. Examples are the revitalization of the Māori language spearheaded by Hana Te Hemara in 1973 and the inclusion of tikanga Māori in the Education Act of 1989.[23] In Māori food systems, the revitalization of māra kai is a vital space for Māori to enact their rights to practice tikanga Māori and express their aspirations for leading healthy lives and flourishing as a collective.

Mana Whenua and Mana Moana: Authority over Lands and Resources

In this study, the influence of Māori on their ancestral territories encompassing both land and sea refers to the degree of customary authority that Māori have over their territories to enact their own authority. Thus, mana whenua refers to the people who have localized power.[24] This term is rooted in the words "mana" (authority) and "whenua" (land). Mana whenua relates to the mana held by local people who have "demonstrated authority" over land or territory, including the moana (sea) of a particular area. These Māori terms are a reminder of the power, energy, and vitality that derive from being from the whenua (including moana) and being Indigenous of Aotearoa. Thus, for Māori research partners knowing their whakapapa is paramount in establishing authority or mana over the people who occupy the whenua.

The concept of whakapapa, in connection with whenua, helps illuminate the influence of mana whenua in asserting the degree of Māori peoples' autonomy and self-determination over their food systems. Whakapapa plays a crucial role in Māori claiming and having influence over the whenua and moana because authority is established through the ability to prove whakapapa by reciting land and sea-usage stories and bloodline connections from an ancestor. According to Elizabeth Ngarimu of Ngāti Porou, "You can't claim land without proving your whakapapa. When my people went to the Native Land Court to gain title to this land, they had to prove that they whakapapa to this whenua."[25] The whenua is the resource that sustains the foods of the land and sea and, therefore, sustains the people. Thus, asserting mana over whenua and moana is pivotal for Māori in securing access to the land and sea and for the governance of their natural resources as the basis of a sustainable livelihood. It also makes it possible to exert absolute authority and to control the course of their own lives and the well-being of their communities.

Customarily, land tenure was vested in the community, and the main proof of entitlement was continued occupation and use, or ahi kā. This Māori land custom continues in modern Aotearoa, as Māori tribal leader Dr. Apirana Mahuika affirmed in his public statement on Māori authority over the land in August 2014: "Nōku te whenua, kei a au te kōrero—Nōku te whenua ko au te Rangatira (The land is mine, I have all the say. The land is mine; I make all the decisions)."[26] Whakapapa stories about Māori-land connections or ahi kā become powerful political statements asserting a person's or family's long-term occupation and use of a piece of territory, which ultimately influences land rights and entitlements. Ngarimu described the whakapapa link to the whenua of her own family: "Ngāti Porou is the iwi we all come under. Growing up here, we always had big gardens; we were and are a big family. Mum, dad, nanny, grandparents, great and great-grandparents all lived here holding ahi kā [keeping the home fires burning]. Currently, today, as a whānau, we're about 136, from our parents, the siblings, and our thirteen children and grandchildren and great-grandkids.... And that's not even counting the partners. Under Pākehā [a white New Zealander] law, my great-grandmother had to go to the Native Land Court to put the title to this land. This land is ours."[27]

Symbolically, whenua, as mentioned in chapter 3, means both land and placenta. In customary Māori practices, after a Māori woman gives birth, the pito (umbilical cord) and the baby's placenta are buried back in the earth. They are usually buried in a place of ancestral significance so that children can return to it to trace their whakapapa later in life. The action of returning the whenua (placenta) to the land reinforces the relationship between newborns and their tūpuna (ancestors) and with the whenua. Through these physical ties with and presence on the whenua, whakapapa is the instrument for Māori asserting mana whenua and mana moana (autonomy and land rights) over their ancestral territories.

However, since colonization, Māori had to endure the disruption to this human-whenua relationship, much to the detriment of the well-being of Māori. Fred Tito of the Wai A Ariki Onerahirahi (Food Forest) garden stated, "Much of Māori land was lost in the nineteenth century and against the will of my people. We are still experiencing trauma. We are in the twenty-first century and continue to experience the effects of losing our tūrangawaewae—our sense of belonging, foundation, and stability. Hopefully the tide is turning and there can be a better understanding of the importance of whenua."[28] Fred whakapapa, or has a direct lineage to, the Te Parawhau and Te Uriroroi subtribe of Ngāpuhi and also connections to Ngāti Whātua in the country's North Island. Tūrangawaewae is a portmanteau bringing together tūranga (standing place) and waewae (feet), meaning the place for the feet to stand. It refers to the foundation of being Māori, their identity, and their place in society.[29] Tūrangawaewae represents the bonding link between Māori and the whenua, the place for the feet to stand proud, because that place represents the people's roots and the sense of belonging to a place and home.[30] I learned that Māori, as tribal peoples, rely on a holistic view of the human-Nature-spiritual interdependence with the environment. Therefore, losing land disrupts their intrinsic spiritual bonds with Papatūānuku and extended non-human kin. It was Māori peoples' desire to reclaim mana whenua that motivated their activism in the 1960s and 1970s to stop the sale of Māori land; key examples of this activism are the two major lands protests—the Land March in 1975 led by Whinia Cooper and the occupation of Bastion Point in 1977.[31] The loss of ancestral lands continue to be a key issue for Māori who want to retain their traditions of growing food and use their agricultural knowledge, innovation, and practices to protect and enhance the well-being of their ancestral lands.

More recently, Aotearoa has witnessed Māori youth reclaiming their ancestral lands to restore and preserve their tūrangawaewae in the Māori village of Ihumātao so that future generations will have a place to stand. Located in the south of Auckland City, Ihumātao became a space of Māori resistance to land dispossession in 2016. It is one of the first places where Māori settled, farmed, and thrived as a collective as early as the fourteenth century and is considered sacred land. It is an ancestral landmark where Māori once cultivated vibrant kūmara, fruits, and vegetables. Since 1841, the Te Tiriti o Waitangi (Treaty of Waitangi) with the British Crown has guaranteed Māori the full, exclusive, and undisturbed possession of their lands, estates, forests, fisheries, and other properties. Yet increasing dispossession by settlers frequently violated the treaty. In 1863, for example, the Ihumātao people had their land confiscated by the New Zealand government under the New Zealand Settlements Act. The land was sold by the British Crown to a private owner, the Wallace family, who farmed it until late 2016.

In 2016, Ihumātao was sold to Fletcher Residential, who acquired the site as part of a housing development project. A land battle between Māori and the housing developers started.[32] Māori groups such as Save Our Unique Landscape (SOUL) occupied the land to block plans to develop it into market rate housing. As of this writing they continue to occupy the land under the leadership of SOUL founder Pania Newtown, a direct Māori descendant of Ihumātao. Māori protesters, most of them between fifteen to twenty-four years old, are actually growing traditional foods such as kūmara to feed themselves, their families, and the broader community at Ihumātao on the land.[33] Young Māori have been very vocal during these protests about how they are envisioning access to and use of their ancestral land to be self-sufficient, including setting up water storage and solar panels to preserve their food systems and ways of life. For Māori, reclamation of their ancestral lands is central to movements that call for self-determination, such as hikoi (political protest movements) against major land confiscations that threaten their physical and spiritual well-being.[34]

Kaitiakitanga: Trusteeship, Guardianship of the Land

Understanding oneself as being part of an interrelated web of life offers a vested interest in taking care of Nature, an ideology Māori Marsden defined as kaitiakitanga.[35] The Māori principle of kaitiakitanga broadly translates to English as "guardianship of the land," but, as with other Indigenous terms, it goes beyond this meaning. Kaitiakitanga derives from the word "tiaki," which means "to protect, nurture, and watch over." The prefix "kai" denotes the one who performs this action, transforming the world to a nurturing state of protection.[36] Within this context, the traditional Māori food system only uses agroecological practices such as animal manure, crop rotation, and planting and harvesting according to the rhythm of Nature, respecting the natural cycles of environmental systems. It is no surprise, then, that in Māori thinking, industrial farming that forgoes these mindful practices has a negative impact on their soils. Consider how the intensification of industrial farming—converting arable land to farmland used for intensive sheep and beef farming and monocropping, and the application of synthetic fertilization—distorts organic matter that enriches the soils and diverse plants that grow in it.

This distortion inevitably results in the destruction of Indigenous vegetation, soil biodiversity, and landscapes that previously supported agroecological food systems. Māori and other Indigenous peoples have been facing this loss since the arrival of European settlers. To counteract this environmental injustice, research partners mentioned that they are promoting and asserting the principle of kaitiakitanga. For example, "the moral obligation and duty of Māori is to be a kaitiaki (guardian, protector) of the land and the environment," said Buchanan Beech-Cullen of the Wai A Ariki Onerahirahi (Food Forest) garden.[37] To fulfill their role, Māori enact kaitiakitanga through the application of sustainable environmental principles. One such norm is rāhui[38] (restriction), a form of tapu[39]—a restriction of the use of natural resources designed to protect the well-being of Papatūānuku. Buchanan Beech-Cullen referenced one type of rāhui: "A restriction imposed on Māori land to prevent you from replenishing the food in that particular area. This is a principle I learned when growing up with my grandparents." Kaumātua Rereata Makiha provided another example: "Pigeons were a common edible commodity back in pre-colonial Aotearoa, so if Māori wanted to look after that population of pigeons, for example, they could put a rāhui in particular areas so you weren't allowed to harvest any pigeons from that area. Rāhui had that purpose."[40] The narrative above provides a window into the food security policy approach of Māori and underscores that the principle of kaitiakitanga assists Māori in sustainably caring for the environment, promoting an environmental policy that regulates the preservation of healthy soils and food resources.

Manaakitanga: Acts of Giving and Caring

Mate Heitia of the iwi of Ngāti Awa, Ngāti Pukeku and Ngai te Rangi on the East Coast of the North Island of Aotearoa explains that manaakitanga (generosity and care for others) derives from two words—"mana" and "aki." Mana is a condition that holds everything in the highest regard and aki means to uphold or support. The essence of "manaakitanga," then, is to care for, demonstrate hospitality, show respect and generosity, and support for others. She further discusses the importance of food rituals such as hākari (ceremonial feast) in conveying teachings about manaakitanga encoded in food: "Hākari is important for us because it has to do with our hospitality with guests. Hākari strengthens our relations with our community and other iwi because kai brings us together. Kai tahi tātou I te hākari—we will eat the feast together."[41] The importance of

Figure 15. Lionel Hotene, a Māori gardener holds a bunch of red kūmara recently harvested for a hākari to celebrate the Winter Solstice. Photo: Mariaelena Huambachano.

hākari in Māori culture goes beyond the link between land and food; it manifests the hospitality and leadership of, for example, a rangatira (chief), of a marae (meeting place), a whānau (family), hapū (sub-tribe), or iwi (tribe).

For hākari, the hosts cook extravagant food in attempt to provide the biggest feast possible, to assert mana (prestige, authority) and manaakitanga such that the guests cannot outdo them in the future.[42] I asked Māori scholar Aroha Mead, who has tribal affiliations to the tribes of Ngāti Awa and Ngāti Porou, about manaakitanga. She referenced a famous waiata (song) from the tribes of Ngāti Awa and Tuhoe: "Taku rakau," a song about iwi whose land was confiscated by the British Crown. The Māori lyrics, she said, explain how these waiata make the connection that without land there is nothing to serve guests, and thus mana of the rangatira, of a marae, a whānau, or iwi is diminished. She said that in Māori traditions, being generous hosts and feeding your manuhiri (guests) is important. Food is a vehicle to express manaakitanga to ensure the nurturing of relationships and to establish the comfort and well-being of guests and host.[43] Various customs convey the essence of manaakitanga, such as the traditional Māori pōwhiri (formal welcome).[44] Every stage of the pōwhiri focuses on acts of giving and caring for (manaakitanga), and ends with the sharing of kai (food) to help everyone move from the heightened, spiritual state of the pōwhiri back to ordinary activities. In this context, food is the medium to express manaakitanga, for showing respect and kindness to people. It is also for establishing and nurturing relationships by being mindful about the comfort and well-being of manuhiri and respecting their mana no matter their standing. It is paramount to understand the principle of tikanga to understand that manaakitanga is part of tikanga Māori. In the process of cultivating food plants, Māori articulate values of manaakitanga, which are active expressions of customary responsibilities to protect and enhance soil health. Māori research partners' relationships with non-human kin across and within their food landscapes are vital for their health and well-being. Thus, manaakitanga is part of the foundation for cultivating relationships based on kindness, aroha (love), and empowerment, connections that strengthen the body and soul and are the backbone of strong community networks. The principle of manaakitanga is now especially visible in public concern for and debate around both land and water.[45]

These Māori traditions and values, which form the core component of this book, bring attention to the way in which Māori are asserting mana whenua to demand access to and use of their ancestral land to be self-sufficient and to restore the mauri of soils through their own values (tikanga, manaakitanga, and whakapapa). These demands demonstrate the determination of Māori research partners and their continued struggle to reclaim the physical and spiritual well-being of current and future generations of Māori in Aotearoa. Such a strength resonates with the grit and determination of Quechua research partners to uphold their traditions and bolster food sovereignty to continue feeding themselves and lead sustainable futures. All this flows into the goal of "rematriating holistic/collective well-being" within these two Indigenous groups and beyond, as discussed in the next chapter.

6 Rematriating Holistic/Collective Well-Being

THE CHAKANA/MĀHUTONGA, AN INDIGENOUS FOOD SOVEREIGNTY FRAMEWORK

Iti noa ana, he pito mata.
With care and nourishment, a small kūmara will produce a harvest.

—Māori whakataukī (proverb)

Huk muhuqa kausaymi, Pachamamaq qowasqanchismi.
Seed is life; it is a gift from Mother Earth.

—Author's fieldnotes

In 2020, the global COVID-19 pandemic shed a harsh light on the disproportionate impacts of the lack of affordable, accessible, and nutritious food on vulnerable groups such as low-income communities; Black, Indigenous, and people of color (BIPOC); and immigrant households.[1] As governments imposed lockdowns and borders closed, frenzied people in Aotearoa, Peru, and the United States flocked to supermarkets amid fears of food scarcity and rising food prices, only to find lines that wrapped around the store and shelves plastered with signs that read "out of stock" or "limited quantities" on products such as fruits, vegetables, poultry, flour, and rice. In Aotearoa, despite the Māori's rich agricultural traditions and deeply rooted ancestral foodways, systemic racism and injustices that dispossessed them of their lands and prevented them from managing their resources effectively forced them to depend on food banks and to rely on non-Indigenous global food systems for sustenance in this time of crisis.

The Māori experience resonated with other Indigenous peoples around the world, for example in Indonesia, Canada, Brazil, Turtle Island and South Africa, who faced challenges with food security, food sovereignty, and seed sovereignty, all of which long predate the pandemic.[2] Yet some groups remained resilient, building and strengthening self-sustaining communities, relying on their own traditions and methods. When I called relatives in Aotearoa to ask how they were faring in March 2020, I learned that Māori food-growers, chefs, youth, and community leaders from various tribal groups throughout the country had collectivized to implement a rapid response to COVID-19. They set up community checkpoints at regional boundaries to protect vulnerable Māori populations such as the elderly and children in communities with minimal healthcare infrastructure.[3] Māori at urban māra kai (food gardens) across the country mobilized to assemble boxes of kai (food) for food-insecure communities.[4] They took responsibility and cared for their people by exercising tino rangatiratanga (self-determination) and upholding manaakitanga (hospitality) and tikanga Māori (ethical values and practices) among other values and principles. This work inherently enacted Māori socio-ecological values, ethics, customs, and the right to food—that is, our human right to access healthy and culturally appropriate food.[5]

When I called my Quechua research partners in March 2020, Sonia Quispe of Choquecancha answered my call in Quechua: "Allillancho Mariaelena!" (Hello, Mariaelena!) I asked how her community was coping with Peru's lockdown and supply shortages.[6] She seemed unconcerned as she said that they were "doing fine. Farming the land and getting ready for harvesting season." Her tone only changed when she asked about me. She said they had heard about food shortages and panic-buying in urban cities. "We are worried about you," she said. "Do you need food? We have plenty." I had been worried about her health and well-being and that of the rest of the people in the highlands of Peru. They were undeniably vulnerable because of colonial-driven marginalization, with limited or no access to basic public services, such as education and health care.[7] I envisioned city dwellers flocking to the highlands, fleeing the crowded cities, and knew that Peru's health system would not provide ventilators for those who fell sick or personal protective equipment for those who cared for them. But Sonia reminded me that these communities have vital tools to be food secure: Indigenous agroecological knowledge, traditions such as ayllu to govern their ancestral lands, and values and methods to work in unity to ensure everyone has nutritious food. And they were right to be worried about me. I faced empty grocery shelves and had little means of growing my own food. Sonia's concern for my well-being in an urban area underscored the urgency to bring Indigenous traditional ecological knowledge (TEK), ancestral foodways, and the resilience of Indigenous holistic philosophies of life into consideration as a potential solution to the food crisis faced worldwide.

Watching the chaos of scarcity and panic in urban areas unfold as the world entered the terrifying unknowns of a global pandemic, I wondered, "Is this the only means for people to access food in a city?" It seemed clearer than ever that the system operating around me was inferior to listening to and learning from Indigenous peoples' TEK in preserving foodways. The need for an alternative to the malfunctioning food system seemed to permeate those times. Our dysfunctional food system prioritizes intensive farming promoted by wealthy, industrialized nations that utilize large-scale, intensive production of crops and animals and rely on sophisticated, scientific-technological approaches to reducing world hunger. These same ineffective approaches to food production have been central causes of Indigenous peoples' struggle for survival as they threaten the preservation of Indigenous agricultural foodways that are steeped in TEK and deeply connected to cultural identity, sovereignty, rights, and fundamental freedoms.[8]

Much like climate change, the COVID-19 health crisis highlights the imperative to reshape our current food systems to address humanity's pressing challenges of global hunger and the urgent need for access to healthy, safe, and diverse diets. For some Indigenous peoples, it grounds calls to restore their holistic philosophies of life, food traditions, sovereignty over ancestral lands, recognition of Indigenous TEK, and access to treaty-guaranteed food gatherings such as fishing and hunting sites.[9] This call to action provides an opportunity to consider this question: how can Indigenous peoples' philosophies—in this case, those of the Quechua and Māori—contribute to fostering a more inclusive, equitable, and healthy food system in their own communities and at a broader scale? In this chapter, I provide one possible answer to this question through a composite Indigenous Food Sovereignty framework, the Chakana/Māhutonga framework, drawing from Quechua and Māori research partners' shared similarities in their epistemologies and ontologies discussed in chapter 3 and core values and principles discussed in chapters 4 and 5. I aim to add evidence of how two Indigenous communities—Quechua and Māori—are bolstering food sovereignty and well-being, holding tight to their traditions, philosophies, and values that may resonate with other Indigenous peoples and thereby contribute to the restoration of cultural foodways and working landscapes on the local and global scale. This Indigenous framework is a political act of resistance to colonial foods and seeks to reposition Indigenous TEK and holistic/collective well-being ideologies at the heart of sustainable food systems.

Below I provide the contextual background of the Chakana/Māhutonga. I then explain how Quechua and Māori have operationalized the Chakana/Māhutonga to realize rematriating holistic/collective well-being—restoring, reclaiming and reaffirming their Indigenous philosophies, laws, cultures, and economies of well-being enmeshed with values, principles, and ethics. It likewise supports their broader goals of promoting sustainable food systems, planetary health, and the reclamation and continuation of tribal sovereignty. I do this through a relational case study of the Papatūānuku Kōkiri Marae, a Māori urban community garden, and the Andean seed keepers, or "women of Choquecancha," a subsistence farming community in Peru. I conclude with a discussion on how the Chakana/Māhutonga offers pathways for a paradigm shift from the contemporary global food system to embrace living in harmonious relationships between human society and Nature, braiding all of humankind together in nets of reciprocity and kindness and pointing us toward a viable, healthy food system and future.

AN INDIGENOUS FOOD SOVEREIGNTY FRAMEWORK

"Chakana" in Peruvian Quechua and "Māhutonga" in the Māori language are the terms for what is known in English as the Southern Cross constellation. This constellation is one of the striking astronomical associations of Quechua and Māori peoples. Visible throughout the year in their southern skies, the Chakana/Māhutonga watches over the progress and proliferation of the

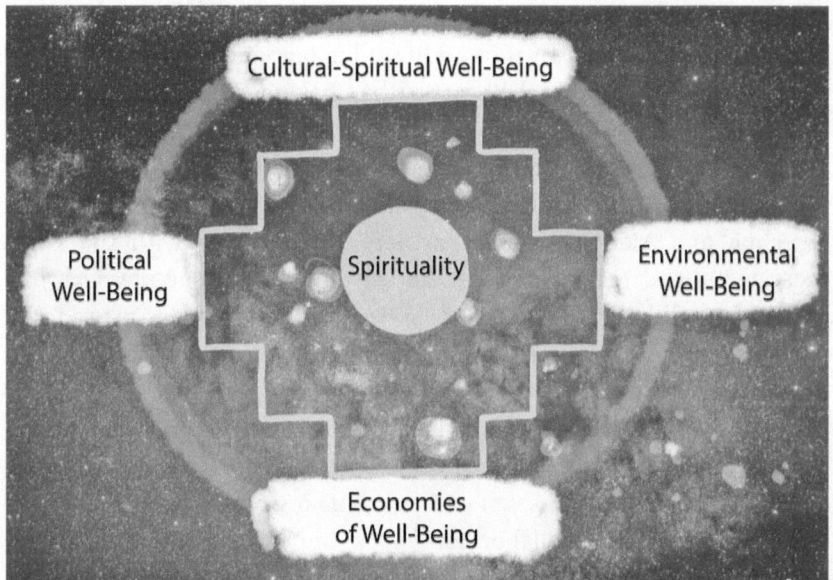

Figure 16. The Chakana/Māhutonga—An Indigenous Food Sovereignty Framework. Illustration: Sam Bradd.

communities it has guided since eons ago through mystical intuition, traditions, and agricultural knowledge that Quechua and Māori research collaborators encode in their lifeways.[10] It only seemed fitting, then, that a model geared toward restoring Indigenous foodways should be named after that which shaped them: the Southern Cross constellation.

I adopted the Chakana/Māhutonga metaphorically. I framed the ontological and epistemological similarities between Quechua and Māori research partners and their core values and principles in four areas—cultural, ecological, economic, and political—and placed them in each of the four quadrants formed by the constellation's four bright stars. These four interdependent quadrants show how Quechua and Māori practice holistic/collective well-being. It acknowledges a holistic and circular process where there is no beginning or end in preserving TEK and cultural foodways. In exploring new ways to frame sustainable food systems, Quechua and Māori collaborators pointed out that because of the dynamic interplay of the Chakana/Māhutonga, when one quadrant is impacted, either positively or negatively, the others suffer or flourish accordingly.

Thus, to achieve impactful solutions, each quadrant of the Chakana/Māhutonga framework must be addressed in tandem with the others.

I placed *spirituality* at the heart of the Chakana/Māhutonga, infusing every single quadrant, because community members acknowledged it as the portal of energy and spiritual vitality contained within all human and non-human kin vital for their flourishing. Spirituality is embedded in Quechua and Māori research partners' relationships with the land, ecosystems, and food traditions that pivot around their physical and emotional well-being. For example, prayers and food rituals are used as a medium to connect and maintain equilibrium among the human, natural, and spiritual worlds. I discuss the community suggestions underpinning the surrounding, interrelated quadrants below:

Cultural-spiritual well-being underscores "food for reestablishing identity and reviving cultures of well-being." During my time spent helping Quechua and Māori collaborators work the land, we shared in the experience of intergenerational TEK through a nurturing approach with all human and non-human kin—plants, rivers, and biological organisms. Sentiments of love are tangled with values and principles of respect, care, solidarity, and kindness. Working in these environments and in the company of those who share in a reverence and unique TEK of soil health transformed me. Through the tending of seeds and plants that hold ancestral memories, I became more mindful of the existence of all living beings and heard the voice and vibrations from different realms. Like my collaborators, I was in tune with all of my divine senses. We experienced a sense of knowing the land from within ourselves, and a sense of belonging because we felt like a part of it. We understood the life that grows from Pachamama/Papatūānuku (Mother Earth) and her gifts in the form of food, which in turn ignited feelings of affection, respect, and duty to nurture such a precious gift. I believe this work would transform anyone.

In this study, the analysis of the relationship between cultural-spiritual and food was integral to understanding Indigenous Food Sovereignty from a Quechua and Māori perspective. *Indigenous* Food Sovereignty, as discussed in chapter 1, is distinct to food security and food sovereignty. It is grounded in a relational ethics approach to preserving sustainable food systems. It reaffirms Indigenous relationships with traditional foods and recognizes traditional lands and waters as necessary for healing and sustaining the health of Indigenous communities. As Secwempec scholar Dawn Morrison puts it, "Food is a gift from the Creator. In this context, the right to food is sacred and cannot be constrained or recalled by colonial laws, policies, or institutions."[11] Food is indispensable in shaping Quechua and Māori lives, identities, and futures. From it, they derive their self-worth, individually and collectively, from traditional livelihoods such as rotational agriculture, fishing, pastoralism, and high-mountain agriculture. Thus, this quadrant focuses on reconfiguring the global human-Nature-spiritual relationship to promote resilient and sustainable food systems akin to those of Quechua and Māori. It urges humanity to stop treating Pachamama/Papatūānuku as a commodity to be exploited and instead to love and respect her and understand that humans are embedded within Nature and not disconnected from or superior to it. This quadrant works in tandem with the other three to emphasize the significance of spirituality in Indigenous food systems and modify human-Nature behaviors to restore Indigenous philosophies, food sovereignty, and cultural knowledge in order to ultimately pursue environmental and food justice.

A cultural-spiritual well-being requires the recognition of another quadrant of the Chakana/Māhutonga, *environmental well-being*. This quadrant focuses on intergenerational justice to ensure the growing of food that promotes a harmonious human-Nature-spiritual balance for generations to come. As Māori philosopher Krushil Watene puts it, "Well-being and justice begin at the intersections of widely inclusive relationships—not least where our relationships with each other and the natural environment meet."[12] The quadrant of environmental well-being focuses on re-centering environmental governance around Indigenous values, ethical principles and practices, and intergenerational well-being and justice. This quadrant aims to achieve them by promoting a relational ethics philosophy grounded in the understanding that our relationships and connections with the rich and endlessly varied diversity of biological beings—plants, animals, insects, landforms, and deities such as the mountains and rivers—shapes our lives and futures.

Reciprocal relations invoke responsibilities and intimate, mutual respect between people and place that are part of everyday, local practices. For example, Quechua and Māori fulfill responsibilities by upholding their duty to safeguard healthy ecosystems just as deities such as Rongomātāne, the

Māori god of agriculture, and Inti, the Quechua sun god that brings forth crops for humanity's subsistence and oversees elements of Nature. Quechua and Māori are also guardians of biodiversity and agrobiodiversity[13] and protect local ecosystems and Pachamama/Papatūānuku from human exploitation. A fundamental aim is to restore and preserve the mauri (spirit, life essence) of all ecosystems and their evolving relationships with the land. Māori and Quechua regulate human activity with the environment through TEK methods, principles, and policies such as rāhui,[14] the ban or restriction on taking food from a specific area; discouraging wastefulness; and ayni,[15] the principle of reciprocity that promotes only taking from the land what is needed. The seasonal timing for food collection is emphasized through the use of their Indigenous agricultural calendars: the Māori maramataka[16] (lunar calendar) and the Quechua Inti (sun) and Quilla (moon)[17] calendars. Thus, the goal of this quadrant is to maintain a harmonious balance in the development and environmental protection of land, water, and sky, on which humans depend for both a healthy life and a strong spiritual connection.

The *political well-being* quadrant, thus, focuses on reclaiming Indigenous peoples' right to food and food/seed sovereignty that has been affirmed in an array of instruments created by international governmental and nongovernmental alliances. One such instrument is the United Nations Declaration on the Rights of Indigenous Peoples (UNDRIP), which specifies the range of rights required for the full exercise of the right to food and food sovereignty, paying particular attention to the connections between the right to cultural self-determination and the right to maintain and protect seeds and land.[18] My research collaborators cited the moral obligation and accountability that they feel for preserving the dignity of Pachamama/Papatūānuku as driving forces for enacting self-determination. This includes demanding recognition of Indigenous rights as acknowledged in treaties such as the Te Tiriti o Waitangi (Treaty of Waitangi), international covenants such as the UNDRIP, the Convention on Biological Diversity,[19] and the United Nations Declaration on the Rights of Peasants and Other People Working in Rural Areas.[20]

The philosophy and practice of guardianship and protection with all kin relations found in many Indigenous societies help to transform environmental governance into an Indigenous climate justice strategy to counteract the deterioration of Mother Earth. An example of such an undertaking is the formal recognition of the Whanganui River, an ancestor of the Māori people of Whanganui, as a person in 2017. This recognition is rooted in the mutual relationships between the Māori people and the Whanganui River, expressed in Māori language as "Ko au te Awa, ko te Awa ko au" (I am the River, and the River is me). The "Te Awa Tupua" (Whanganui River Claims Settlement) Act of 2017 led to significant changes in status quo environmental management practices. The river and all its tributaries were recognized as a single entity, Te Awa Tupua, as were its rights and interests as the owner of its own riverbed. The law acknowledges the river as a living whole that stretches from the mountains to the sea, including both its physical and metaphysical elements. The crown and the Whanganui people serve as legal custodians in the same way that legal guardians represent children today in loco parentis.[21]

The river itself can sue and be sued as necessary and is represented by a two-person guardian, Te Pou Tupua, comprised of one representative of the Crown and one representative of the Whanganui people. The people who comprise Te Pou Tupua must act and speak to benefit the river's health and well-being. This covenant draws on deeply divergent forms of order—Western legal and ancient Māori cultural—to protect the well-being of the Whanganui river and, by extension, the Māori people of Whanganui.[22] Other examples of accomplishments in advocating for the rights of Mother Earth and environmental personhood include the government of India's vesting of the Ganges and Yamuna Rivers with the legal status of a person after a battle to stop its pollution in March 2017.[23] In 2008, Ecuador became the first country in the world to include "Rights of Nature" in its constitution.[24] Such efforts highlight the importance of the political well-being quadrant for Indigenous peoples' ability to reject the dominant Western view of Nature. Indigenous activists are at the forefront of advocating for political well-being, for their rights as Indigenous peoples, and for their non-human relatives.

The final quadrant, *economies of well-being*, highlights the importance of food for thriving and flourishing communities. It addresses the "rematriation of economies," which entails the reclamation and reassertion of Indigenous traditional and local economic systems as well as the understanding that for some Indigenous peoples, the land held in trust is their wealth. Thus, a focus only on the supply aspect of food procurement does not adequately address human societies' histories and relationships with food. Economies of well-being transcend economies of competition in their consideration of a relational ethics philosophy entrenched in Indigenous cosmovisions/epistemologies and ontologies. This approach informs socio-ecological principles such as reciprocity and solidarity as facilitators of dignified livelihoods, a healthy environment, and food sovereignty. It prioritizes the dignity and well-being of land and soil as the fundamental basis for how we think of economic growth, trading, and transactions.

As Potawatomi scientist and plant ecologist Robin Wall Kimmerer explains in her book *Braiding Sweetgrass*, food is a gift from the Creator, and the fundamental nature of gifts is that "they move, and their value increases with their passage. . . . The more something is shared, the greater its value becomes. This is hard to grasp for societies steeped in the notion of private property, where others are, by definition, excluded from sharing."[25] The Quechua and Māori food sovereignty case studies exemplify the rematriation of economies of well-being prioritizing relational equilibrium, a state in which all parties engage in a cycle of trading and exchange that is fair and just until a harmonious relational balance occurs between them. All Māori and Quechua research collaborators highlighted the importance of developing local and intertribal trading food systems, beginning with taking care of local land where food is grown, supporting local growers, and reviving the accessibility of foodways at a global scale. As a result, these communities are promoting holistic/collective philosophies of well-being in urban and rural settings through stewardship of land and water resources, intergenerational knowledge, and justice through peer-to-peer mentoring, renewal of Indigenous food traditions, and multigenerational empowerment.

The following case studies show how the interrelated quadrants of the Chakana/Māhutonga work within a Quechua and Māori context for the rematriation of holistic/collective well-being, fostering coordination both locally and internationally of an Indigenous Food Sovereignty framework for restoring the health of food systems in order to end hunger. One of the main components of this Indigenous Food Sovereignty framework is to recognize Indigenous knowledge as valuable and that Indigenous peoples are important actors in the dynamic transformation of current food systems.

CHAPTER 6 141

THE QUECHUA COMMUNITY OF CHOQUECANCHA IN PERU

I vividly recall my first visit to Choquecancha in April 2014: after a day of hiking deep in Peru's highlands, I arrived in this approximately 1100-person Quechua community in the district of Lares, located 3,850 meters—or 12,600 feet—above sea level. The landscape is green, the air is clear and fresh, and Andean engineering ingenuity abounds through the Inka terraces built and maintained by local communities. The main source of livelihood in Choquecancha is farming corn, native potatoes, and other Andean crops and livestock, most of which they eat themselves. The people of this village refer to themselves as the "guardians of corn" after the unique variety of corn that is still preserved there. The people of Choquecancha are also skillful weavers and for generations have passed on knowledge about both seed preservation and loom-woven textile art. I went two years without a visit because of the COVID-19 pandemic but returned in July 2022 to find that there they were again, waiting for me at the top of the hill with a warm "Allillancho Mariaelena!"

By now, the people of Choquecancha are used to my comings and goings, and although I can easily reach it by a long bus ride, I still prefer to hike there when I visit. The path to Choquecancha is long, steep, and narrow, but taking it means that from far away I see a group of women wearing colorful, traditional Quechua polleras (long skirts) and llikllas (shawls). They always wave to me joyfully as I approach. When I reach the top of the steep Inka slopes, these women, community leaders of Choquecancha, embrace me warmly. The first thing Petronila Quispe, Sonia Ttito, and Maria Ttito ask me is always the same: Are you hungry? Before I can answer, they whisk me to Sonia's home where the rest of women seed keepers and weavers are waiting for me. There I immediately smell the scents and flavors of Andean cuisine—wild herbs, ají (chili) peppers and roasted corn. Then I know that I am back in the homeland. One of the women quickly comes out of the kitchen to greet me with a plate of cancha (roasted corn), one of the traditional welcome snacks in the Andes.

Much of the farming work in Choquecancha springs directly from the cultural/spiritual well-being quadrant of the Chakana/Māhutonga. An example is spirituality, which plays a vital role in Quechua food systems

Figure. 17. Women of Choquecancha wearing the llikllas (shawls) that they knitted themselves, and waiting at the top of the hill for visitors like me. Photo: Mariaelena Huambachano.

because Quechua research partners understand that all life springs from the land, and the life force energy of a plant or animal has been sacrificed to feed another being. Therefore, rituals and ceremonies express care, love, and gratitude to the land and the non-living beings. Despite artificial, synthetic, and technologically produced forms of food disregarding the spiritual dimension of local and Indigenous food systems, Quechua communities remain true to their cultural lifeways and traditions. Spiritual energy is ubiquitous in the highlands, and the area's energy is felt strongly by everyone all year round. The month of August is of great significance for the Runakuna because it is the month when Pachamama, the feminine representation of the natural world and force on Earth, is the most fertile.

In August 2023, during my annual visit to Peru, I experienced one of the largest ch'alla to Pachamama in Cusco. Paqo[26] Juan de Dios Cruz of

Figure 18. A welcome lunch with the women of Choquecancha: potatoes, seasoned herbs, salad, and chicha de jora (fermented corn drink). Photo: Mariaelena Huambachano.

Ccachin explained to me that ch'alla traces back to the Q'ero peoples of Peru, a small community of farmers, weavers, and healers. After the Spanish conquest, they sought refuge high up in the mountains to preserve their ways of life. In August, the paqo of the Q'ero people would perform a ch'alla for Pachamama and other deities on behalf of the Runakuna. Paqos are revered in the Andean world as the gatekeepers of Andean knowledge, beliefs, and traditions. A role given to both men and women, it includes the responsibility of assembling the ch'alla and conducting it in August. The ch'alla is a joyful event. Some community members prepare a "pachamanca," a traditional Andean dish cooked in a huatia (earth oven). Others bring chicha de jora, a type of corn/maize beer, which in the rural highlands of Peru is made of fermented yellow maize called jora and served in decorative clay jars. Others play the quena (traditional flute of the Andes) and charangos (small Andean threaded musical instrument)

Figure 19. On August 1, 2023, at the ruins of Saccsayhuamán in Cusco, we gathered in ayllu to perform despacho (offerings) to Pachamama. At the center of the photo an Andean priest holds a bouquet of colorful flowers, a Quechua sabedora (knowledge holder) holds a conch shell, and two Quechua men stand next to a big jar of chicha de jora (an Andean beverage made of fermented corn). This celebration is called Pachamama Raymi. Photo: Mariaelena Huambachano.

outside their houses and in the chakra. In 2018, I attended a ch'alla in Ccachin. The ritual began at 10:00 p.m. In ayllu (community), we went "challeando" (a word that reflects the blending of Spanish and Quechua languages): dancing to the sound of the flute and charangos. The sound of the quena, drums, and charangos provided the ceremony with a delightful and spiritual ambiance. Paqo Juan de Dios conducted the ceremony, which involves taking the bundle of gifts for Pachamama to the top of the mountain to bury in a pukara (sacred place).

According to Paqo Juan de Dios, it is always preferable that a paqo from the ayllu where the offering to Pachamama is taking place conduct the ceremony. He described a case where a community's llamas died soon after a paqo from another ayllu substituted for the main paqo, who was unwell. Just before midnight, Paqo Juan de Dios placed a generous piece of Andean textile on the ground. He gently and methodically placed all the offerings—coca leaves, corn, potatoes, biscuits, candles, animal fat, confetti, wine, and flower petals—on the cloth, then packaged them into a bundle. Facing the east where the sun rises, he elevated the bundle over his head, and we clasped hands around him. Then we all followed him in a joyful procession accompanied by the sound of the drums and people singing in Quechua. Paqo Juan de Dios asked us to wait for him while he went to the top of the mountain to bury our offerings. The ritual concluded a few hours later when Paqo Juan de Dios returned from the hill empty-handed, saying that Pachamama and our non-human relatives had welcomed our offerings. The ritual strengthens the human-Nature connection and invokes teachings about ecological sustainability grounded in a "caring or nurturing approach" to biodiversity, individuals, and community. It reflects the importance of spirituality much as mauri (life essence) does for the Māori. Food traditions and rituals underscore the significance of Indigenous foodways for staying intimately connected with the land—Mother Earth fosters a sense of belonging and love of and respect for the existence of all beings.

In the Chakana/Māhutonga, the political well-being quadrant underscores the self-governance communal system, ayllu, and its internal regulation by an ethic of cooperation known as ayni as vital values engrained in Quechua peoples' history and traditions. According to Petronila Quispe of Choquecancha, "Within the ayllu, all members have the understanding that there is no private ownership of land. It all belongs to the community."[27] In Choquecancha, understanding and recognizing ayllu norms helps to avoid conflicts that may arise due to unequal land ownership and protects the production and natural resources of the ayllu. The ayllu of Choquecancha is an egalitarian society without established political or religious positions; instead, the leadership roles rotate between members on a two-year basis. Yanantin-masintin (principles of duality and complementarity), which institute gender equity, play a vital role in the farming practices of the Runakuna of Choquecancha. Both men and women work the land together and use traditional agroecological practices to preserve agrobiodiversity, wildlife, and healthy ecosystem services such as water. The egalitarian, interrelated values of yanantin-masintin are rooted in their everyday life practices such as cultivating seeds together, when men and women carefully select both male and female seeds for pollination. In farming, male and female activities are conceptually distinct and complementary. As the world's attention falls on redesigning food systems to deliver safe and healthy food, livelihoods, and environments for all, it is equally essential to ensure that gender equity rights are respected and the dismantling of food patriarchy.

Regarding environmental well-being, drawing from their intimate and distinctive traditional ecological knowledge of their environments and food landscapes, Quechua research partners employ innovative agricultural methods like food systems preservation techniques to avoid food shortages in the rainy season, the months of January and February. When I asked if any of my Quechua research partners had ever experienced food shortages, none had. No one had any knowledge of their community ever experiencing food shortages, which they attribute to their food knowledge. One day while I was working alongside Crisostomo Quispe of Choquecancha in his family's chakra he gave me a glimpse of the system that ensures they never starve. He showed me a type of potato, the chuño or ch'uñu,[28] that his family would eat in the rainy season. The crop is one of the most important legacies of the Andean civilization. I asked Crisostomo if all families in the ayllu grow ch'uñu. He nodded. "We grow them in ayllu to ensure there is equity in what we grow and eat and foremost no one starves."[29] The term ch'uñu, I learned, is actually both a potato crop variety bred in high agroecological zones that is highly resistant to severe weather conditions and a food preservation method. Ch'uñu is a traditional freeze-drying method consisting of placing small potatoes close together on flat ground and allowing them to freeze. Overnight temperatures in winter (mid-June to mid-September) reach around −5°C (23°F) at elevations of over 3,800 meters (12,500 feet). During the day, the potatoes are left to dry and trampled by foot (called "dancing" on the stack) to eliminate any remaining water. This also removes the skins, enabling subsequent freezing and drying. This process is repeated for three to four days, depending on weather conditions. Afterward, the remaining skin is peeled off by hand. Ch'uñu is used not only in Choquechancha but also in soups and stews in the highlands of Peru and around the country to ensure that no one goes hungry.

The Papatūānuku Kōkiri Marae in Aotearoa New Zealand

On a hot and humid summer day, I drove past the south of Tāmaki Makaurau, the Māori name for Auckland City, to arrive at the Papatūānuku Kōkiri Marae, a self-sustaining urban marae (communal space) in the heart of the city. A Māori rock carving in the shape of Rongomātāne (god of cultivation) opposite a sign that read "zero carbon" greeted me. Barefoot kids, out of school for summer, ran around at the entrance of the garden, and one of them smiled and greeted me with "Kia ora!" Not far from the māra kai (food garden) entrance was a vibrant green field with a small nursery and patches of salad veggies and kūmara (sweet potatoes) in which forty hands and feet were busy planting. The field was full of volunteers: school kids, kuia (elderly Māori women), and koroua (elderly Māori men) were giving instructions on how to grow food. Lionel Hotene, who oversaw the māra kai, waved at me from a distance. "Kia ora Lionel!" I greeted him. "This is a beautiful field, alive and filled with good energy everywhere you turn."

I met Lionel Hotene and his wife Valerie Teraitua in 2012 during a workshop about growing Māori food at the Papatūānuku Kōkiri Marae. We continue to work closely in supporting the aspirations of Māori to be food secure, fostering Indigenous networks across the Pacific to preserve cultural knowledge about foodways. Lionel explained that Mere Knight of Ngāti Porou (Māori tribe on the East Coast) had established the Papatūānuku Kōkiri Marae in 1984 with a twofold aim: "To recover mātauranga Māori of our ancestors about sustainable kai production to feed ourselves, families, and communities, and to service the needs of Māori from children and youth to elders in South Auckland."[30] He grinned as he continued: "We are doing it. We are achieving nana Mere's vision. Whānau [families] are coming together to learn and work in the māra kai, participating in more cultural events, using their te reo [Māori language], and practicing tikanga [customary values and practices] with confidence."

During a series of interviews, I conducted with Lionel between 2014 and 2020, he emphasized the importance of "spirituality" at the heart of

Figure 20. Top: the logo of the Papatūānuku Kōkiri Marae located at the entrance of the māra kai (food garden). Bottom: the māra kai of the Papatūānuku Kōkiri Marae. Photos: Mariaelena Huambachano.

Figure 21. Some of the fresh produce that grows in the māra kai (food garden) of the Papatūānuku Kōkiri Marae: kūmara, peruperu potatoes, corn, pumpkin, beans. Photo: Mariaelena Huambachano.

the Chakana/Māhutonga. As he put it, "All elements in our food garden, such as seeds and plants, have a mauri [life force, spiritual essence], and this is why it is important to do a karakia [prayer] to ask and obtain consent from our non-human kin to enter into their realm to work on the food garden." Conversely, he said, this spiritual element is absent in industrial food production. "The spiritual connection is missing in foods—the spiritual connection between us as people to the land and the atuas [spiritual beings]—and, sadly, to the detriment of our peoples." Lionel highlighted the vital role of the culture of well-being quadrant in reviving Māori cultural knowledge. To counteract the dismissal of spirituality in the contemporary food system, he explained, cultural traditions such as the karakia have been reinstated in the Papatūānuku Kōkiri Marae. Every time someone enters the garden to work, a karakia is recited. He described how a kaumātua (Elder) had recited a special karakia on a recent day to the god of agriculture, Rongomātāne, as the gardeners planted food crops, "because he [referring to Rongomātāne] is considered the creator and protector of vital Māori crops such as the kūmara."

In accordance with the culture of well-being quadrant, the Papatūānuku Kōkiri Marae grows kūmara, lettuce, tomatoes, beetroots, kale, and other vegetables. The kūmara dominates, in line with the objective of reestablishing the relationship between Māori and their ancestral foods. The Papatūānuku Kōkiri Marae grows six varieties of kūmara, kamokamo (a type of squash), and three kinds of taewa (Māori potatoes),[31] including one variety called peruperu potatoes. Lionel told me that the name peruperu acknowledges the whakapapa (genealogy) of this food crop, which is originally from highlands of Peru but is now nurtured by the hands of the Māori people in Aotearoa. Papatūānuku Kōkiri Marae also embraces an egalitarian approach wherein both men and women have vital roles to play, ranging from growing food crops to cooking and teaching about Indigenous agroecological practices such as crop rotation, planting in companionship (polyculture), and collecting and storing seeds like those of the kūmara in traditional pātaka (storehouses).

Valerie Teraitua described her vision for the Papatūānuku Kōkiri Marae to become a hub of continued learning, sharing, and teaching of Māori and Indigenous knowledge. Here te reo Māori (Māori language), tikanga, and practice would support Māori aspirations to be self-sufficient and self-determined. She told me that Māngere, where the Papatūānuku Kōkiri Marae is located, once a place of abundance, had become a place of insufficiency where the abundance is the amount of foreign-owned fast-food restaurants. The Papatūānuku Kōkiri Marae has begun to reverse this by enacting the principle of tino rangatiratanga (self-determination) through the reclamation of their tūrangawaewae, which falls under the culture of well-being quadrant of the Chakana/Māhutonga. According to Lionel and Valerie, one way to reclaim tūrangawaewae is through restoring soil health by implementing mechanisms that resonate with their Indigenous worldviews and aspiration to restore Māori food systems. The Hua Parakore Certification, an Indigenous verification and validation system rooted in Māori values, principles, and practices when growing kai, is such a mechanism.[32]

In 2011, the Papatūānuku Kōkiri Marae embarked on a journey to attain the Hua Parakore Certification, which it received in July 2015.

Figure 22. Mariaelena Huambachano on July 4, 2015, signing the Hua Parakore Korowai, a certificate that validates and verifies that the choice and activities used by the Papatūānuku Kōkiri Marae resonate with the caretaking of resources and production of a pure product, chemical-free and with non-GMO ingredients.

Uncle Percy Tipene, one of the founders of the Hua Parakore, invited me to the community ceremony that recognized the certification. On July 4, 2015, the Papatūānuku Kōkiri Marae was officially recognized as a "Hua Parakore māra kai," a Māori organic food marae.

At the event Lionel described the principles of the Hua Parakore Certification as follows:

> *Whakapapa:* A reminder of Māori ancestral links to soil—to Papatūānuku.
>
> *Wairua:* Enhancing the human-Nature-spiritual essence to empower Māori to develop sustainable soil-management approaches.
>
> *Mana* (authority): Upholding the practice of manaakitanga (hospitality) and sovereignty through the provision of healthy foods.
>
> *Maramatanga:* In the context of the Hua Parakore, this means knowledge and enlightenment about Papatūānuku, the wairua (spirit) and mauri (life essence) of the soil and food gardens.
>
> *Te ao tūroa* (natural order of the living world): Underscores interconnectedness and mutual interdependence with one another and of the need to preserve healthy, socio-ecological relationships.
>
> *Mauri:* Understanding Papatūānuku and her complex-life-supporting capacities to preserve the life essence of food crops.

According to Lionel, "all are welcome to the Papatūānuku Kōkiri Marae to learn, reconnect, and follow the teachings of our tupuna (ancestors) to thrive as whānau, hapū, and iwi. We pride ourselves in being a marae that is ethnically diverse. We are very lucky to welcome many people who come from different tribes and ethnic backgrounds." Under the care of Lionel and Valerie, the marae has also expanded its community services to offer various educational programs such as the Kai Oranga program in conjunction with Te Waka Kai Ora, the National Māori Organics Authority of Aotearoa. They offer free te reo Māori classes, fitness sessions such as the popular Zumba dance classes led by Valerie, and community events and meetings including youth leadership programs, cooking classes, and community dinners, among other activities.

Much of the agricultural work conducted at the Papatūānuku Kōkiri Marae springs directly from the Chakana/Māhutonga's environmental well-being quadrant. Recognizing the depletion of Earth's natural resources and the urgency for ecological wellness, the marae is partnering with Māori

Figure 23. The Hua Parakore sign in the Papatūānuku Kōkiri Marae's māra kai (food garden). Photo: Mariaelena Huambachano.

residents in the south of Tāmaki Makaurau (Auckland City) to restore many varieties of traditional Māori foods such as the kūmara. As Lionel says, they are doing it "the Māori way," using the Indigenous Māori maramataka, the lunar calendar. Indeed, I learned that community members and volunteers at the Papatūānuku Kōkiri Marae are growing kai within a te ao Māori (Māori world) framework, using Indigenous agroecological techniques and practices such as the hua parakore and maramataka as the foundation of restoring the health of the soil, our own health, and our well-being. I still visit the Papatūānuku Kōkiri Marae to this day, and I leave each visit fed both physically and spiritually by a community that welcomes me warmly, puts me to work, and sends me home with nutritious and chemical-free foods such as kūmara, peruperu potatoes, beans, and lettuce. At the Papatūānuku Kōkiri Marae, no stomach or spirit goes hungry, and it is through their traditional and sustainable foodways that the rest of the world can also come to know this holistic sense of fullness.

A Bountiful Harvest: Lessons Learned from the Māori and Quechua Peoples

The dominant industrial food system is alien to the lively and vibrant native ways of knowing and being that are embedded in Indigenous peoples' cosmovisions and foodways for the achievement of holistic/collective well-being. Pachamama/Papatūānuku transcend understandings of the land as an agricultural space necessary for human and non-human physical and spiritual sustenance. Rather, Pachamama/Papatūānuku *represent* the land and sea where all the humans and other-than-humans flourish as a collective. Accordingly, food is not a commodity: it is a gift that holds cultural and spiritual meaning because it is nourished on the land, with Papatūānuku/Pachamama and non-human relatives ultimately promoting the well-being and sustenance of all humanity. The two case studies I offer here illustrate the ways in which Quechua and Māori are enacting their right to food and reclaiming Indigenous Food Sovereignty in order to reindigenize their diets, preserve ancestral knowledges, and regain control over their health and well-being.

Both Quechua and Māori follow distinctive norms and rules in relation to Pachamama/Papatūānuku and the use of natural resources. Furthermore, understandings of customary law and socio-political processes for fostering long-term human-Nature relationships are highly localized. For example, Quechua communities work in ayni on seed preservation and pollination and as stewards of the land in the chakra. Similarly, through acts of self-determination (tino rangatiratanga), Māori assert their rights to be the stewards of their homelands. Yet, the Māori and the Quechua share a holistic/collective well-being approach to living well, rooted in their respective cosmovisions and worldviews, which forgoes notions of human superiority in favor of connectedness, values, and ethics.

Despite the differences in the specific details of their respective approaches, I learned that Quechua and Māori collaborators deploy the Chakana/Māhutonga as an Indigenous-led framework for the *rematriation of holistic/collective well-being* steeped in Indigenous traditions, resilience, resurgence, and social-ecological justice. Indigenous Food Sovereignty drives holistic/collective well-being in both Choquecancha and the

Papatūānuku Kōkiri Marae. Quechua and Māori research partners' practices of autonomy, self-sufficiency, community empowerment, gender equity, and solidarity lie at the heart of their philosophies of well-being that go beyond the individual rights-based approach to food, and are encompassed by Indigenous Food Sovereignty.

As discussed in chapters 4 and 5, collective/well-being philosophies of Quechua and Māori research partners are elicited by their respective notions of well-being, referred to as "allin kawsay" in the southern highlands of Peru and "mauri ora" by some Māori collaborators. Both are underpinned by cultural and environmental values and ethics that are incompatible with the dominant Western paradigm of economic growth endorsed by industrial food production.[33] In summary, the examples of Choquecancha and the Papatūānuku Kōkiri Marae show how Indigenous peoples such as Quechua and Māori are advancing a well-being agenda that urges a paradigm shift from industrial food production to one that focuses on Indigenous philosophies, TEKs, values, innovation, and methods for achieving holistic/collective well-being.

In this fight to reclaim Indigenous Food Sovereignty and rematriate holistic/collective well-being philosophies, we can't overlook the valuable role of the heritage seeds often discussed as the foundation of the food sovereignty movement. Heritage seeds are living relatives, and most are passed down through generations of Indigenous gardeners carrying cultural knowledge and tools for education and reclaiming health.[34] They need to be protected from patent or genetic modification. As sociologist Jack Kloppenburg asserts, "If there is to be food sovereignty, surely it will be facilitated and enabled by a struggle for seed sovereignty."[35] Food sovereignty efforts, both local and global, are expanding and seeking to prevent multinational food corporations from gaining more control over seed resources. There are seed-saving initiatives in Peru, Aotearoa, and the United States. Slow Food Peru, for example, is a growing network of small-scale Indigenous and non-Indigenous farmers and seed keepers in Peru.[36] They are working to provide education to tribal folks and city dwellers about the biological and cultural heritage of diversity and to advocate for food sovereignty legislation that acknowledges the importance of traditional seeds and their link to land and traditional knowledge. The aim for a new food sovereignty legislation is to support the work of those who cultivate diversity of seeds and to offer opportunities in support of farmers who are guardians of registered varieties of seeds.

For example, in Turtle Island, the Seed Keepers Network connects Indigenous seed keepers who coalesce to educate tribal people about seed planting and saving and who push institutions that have collected or inherited seeds to rematriate them to their communities of origin.[37] Similar efforts from Māori include the revitalization of te reo Māori language, Land March protests, and the pockets of māra kai (food gardens). Examples of such work taking place in Peru include the establishment of the Indigenous organization CHIRAPAQ (Centre for Indigenous Cultures of Peru), located in the regions of Ayacucho and Lima and which, for the past thirty years, has been promoting Indigenous rights and Indigenous Food Sovereignty. I am also leading a seed rematriation project in partnership with the Quechua communities of Choquecancha, Ccachin, and Pampacorral in the region of Lares in Cusco as a means of improving health, promoting culture, and reducing the impacts of climate change.

As humanity continues to live through the threats of climate change, environmental degradation, and new pandemics, it is critical that we turn away from the dominant, industrial approach to food production. It is only when we recognize the vital role Indigenous peoples play in building healthy food systems and advancing sustainable development goals that we will begin to live in harmony with Pachamama/Papatūānuku (Mother Earth) and receive her nurturing in return.

Conclusion **We Want Foods That Tell Our Story**

RECLAIMING AND CELEBRATING
INDIGENOUS FOOD SOVEREIGNTY

Imagine a garden: a vast, lush expanse sprawling to the edges of the Earth where the land meets the sky. It's brimming with neat rows of potatoes, kūmara, and corn running from east to west. They face the sun because they thrive in light, and they're nestled in gravel soil, which warms up quickly and retains heat. The crops are flanked by shimmering waterways that stretch out into the horizon, healthy and life-giving. On one end of the garden are the Quechua Runakuna; on the other end, the Māori. As they tend these crops and plant medicines embracing agroecological farming practices not to cause harm Pachamama/Papatūānuku (Mother Earth)—methods such as polyculture (intercropping), natural fertilizers, and foot plow tools such as the chakitaqlla[1] and kō[2]—they work down the rows toward each other.

The rows are like the common foodways of these two Indigenous groups. Springing from distinct bodies of knowledge and traditions, these foodways, deeply rooted in their local wisdom or TEK, nonetheless bring these two groups together such that they meet in the middle. In that middle, main food crops are cultivated alongside other food plant relatives to enrich agrobiodiversity. Strict protocols influenced by agricultural calendars—the maramataka and the Quilla/Inti—indicate optimal times for planting and fishing, allowing each seasonal planting to live its full life cycle as prescribed by the natural world. Nurturing hands sustain the life of diverse varieties of seeds and medicinal plants, and rituals and ceremonies express gratitude and celebrate each life cycle. Embracing economies of well-being that do not solely focus on economic growth but also seek equity for all through the promotion of values and principles of reciprocity, gratitude, and equality and guiding ethics of engagement with one another and surroundings, they are building sustainable economic systems. Life is pulsing in this garden, and its caretakers obey not human laws of time but the rhythm of Nature, the sacred heartbeat of the world. They follow the movement of light in the sky and the rotation of seasons through the year. They uphold the moral obligation to naturally regenerate, preserve, and honor the land, Pachamama/Papatūānuku, and the network of human and non-human relationships.

In the twenty-first century, the harmonious human-Nature way of life that Quechua and Māori farmers seek may sound impractical and even utopic, but it can be the seed from which humankind germinates the restoration of the currently inadequate global food system in a way that fosters food security and nutrition, soil fertility, biodiversity, and fair and equitable access to good, healthy food. Reimagining is an essential step in reclaiming and restoring sustainable food systems. Indeed, as the international food sovereignty movement continues to expand, reimagining has become an essential strategy among Quechua and Māori farmers for such reclamation and in reviving Indigenous TEKs as pathways for their cultures to persist and thrive. The rise of today's Indigenous Food Sovereignty movement is part of a political project of resistance and of resurgence to structural violence and historical trauma inflicted by discrimination, violent and capitalist dispossession, and exploitation of the resources found on their lands and territories on which they depend for their economic, spiritual, cultural, and physical well-being—land, labor, water, and seeds. This truth resonates with many minority groups and peoples of color, such as African Americans, South Asians, and Latin Americans, whose ancestors' voices and knowledge contributions to improving food systems are ignored or silenced.

As I write this, we stand at a crossroads for a very fragile world plagued by concerns about environmental degradation, climate change, and the fallout from the global COVID-19 health crisis that continues to sharpen existing threats to human livelihood, particularly to the world's food insecurity. Yet, Indigenous peoples' TEK and philosophies of well-being still see little uptake within mainstream food and environmental policy in charting global solutions. *Recovering Our Ancestral Foodways* demonstrates that we can take this opportunity to embrace a different approach to how we relate to Nature found in millenarian Indigenous holistic philosophies, TEK, innovation, and practices. All these elements are still latent in the lives of my Quechua and Māori research partners. In over a decade of research, I have learned while the TEKs of Quechua and Māori are highly localized, both center on a philosophical strand—if the land is healthy, our foods and our bodies will be health—entrenched in their Indigenous cosmovision. I theorize this fundamental commonality as holistic/collective well-being, known as "allin kawsay" in the highlands of Peru and as "mauri ora" among some Māori collaborators in Aotearoa. I would describe *holistic/collective well-being* as a dynamic, Indigenous-centric, socio-ecological philosophy for living well that presents a treasure trove of ancestral knowledge and traditions passed on with affection, love, and spirituality from one generation to the next. These Indigenous philosophies promote intergenerational justice, biodiversity, social equity, and economies of well-being that are linked to their respective sustainable foodways.

Recovering Our Ancestral Foodways has underscored that Indigenous TEKs of foodways and ideologies of well-being are context-specific. So, we cannot and should not generalize or assume that there is a unified concept of well-being or living well. Nor it is transferable across cultures. Language is at the heart of Indigenous cultures, and they speak more than 4,000 of the world's languages; thus it is impossible to find a well-being concept that suits all societies. For example, as discussed in chapters 3 and 4, although sumak kawsay is widely understood as "living well" or "buen vivir"[3] in the Anglo-Eurocentric academic literature exploring Indigenous philosophies of living well in South America, it is not the concept acknowledged by the Quechua Runakuna who took part in this study. They follow "allin kawsay." In Aotearoa, there is no one single concept used to describe a Māori philosophy of living well; mauri ora was only the most common term I heard. I highlight all of this to emphasize the diversity of epistemologies and to offer a reminder that there is no one

Indigenous view of living well. Indeed, there is no precise terminology within a Peruvian context and the broader Latin American buen vivir discourse. Buen vivir finds its roots in the Spanish translation of various Indigenous traditions of good living or living well that have existed for centuries in South America, as I discussed in chapter 3. There is not a single definition because it emerges from within each Indigenous society's cultural, historical, and political contexts and aspirations, which adds regional nuance to the Spanish concept of buen vivir.

Hence, this book proposes "holistic/collective well-being" to highlight the diversity of Indigenous TEKs, ontologies, ethics, traditions, and value-laden food systems entangled in their respective Indigenous philosophies of life. At the root of holistic/collective well-being is a quest for a harmonious living between humans, the spiritual world, Nature, and society. Both Quechua and Māori research partners argue that achieving holistic/collective well-being depends on reconfiguring our understanding and practice of the quality of our relationships and responsibilities to human and non-human beings. Because these ideologies for living well forgo notions of human superiority in favor of interconnectedness, values, and ethics, I posit that they are prime models for reframing the narrative of the global food system. Food is not a commodity, but it has cultural-spiritual value. It is a treasured gift that we must look after, and an expression of holistic/collective well-being.

In this book I have asked how Indigenous peoples' philosophies—in this case, those of the Quechua and Māori—can contribute to fostering a more inclusive, equitable, and healthy food system in their own communities and at a broader scale. In over ten years of research, I found a new pathway to rebuilding food-sovereign communities through a paradigm shift in food systems. I call for uplifting Indigenous-based food sovereignty frameworks such as the one proposed in this book—the Chakana/Māhutonga (Southern Cross Constellation), a composite, relational, and restorative Indigenous Food Sovereignty framework. The Chakana/Māhutonga emphasizes that Quechua and Māori communities have richly diverse TEKs that offer context-specific solutions for improving our food systems. These solutions, outlined in-depth in the Chakana/Māhutonga's four quadrants, include reconfiguring our relationship with our Earth Mother and becoming agents of social change who participate in eco-culture restoration projects such as Indigenous Food Sovereignty and soil health. They include moving from economies of competition to economies of solidarity, care, and well-being of both people and Nature as the basis for the sustainability and resilience of future food systems.

I argue that this Indigenous Food Sovereignty framework has the potential to "rematriate"—to lead, restore, and regenerate—Indigenous food systems. With it, we can advance an Indigenous holistic/collective philosophy of life promoting socio-ecological values embedded in the Chakana/Māhutonga and the Khipu Model with anticolonial laws, research paradigms, and policies. By utilizing the Khipu Model to dig deep into the theoretical and intellectual foundations of Quechua and Māori research partners' philosophies of well-being and sustainable food systems, this book has revealed rich narratives, land-based wisdom, and lived experiences unique to the Quechua and the Māori. The Khipu Model confronts and challenges mainstream research; it is a counter-story that highlights the vital roles of epistemology, ontology, and accountability in the process of conducting research with Indigenous communities. The Khipu Model and the Chakana/Māhutonga call for conducting research through working *with, by,* and *for* the benefit of Indigenous communities to enrich the study of Indigenous TEKs. The Khipu Model joins in the efforts and voices of Indigenous peoples globally seeking to reclaim and restore the importance of Indigenous TEK and teachings to revitalize cultural and environmental stewardship practices and prioritize Nature-based solutions.

In this book I have posited that Indigenous Food Sovereignty is a movement, method, and framework for rematriating holistic/collective well-being. For Quechua and Māori collaborators, Indigenous Food Sovereignty is about their right to live in dignity, honoring relationships with foodways to produce nutritionally and culturally appropriate food and plant medicines from the land on which they live and depend to sustain themselves, their families, and their communities. Thus, *Indigenous* Food Sovereignty is distinct from other food sovereignty movements of the last four decades. Whereas human-rights-based food sovereignty enacts the right to food as a human right, Indigenous Food Sovereignty is a holistic/collective approach to the right to preserve the integrity of the non-human kinship-centric system in addition to food as a human right. Rather than adding social justice components to an environmentally sustainable food system, Indigenous Food Sovereignty involves building a food system on a social justice foundation. Values such as reciprocity, generosity, intergenerational knowledge, gender equity, and agency are deployed to correct historical and structural injustices. In ways that are distinct for each Indigenous group, Indigenous Food Sovereignty underscores Indigenous rights to self-determination, cultural knowledge, and sovereignty. These elements allow Quechua and Māori to operationalize the rematriation of a holistic/collective approach when cultivating, hunting, fishing, gathering, preparing, sharing, and gifting (recirculating) food.

The book's findings evidence how the practice of an Indigenous holistic/collective philosophy of life as it pertains to food sovereignty can positively influence individual and community wellness outcomes and facilitate social and environmental justice. This discussion suggests the necessity for and potential of future lines of research on the value of Indigenous TEK and holistic philosophies of living well. It urges us to question: what would our food systems look like if they were designed to promote holistic/collective well-being? The book calls for new insights and perspectives on food sovereignty, self-determination, equity and justice, and ecological health as the center of food security and nutrition and the reshaping of mechanisms to increase the possibility of success.

International organizations advocating for the recognition of Indigenous peoples' rights and the rights of Nature offer hope for a global development agenda.[4] As a growing number of non-Indigenous peoples want to support the struggles of Indigenous peoples for food sovereignty and to preserve their holistic philosophies of life, implementing good allyship practices is paramount. These practices include understanding Indigenous cosmovisions, the United Nations Declaration on the Rights of Indigenous Peoples, and recognizing the validity of Native science. It also requires a more inclusive, participatory, food systems knowledge approach in which the voices and land-based knowledge of vulnerable societies, low-income communities, and communities of color are heard, acknowledged, and incorporated into policymaking. Failure to understand good allyship has not only hindered Indigenous aspirations to build vibrant, resilient, and sustainable food systems; it also serves to create and entrench further inequities and injustices.

DANCING IN GRATITUDE: CELEBRATING SEEDS OF HOPE AND WELL-BEING SPROUTING WORLDWIDE

This book is also a celebration of all the achievements made thus far by Indigenous peoples in Aotearoa, Peru, and around the globe in rematriating cultures of holistic/collective well-being and planting seeds of hope through restoring and elevating Indigenous Food Sovereignty and local food systems. In over a decade of research for this book, I had the opportunity to travel, visiting and taking part in intertribal food summits, Indigenous food/seed sovereignty conferences, and Indigenous gastronomical events with Indigenous communities in Mexico, Ecuador, Chile, Peru, Aotearoa, Norway, Australia, South Africa, and on Turtle Island (North America). In all these gatherings, as an Indigenous scholar, I connected and re-connected with Indigenous peoples of all ages and from all corners of the world, grassroots organizations, and civil society, forming long-lasting friendships and collaborations with many of them. These events and discussions around how to holistically heal and restore the health and well-being of the land, our bodies, and our diets through our Indigenous philosophies of food sovereignty were invigorating. They illustrated how, beyond Aotearoa and Peru, traditional Indigenous farmers and urban, local, small-scale farmers around the world continue to sprout new discussions, activities, and actions restoring soil health through weaving together holistic kinship relationships, respecting agency, and standing firm on the ground, expressing gratitude, respect, and love for the soil they sow.[5]

The visibility of an Indigenous Food Sovereignty movement is inspiring! There is a growing international Indigenous Food Sovereignty movement as Indigenous peoples are building empowering food sovereignty initiatives and making connections with each other across the globe. They do this by upholding relational philosophies of well-being and traditional methods for restoring, in a holistic/collective manner, the soil and ecologies on which we all depend—and promoting this as a life-affirming and vital strategy in reclaiming vibrant Indigenous food systems that bolster food-secure and sovereign futures for all. Here are just a few examples based on my first-hand experience in Aotearoa, Peru and Turtle Island. In the rural areas of Aotearoa is the grassroots organization Rapua E te Iwi nga Kai o nga Atua (People, look for the food of the gods for wellness), known as REKA,[6] which established an educational food garden in 2008 where Māori children learn about the foodways of their ancestors. In an urban setting, Waitakere, located on the east side of the Auckland region, has also become an active, urban, food sovereignty hub with seasonal food-foraging expeditions to the Waitakere Ranges and bountiful birdlife and fruit trees.[7]

In Peru, in 2019, the youth in the Slow Food Peru network organized the Latin American Congress of Young Farmers, also called SISAY ("blooming" in the Quechua language). The goal of the organization is to empower young people to become leaders of responsible farming and healthy food in their communities.[8] Another example in Peru is "Generación con causa" (Generation with a cause). The Generación con causa is a movement of Peruvian chefs from Lima and various regions of the country whose mission is to maintain the tradition and heritage of Peruvian cuisine and bolster food sovereignty.[9] Indigenous chefs globally are championing Indigenous foodways and culinary traditions as ways of rematriating the richness and diversity of wild and domesticated foods and revitalizing Indigenous cuisine. For example, Māori chefs such Peter Gordon and Monique Fisko in Aotearoa are transforming New Zealanders' perceptions of Māori foods and culinary traditions. These chefs are prioritizing purchasing ingredients from Indigenous producers, revitalizing Indigenous cuisine, and promoting through their culinary contributions the vast diversity of local and Indigenous food cultures.

In July 2021, I sat down with Peter Gordon in his newly opened restaurant, Homeland, located at the heart of Auckland's central business district, to talk about Indigenous foods and gastronomy. Peter described his vision for Homeland to serve as the food embassy of Māori, the Pacific, and beyond. He imagined that Homeland would connect directly with local food growers and producers such as the Papatūānuku Kōkiri Marae (an urban food garden) not only to cut costs but also so that native Māori foods could once again become treasured foodways. Peter and those who work with him seek to foster an appreciation and love of traditional Māori recipes that have been difficult to prepare due to the lack of accessibility of pre-contact food plants such as kawakawa tree (plant medicine), pikopiko (new fern fronds), and the now widely available kūmara (sweet potato) grown by Māori. One way to do this is through Homeland's "Community Wednesdays," a fortnightly event in which an array of people engaged or interested in revitalizing Indigenous foods gather at Homeland to enjoy a cooking demonstration and hands-on class with a focus on Māori ingredients or themes. Grassroots organizations, school groups, local producers, charities, and small food businesses have all taken part. The one I attended included a lesson on how to cook fish head soup. For me, and perhaps for others, it was a rekindling of childhood memories. As Peter pointed out, it has a broader message: a reminder "that our ancestors did not waste food."[10]

This Indigenous Food Sovereignty work extends far beyond Peru and Aotearoa. In the United States, the Indigenous Seed Keepers Network—an organization linked to the Native American Food Sovereignty Alliance—hosts seed exchanges in workshops instructed by Mohawk seed-keeper Rowen White in intertribal food summits and conferences, as well as other places. The organization educates people in tribal communities about seed saving and seed sovereignty, and how to preserve native seeds and share them within the community.[11] Native American Chefs Sean Sherman (Oglala Lakota Sioux), Elena Terry (Ho-Chunk), Maria Gladstone (Blackfeet, Cherokee), Carlos Baca (Diné/Tewa/Nuche), Claudia Serrato (P'urhépecha/Xicana), Loretta Barret Oden (Potawatomi), and Neftalí Durán (Oaxaqueño) are among those playing key roles in the Indigenous Food Sovereignty movement. These chefs are sparking conversations about and movements supporting Indigenous Food Sovereignty and food justice among producers and among consumers, ultimately shaping and re-shaping market economies. The resulting Indigenous Food Sovereignty networks also embody a lively socio-ecological and market-based economy that enables economies of well-being and Indigenous entrepreneurship by reducing the physical and social distance between producers and consumers.[12]

I also learned through my relationships with Quechua and Māori collaborators that resilience, determination, love of, and respect for Pachamama/Papatūānuku are key drivers in rematriating holistic/collective well-being. This thinking resonates with other Indigenous peoples globally, such as many Native Americans. As čišaaʔatḥ (Tseshaht)/Nuu-chah-nulth Indigenous Food Sovereignty scholar Charlotte Coté maintains, to address food insecurity and realize community wellness requires "revitalizing Indigenous foods systems and practices through the reaffirmation of spiritual, emotional and physical relationships to the

Figure 24. Left: a sign in the Māori language conveying Māori resilience; the English translation means: "hold fast to your Māoritanga (being Māori)." Right: a sign in Spanish honoring the potato, a highly prized food crop of Peru, as a reminder of the vibrant biodiversity of the country. It highlights the huayro, a variety of potato widely consumed in Peru. At the center of the image is a phrase translated as "your roots [referring to the potatoes] are the foundation of our origins [referring to Peruvians]." Photos: Mariaelena Huambachano.

lands, waters, plants, and all living things that have sustained Indigenous communities and cultures."[13] Coté's call to action resonates with my Quechua and Māori research partners and illustrates the imperative to seek justice for the fertile ground from which all of their existence springs, both physically and spiritually, to ensure that Mother Earth, humans and non-human kin, and deities like mountains and rivers flourish together.

The garden that began this chapter does not have to be an ideal or a fantasy; that vibrancy and abundance of nourishment for both body and soul can be a reality if we return the nurturing of the land and the production of that which nurtures us to the foodways of the Indigenous peoples and local communities. The blossoming and embellishment of the Indigenous Food Sovereignty movement encourage us to continue reimagining healthy food systems and working collectively to reposition holistic philosophies of well-being and Indigenous Food Sovereignty at the heart of sustainable food systems. We must hold fast to our traditions, values, and creativity in order to forge sustainable futures.

Glossary of Māori and Quechua Terms

This glossary provides definitions for the Māori and Quechua words that are used throughout this book. The meanings reflect the context in which the words have been used. Therefore, caution must be exercised when using the words in a different context. Definitions of the Māori words have been sourced from the Dictionary of the Māori Language by Herbert Williams and Te Aka Māori-English, English-Māori Dictionary. Similarly, definitions of Quechua words have been sourced from Spanish-Quechua, Quechua-English Dictionary by Odi Gonzales, Christine Madie Janney, and Emily Fjaellen Thompson. A definition of Māori and Quechua words is provided the first time the word appears in the body of this book. When the description is short, it is provided in parentheses directly after the word. When the definition is long, it is provided as a footnote so that the definition does not disrupt the flow of the sentence.

MĀORI

Ahi kā long burning fires of occupation, continuous occupation—title to land through occupation by a group, generally over a long period of time
Aotearoa the Māori name for New Zealand
Atua ancestor with continuing influence, god, demon, supernatural being, deity, ghost

GLOSSARY

Hākari	sumptuous meal, feast, banquet, celebration, entertainment, to have a feast
Hapu	descendants of a common ancestor, sub-tribes
Hui	gatherings
Iwi	tribe, nation
Kai	food
Kaitiakitanga	guardianship of the land, caring
Karakia	prayer
Kaumātua	respected tribal Elder
Kaupapa	purpose, intention, reasons for action
Kina	sea urchin or sea egg
Koroua	elderly Māori men
Koura	freshwater crayfish
Kuia	Māori female elder
Kūmara	sweet potatoes
Mahinga Kai	Māori customary food-gathering sites and practices
Mana moana	authority over lands and resources
Mana whenua	authority and power over land or territory
Mana	spiritual power, prestige, sovereignty and strength
Manaakitanga	to care for, hospitality
Manuhiri	a guest
Māra kai	food gardens
Marae	communal or sacred meeting place
Maramataka	the Māori lunar calendar
Mauri	life principle, life force, source of emotions
Moana	sea, ocean, large lake
Mātauranga	Māori body of knowledge determined from Māori values, wisdom.
Ora	life, embodied mauri
Papatūānuku	Mother Earth, wife of Rangi-nui—all living things originate from them
Pātaka	storehouse raised upon posts, pantry, larder
Patere	a form of chant that gives the Māori great pleasure
Paua	the shell of the paua, abalone
Pito	umbilical cord
Pōwhiri	rituals of encounter
Rāhui	to put in place a temporary ritual prohibition
Rangatira	Māori leader, chief (male or female)
Ranginui	Māori Sky Father, God of the sky and husband of Papatūānuku—all living things originate from them
Rohe	tribal areas/ boundaries

Rongomātāne	the God of agriculture, God of the kūmara and cultivated food and one of the offspring of Ranginui and Papatūānuku
Rongoā	medicine, remedy, cure, medication, treatment, solution (to a problem), tonic
Taewa or rīwai	Māori potatoes
Tangata whenua	People of the land
Taonga	treasure, visible or invisible things considered valuable
Tapu	Restriction, prohibition—a supernatural condition
Te ao Māori	the Māori world view
Te kore	energy, potential, the void, nothingness
Te reo	the Indigenous language of Aotearoa New Zealand
Te taiao	the natural environment
Tiaki	to care for people and place (to guard)
Tika	natural, right, true, correct
Tikanga	Māori customary/ethical practices or behaviors
Tino rangatiratanga	absolute power and authority, sovereignty, self determination
Tipa	scallop
Tupuna	a grandparent or ancestor
Tūrangawaewae	place where one has the right to stand.
Waewae	leg, foot, footprint
Waiata	song, chant, psalm
Wairua	spirit, soul—spirit of a person which exists beyond death
Wairuatanga	spirituality
Waka	canoe, groups of people with links to canoe
Whakapapa	genealogical connections, lineage, descent
Whenua tipu	traditional lands
Whenua	land, soil, placenta
Whānau	kin, extended family

QUECHUA

Apus	Andean deity
Ayllu	community, family
Ayninakuy (short ayni)	to practice reciprocity
Allin kawsay	well-being or harmony between human beings and nature
Ch'alla	Andean ritual
Cchaninchay	solution, value, fair

Chakitaklla	footplow
Chakra	field (agricultural), farming land
Ch'arki	jerky, dried meat
Ch'uñu	dehydrated potato
Chiri	cold
Uchu	pepper, chili
Chiri uchu	typical Andean dish
Chanikuy	to keep food to be shared (value)
Huatia	earth oven
Kañihua	a Peruvian seed, a close relative to quinoa
Mayu	river
Mink'a	system of mutual help, system of communal work
Parakay	a variety of native maize in the Andean highlands of Peru
Pachamama	mother earth
Qochas	lake, lagoon
Runakuna	people of the Andes
Yanantin-masintin	a philosophical principle that explains complementary opposites

Notes

INTRODUCTION

1. There are many theories about the sweet potato's origin. The most accepted is that its birthplace was in the current nation of Peru. In 1968, Peruvian archeologist Bernardino Ojeda Enríquez discovered one the oldest samples of potato and sweet potato—dating to 8000 BCE—in caverns at Chilca Canyon locally known as Tres Ventanas (three windows), in the south-central area of coastal Peru. The caverns were located 65 kilometers southeast of Lima in the low highlands (Sierra) of Huarochirí, Sierra de Lima, in Peru, at an altitude of 2,800 meters. Archaeologists have found prehistoric remnants of sweet potatoes in Polynesia from about 1000 CE to 1100 CE and hypothesized that those ancient seeds came from the western coast of South America. One Polynesian word for sweet potato is kuumala, which resembles kumara, or cumal, the words for the sweet potato in the Quechua language. In Peru, the most common word for sweet potato is camote. It is called papa dulce and batata in other South American countries. Sweet potatoes are known as kūmara in Te Ika-a-Māui (North Island of Aotearoa) where this study took place. They are known as kūmera in Te Waipounamu (South Island of Aotearoa). In the South Pacific, the kūmara is known by various names such as kumaa in the Marquesas Islands and kumala in Fiji, Tonga, Vanuatu, and Tokelau. For a detailed list of the names of the kūmara in the South Pacific, see Roskruge and Semese (2020). For more on the "sweet potato" see Yen (1971); Roskruge (2009); Whitbourne (2017).

2. Chorrillos is a small fishing village. The area around the Morro Solar in Chorrillos was once a pre-Columbian settlement known as Armatambo. The first settlers were fishermen from the Yschma culture during pre-Inka times, and later the Inkas named it Pachakamaq. Thank you to Uncle Julio Bringas Huambachano for this historical account of Chorrillos.

3. I use a capital "I" in referring to Indigenous peoples, Aboriginals, and First Nations, as a sign of respect the same way that English, French, and Spanish, etc. are capitalized. The term "Indigenous" grew out of Indigenous activism in the 1970s when Aboriginal groups organized transnationally and pushed for greater presence of Indigenous peoples in the United Nations (UN), and the UN later adopted the term. Aboriginal leaders adopted it in the 1970s after the emergence of Indigenous rights movements around the world as a way to identify and unite their communities and represent them in political arenas such as the United Nations. For more information on how this term was developed, please see Indigenous Foundations (2023).

4. Ariqipa in Quechua and Are'kipa in Aymara.

5. Chakra is a Quechua word that broadly translates to farm, land sown with seed, and agricultural field. Other spellings in Spanish are chacra, chagra, and chajra; chacra is the most commonly used. The term has no connection to the homonym that yoga practitioners use to point out focal points in meditation practices. For more on the Andean chakra see Perrault (2005).

6. It is called yunza in the Coastal region, sacha cuchuy in the Andean, and umisha in the Amazon region. In English yunza is translated as a wild grass cutter. Yunza is celebrated differently across Peru. My own family used to gather at my Aunt Juanita's backyard, where we had danced in ayllu (community), holding hands around a beautiful capulí tree that was decorated with colorful balloons, flowers, and sweets. Capulí is a fruit tree that is native to the Andes of Peru; its leaves are long and green, and in February the capulí tree is the preferred tree for the yunza carnival.

7. Sadly, in August 1986 our planned family visit to grandmother's chakra was abruptly cancelled when my family was advised against travelling to Acarí due to the activity of a Peruvian revolutionary organization named The Shining Path (in Spanish, Sendero Luminoso). The Shining Path rebellion brought poverty, and political, economic, and social unrest to Peru throughout the 1980s and 1990s. The country witnessed the violation of rural Indigenous peoples' human rights; they were murdered, and displaced from their ancestral lands.

8. In this book, I use the terms foodways and traditional food systems interchangeably. Both terms denote the wisdom and practices of domesticated food plants and animals within Indigenous ancestral lands, and this body of knowledge is entrenched in stories, songs, and recipes. Thus, I highlight Indigenous peoples' distinctive ways of growing, preparing, storing, and sharing foods such as edible plants, food crops, and animals within their geographic area,

and the way they preserve traditional food systems through cultural principles such as respect, reciprocity, and biological sensibility, among other values.

9. The full Māori name is Te Kaokaoroa o Pātetere; it is located in the Waikato region of the North Island of Aotearoa.

10. The Māori man told me that kūmara was the most important crop for Māori in traditional times and about Māori tribal histories that featured the kūmara as deeply ingrained in the whakapapa, or genealogy, of the Māori. When their Polynesian ancestors arrived in Aotearoa, they brought their own traditional food crops, among them the kūmara. Because kūmara flourished abundantly throughout the summer, it was and remains a treasured crop, vital to the Māori people's survival. After his recounting, the Māori man and I playfully argued over the kūmara's origins, each of us laughingly wishing to lay claim to a crop that so clearly belongs to itself and that chose and chooses to lay its roots in both of our respective homelands. For more information on the importance of kūmara for Māori see Roskruge (2009, 2011); Roberts et al. (2004); Yen (1961); Whitbourne (2017).

11. In an Indigenous epistemology agriculture biodiversity, or agrobiodiversity, is an in-depth understanding and value about the diversity of biological beings, including plants, animals, insects, and landforms. This concept acknowledges that spiritual beings—deities such as mountains and rivers—have rights that Indigenous peoples and their descendants must respect, nourish, and preserve. See Harmsworth and Roskruge (2014); McGregor (2004); Gadgil, Berkes, and Folke (1993). For more information on biodiversity and agrobiodiversity see Pilling and Bélanger (2019); IPBES (2019).

12. Huambachano (2012, 2015a, 2015b, 2016, 2018, 2019, 2020).

13. I capitalize Nature to highlight its legal personhood. This means that the environment and animals, non-human persons, have rights. The rights of Nature are enshrined in the Universal Declaration of the Rights of Mother Earth. See Global Alliance for the Rights of Nature (GARN) 2023.

14. See Holt-Giménez (2017) and Nestle (2019) to understand the history of our global food system and the basics of one of its main drivers—capitalism.

15. See the most recent Māori health statistics from the New Zealand Ministry of Health – Manatū Hauora (2023).

16. See Ministerio de Cultura, Peru (2023); FAO et al. (2023).

17. Moeke-Pickering et al. (2015); Huambachano (2018); Campbell (2020).

18. Huambachano (2018); Coté (2016); Morrison (2011); Daigle (2019).

19. A Khipu consists of one long primary cord of approximately one centimeter thick, woven from llama or alpaca wool laces, and with a series of subsequent pendant cords attached to it. Each pendant cord has a particular color, spin, knot, and contains encoded information. See Chirinos Rivera (2010); Urton (2003).

20. See for example Shiva (2016b); Wittman and James (2022); Nestle (2019); Patel (2012); Holt-Giménez (2017); Patel and Moore (2017); Pimbert and Uhnák

(2019); Bezner Kerr et al. (2022); Calvário and Desmarais (2023); Duncan and Claeys (2018).

21. See the scholarship of Turtle Island scholars Melisa Nelson (2019), Charlotte Coté (2022), Kyle Whyte (2016), Dawn Morrison (2011), Valerie Segrest (2013), Michelle Daigle (2019), Tabitha Robin Martens (2018). In Africa see Million Belay (2017), Grace Mudombi-Rusinamhodzi, and Leonard Rusinamhodzi (2022). In Oceania see Hutchings, et al. (2012), Moeke-Pickering, et al. (2015).

CHAPTER 1

1. New Zealand Ministry of Health—Manatū Hauora (2023).
2. Biodiversity is all the different kinds of life you'll find in one area—the variety of animals, plants, fungi, and even microorganisms like bacteria that make up our natural world Legal instruments to pursue global biodiversity are the Cartagena Protocol on Biosafety to the Convention on Biological Diversity (UNEP 2000); the Nagoya Protocol on Access and Benefit-Sharing (CBD, 2010); and the Convention on Biological Diversity's "National Biodiversity Strategies and Action Plans (NBSAPs)" (CBD 2023, updated regularly). The Conference of the Parties, which is the governing body of the Convention on Biological Diversity, regularly releases documents, including the "Convention on Biological Diversity" itself (CBD 2016).

For agrobiodiversity generally, see note 11 in the introduction. Agrobiodiversity is embedded in biocultural heritage, which refers to the customary practices of agrobiodiversity, traditional ecological knowledge, and cultural values as a legacy inherited from our Indigenous ancestors, proving a treasure trove for improving food systems, health, and well-being. For more info on agrobiodiversity and biocultural heritage see FAO (2019); CBD (2023).

3. INEI (2017).
4. See Fitzmaurice (2014); Borch (2001).
5. Wolfe (1999); see also Wolfe (2006).
6. Quijano (1995); Mariátegui (1988); Valcárel (2015).
7. Mutu (2018).
8. Orange (2015); Hutchings and Smith (2020).
9. See Halperin (2018); Esteva (1992).
10. See Rist (2009, 2007).
11. Truman (1949).
12. See Holt-Giménez (2017); McMichael (2009); Stiglitz (2002).
13. Maia (2022); Harvey (2005).
14. FAO, IFAD, UNICEF, WFP and WHO (2022).
15. Whyte (2016, 6).
16. INEI (2017).

17. Australian Bureau of Statistics (2015).
18. Kuhnlein (2017); La Via Campesina (n.d.); Norgaard, Reed, and Van Horn (2011).
19. Kimmerer (2013, 31).
20. This agenda aimed to address the shortcomings of the eight development millennium goals (MDGs) that UN member states signed in September 2000 and agreed to achieve by the year 2015 (UNDEA 2020).
21. UNDEA (2015).
22. Tauli-Corpuz (2015).
23. DiPrete Brown et al. (2020).
24. Also spelled Mino-Biimaadzawin. See LaDuke (1999); McGregor (2018).
25. Nuu-chah-nulth (nuučaańuɫ) or Nootka (/ˈnuːtkə/) is a Wakashan language in the Pacific Northwest of North America on the West Coast of Vancouver, Canada.
26. Chibvongodze (2016); Le Grange (2012); Lefa (2015, 15); Kayira (2015); Qobo and Nyathi (2016).
27. UNWCED (1987, 43).
28. See Muru-Lanning (2016); New Zealand Legislature (2017).
29. Cárdenas and Mestokosho (2023).
30. Whyte (2021).
31. Ricciardi et al. (2021).
32. Berkes (2012).
33. For a discussion of the TEK of Indigenous peoples, please see LaDuke (2005, 1999); Berkes (2012); Pierotti and Wildcat (2000); TallBear (2013); McGregor (2004).
34. McGregor (2004, 386).
35. The right to food, as inseparable from other rights, has been recognized as a fundamental human right since the 1948 Universal Declaration of Human Rights and is enshrined in the 1966 International Covenant on Economic, Social and Cultural Rights. The right to food has also been recognized and incorporated into national law in many countries and is covered in the constitutions of well over one hundred countries. See UNHCR (2010); de Schutter (2012); Knuth and Vidar (2011).
36. See UNHCR (2010, 2).
37. See Altieri and Nicholls (2012); Iles (2005); Montenegro de Wit (2021); Gliessman (2007); Perfecto, Vandermeer, and Wright (2019); Wittman (2011).
38. See The White House (2022).
39. See civil society actors (e.g., HLPE 2019; IPES-Food 2023); social movements (e.g., La Via Campesina n.d.), and intergovernmental organizations (e.g., FAO 2022; FAO et al. 2023).
40. Altieri (1995, 8). There is an extensive literature on agroecology. See Altieri and Nicholls (2005, 2012); Bezner Kerr et al. (2022); Holt-Giménez et al.

(2021); Pimbert and Uhnák (2019); Mburu (2007); Gliessman (2007); Rosset et al. (2011); Wittman et al. (2010).

41. HLPE (2019); UNDEA (2020); La Via Campesina (2017)
42. Pimbert (2017).
43. See Agrawal (1995); Gadgil, Berkes, and Folke (1993); Holling, Berkes, and Folke (2000, 342).
44. FAO (2001).
45. Clapp et al. (2022, 102164).
46. HLPE (2020, xvii).
47. Swaminathan (2012); Zambrano et al. (2022, 825930); Bernstein and Woodhouse (2010); Pinstrup-Andersen (2003: 116); Holt-Giménez and Shattuck (2011); Holt-Giménez et al. (2021); Clapp and Purugganan (2020); Desmarais et al. (2017).
48. McMichael and Scoones (2011, 4).
49. See Hutchings, Smith, and Harmsworth (2018).
50. See Claeys (2015); Desmarais and Handy (2014, 4); Wittman, Desmarais, and Wiebe (2010); Whyte (2016); Manohar et al. (2023, 140).
51. The origins of the term "food sovereignty" are described in many places, including La Vía Campesina's website; see https://viacampesina.org/en/food-sovereignty.
52. Declaration of Nyéléni (2007).
53. Menser (2014, 59).
54. Hutchings (2023).
55. Corntassel (2008, 107, 122).
56. See Coté (2016, 57); Morrison (2011, 100); Daigle (2019); Nelson and Shilling (2018); Segrest (2013); Moeke-Pickering et al. (2015).
57. Morrison (2011, 100).
58. Corntassel and Bryce (2012).
59. Daigle (2019).
60. Wittman (2011); Grey and Patel (2015).
61. This is a summary of my notes taken from presentations about "Introduction to Seed Saving" and "Seed Banking and Selection" by Rowen White and Clayton Brascoupe, members of the Indigenous Seed Keepers Network, at the Great Lakes Food Sovereignty Summit, Jijak Camp, MI, April 2017. For conference information, see https://iacgreatlakes.files.wordpress.com/2017/10/great-lakes-summit-brochure_2017.pdf.
62. The first time I heard about the word "rematriation" was when I attended the Great Lakes Intertribal Food Summit held by the Gun Lake Potawatomi at the Jijak Foundation Camp in southern Michigan on April 22, 2017. Rowen White also explained the concept's role within the seed and food sovereignty movement further in personal communications between 2017 and 2022.
63. See FAO et al. (2023).

64. See UN News (2020).
65. Other terms exist in both contexts.
66. UNGA (2007); UNHRC (2018).

CHAPTER 2

1. This Māori proverb was composed by Mihi-ki-te-kapua, a Māori waita (song) composer of the tribe of Ngati Ruapani and Tuhoe iwi in the North Island of Aotearoa.
2. Grillo (1998).
3. The term mestizo (male) and mestiza (female), broadly speaking, means someone who has both European and Indigenous heritage. Peruvian mestizos have on average 60 percent genes of native origin, that is, Quechuas, Asháninca*s*, and Matziguengas, among others. This is the highest percentage observed among Latin American mestizo populations, according to research presented by the National Institute of Health (INS) of the Ministry of Health. See Instituto Nacional de Salud (2018).
4. Anglo-Eurocentrism is intertwined with English-language hegemony, and advantages garnered by Anglo-European universities were further consolidated during the Cold War era, when English became the dominant academic lingua franca and Anglo-European educational models were considered "standard" if not superior in other countries and regions. See Alcoff (2017, 11); Chakrabarty (2000).
5. In the years between 1994 and 2004, also known as the "Decade of the World's Indigenous Peoples," Indigenous scholars such as Linda Tuhiwai Smith, Graham Hingangaroa Smith, Maria Battiste, James Youngblood Henderson, and Shawn Wilson heavily criticized Western epistemologies and methodologies, calling for a process of Indigenizing Western methodologies. See Battiste and Henderson (2000); G. H. Smith (2005); L. T. Smith (2012); Wilson (2001); Cajete (2000); Chilisa (2012); Kovach (2009).
6. For further discussions of Western tradition of knowledge production from Indigenous scholars, see Bishop (2005); Battiste (2000); L. T. Smith (2005); Chilisa (2020); Buntu (2013).
7. Also known as Quipu, the Spanish spelling and the most common spelling in English academic literature. Early descriptions of the invention of the Khipu system were recorded in the seventeenth century by Indigenous Peruvian chroniclers such as Inka Garcilazo de la Vega and Felipe Guamán Poma de Ayala.
8. Chirinos Rivera (2010); Urton (1998); Medrano (2021).
9. Another example is the Ceiba or tree of life, which was developed by Vivian Jiménez Estrada (2005), an Indigenous scholar of Mayan ancestry.

10. Throughout this book, I capitalize "Elder" as a sign of respect for those who are knowledge holders and authorities in their community and nations' land/sea-based philosophy of living well.

11. According to Mason Durie (2005, 45), tino rangatiratanga "captures a sense of Māori ownership and active control over the future."

12. See Moko Mead (2003); Cajete (2000); Royal (2012); Hikuroa (2017).

13. Pohatu (2005, 5).

14. Rangimarie (1982).

15. Wilson (2009, 73).

16. Weber-Pillwax (2004).

17. Swantz (2008).

18. See L. T. Smith (2012); G. H. Smith (2003); Pihama (2015); Archibald (1992); Bishop and Glynn (1999); Bishop (1991); Buntu (2013); Battiste (2000); Esteva (2015); Mignolo (1999); Henry and Pene (2001); TallBear (2013); Cajete (2000).

19. In Peru, the food baskets consisted of free-range chicken, mandarins, oranges, apples, pears, lettuce, onions, gluten-free bread, pasta, organic brown rice, coffee, and herbal teas.

20. In Aotearoa. the food baskets consisted of kūmara, potatoes, lettuce, onions, tomatoes, organic meat, chicken, free-range eggs, mandarins, oranges, apples, and gluten-free products such as bread, biscuits, and pasta.

21. Wilson (2009).

22. Bryman and Bell (2011).

23. This is a summary of my notes during field work in Choquecancha in 2014.

24. Kimmerer (2015); Archibald (2008).

25. Collis and Hussey (2003).

26. Yin (2009).

27. LeCompte et al. (1993).

28. Between June and September 2014, I visited the Biblioteca Publica de Cusco (the main public library in Cusco, Peru), which is located at an altitude of 2,200 meters (7, 217 feet) above sea level between the charming colonial and precolonial buildings that intermingle across the hills of the city. From the central plaza of Cusco, cobbled streets give way to stone staircases leading to the picturesque town of San Blas, which is within walking distance of the library. Fittingly, among all these beautiful buildings, the Cusco public library has one of the most magnificent research rooms, full of archival data. The library was founded in the 1800s and existed in several different places until it moved to its current location in 1993. The library holds over six thousand volumes on a variety of subjects, especially Andean history. In January 2015, I travelled to Bolivia, specifically to the city of Sucre, a twenty-seven-hour bus ride from Cusco. Sucre is home to the National Archive and

Andean Library. The National Archives and Library of Bolivia were established in 1836 and hold around 114,000 volumes and relevant documents dating from the time of the high imperial court (from 1530 to 1804).

29. G. H. Smith (1997a, 171).

30. L. T. Smith (2012, 12).

31. Pihama (2015); Archibald (1992); Bishop and Glynn (1999); Bishop (1991); G. H. Smith (2003).

32. See L. T. Smith (2012); Pihama (2010); Chilisa (2020); G. H. Smith (1997a).

33. Quijano (2000).

34. Collins (1991); Ladson-Billings (2000); Mohanty (1984).

35. Quijano (2000); G. H. Smith (1997a); Wilson (2009); Bishop (2011).

36. See Wilson (2001); Chilisa (2020); L. T. Smith (2012); Pihama (2015, 5–15).

37. For further discussions on Indigenous research paradigms see Wilson (2001); Chilisa (2020); Royal (2014).

38. Chávez (2022, 129).

39. Freire (2018, 360).

40. Duarte (2017, 175).

41. See D'Cruz, Gillingham, and Melendez (2007); Gilgun (2010).

42. Wilson (2009, 7).

43. Huambachano (2012, 2015a, 2015b, 2016, 2018, 2019, 2020).

44. During my visit to the Awajún people living in Moyobamba, I noted that in Moyobamba, specifically in the area of Alto Mayo, fourteen Indigenous communities are the stewards of Peru's most biodiverse regions, the Alto Mayo landscape's natural resources.

45. This is a summary of my notes during field work in the Awajún Native Community of Shampuyaco in 2013.

46. See Moko Mead (2003).

47. Professor Mānuka Hēnare died, sadly, on January 23, 2021. I was in Aotearoa conducting fieldwork in the tribe of Ngāti Porou when I received the news of his death. In mid-December 2020, I visited Mānuka at the hospice in Auckland, where I had the opportunity to thank him for all the valuable knowledge he kindly shared with me.

48. The Waitangi Tribunal is a permanent commission of inquiry set up by the Treaty of Waitangi Act 1975 to hear and make recommendations on claims brought by Māori, mostly on the dispossession of Māori land relating to Crown actions that breach the promises made in the Treaty of Waitangi. See Waitangi Tribunal (n.d.).

49. See n. 5 above. Other scholars from Latin America, Asia, and Africa have urged the democratization of knowledge, including Indigenous knowledge, in

NOTES

higher education. See Gonzales (2015); Esteva (2015); Shiva (2005); Gathuru (2007); Pimbert (2017).

50. Walter and Andersen (2013).

CHAPTER 3

1. Mate Heitia (Māori), Whakatāne, Aotearoa New Zealand, November 4, 2020.

2. Taewa (Solanum spp.) or rīwai is a collective name for multiple varieties of potatoes (Solanum tuberosum). Taewa is also known by other names, which vary according to tribal dialects around the country, such as peruperu, parareka, mahetau, and rīwai. Many Māori assert that taewa predated the European settlement of Aoteroa and that many varieties arrived with the first European explorers, such as Cook, in 1769 and subsequently with visiting whalers and sealers in the latter part of the eighteenth century. For more information on taewa by Māori scholars see Roskruge (1999); McFarlane (2007); and for non-Māori see Yen (1962, 2–5).

3. Interview with Amauta Condori (Quechua), Cusco, Peru, July 12, 2014. Runakuna is a Quechua word that translates to "peoples of the Andes." I capitalize Runakuna to acknowledge it is a noun used in this book to identify a particular group of people. For example, "the Runakuna of Choquecancha" refers to the Andean/Quechua people of Choquecancha.

4. Latouche (2004, 2007); Illich (1973); Naess (1973).

5. Quijano (1992); Cusicanqui (2012); De Sousa Santos (1977); Escobar (2019); Lugones, 2008.

6. "Sumak" is also spelled "sumaq." Outside of the Peruvian highlands setting, the Indigenous concept of sumak kawsay is widely understood as "living well" and frequently used in non-Indigenous scholars' academic writing about Indigenous philosophies of living well.

7. Choquecancha is located approximately 3850 meters (12,800 feet) above sea level. Rosaspata is approximately 3350 meters (11,000 feet) above sea level. Sacaca is located 3069 meters (10,200 feet) above sea level. Pampacorral is 3055 meters (10,000 feet) above sea level. Ccachin is located at 2921 meters (9600 feet) above sea level. All of them in the District of Lares, province of Calca, Department of Cusco.

8. See Gudynas (2011); Merino (2016); Quijano (1992); Walsh (2010); Lajo (2011).

9. Interview with Gomercinda Sutta (Quechua), Cusco, Pampacorral, July 3, 2014. Translation by author.

10. Interview with Aniceto Ccoyo (Quechua), Cusco, Sacaca, July 20, 2014

11. Interview with Sonia Ttito (Quechua), Cusco, Choquecancha, December 14, 2014. Translation by author.

12. Interview with Marisol Cruz (Quechua), Cusco, Ccachin, December 14, 2014. Translation by author.

13. Interview with Crisostomo Quispe (Quechua), Cusco, Choquecancha, January 22, 2015. Translation by author.

14. Mamakan is a Danish-born, New Zealand-based botanical artist based in the Waitakere City, who, in conjunction with Māori knowledge-holders of rongoā Māori such as Riki Bennett (Ngāti Pikiao), promotes Indigenous traditions and practices of plant medicine.

15. Follow-up interview with Mate Heitia (Māori), Ngāti Pukeku, Aotearoa New Zealand, May 6, 2020.

16. Interview with Hinetu Dell (Māori), Ngāti Porou, Aotearoa New Zealand, April 5, 2015.

17. M. Durie (2001); Marsden (2003).

18. M. Durie (2001); Morgan (2006).

19. M. Durie (2001); Morgan (2006); Marsden (2003).

20. Love (2004).

21. See Morgan (2006).

22. Fresno-Calleja (2017); García (2021); Matta (2019).

23. Merino (2020); Ruckstuhl et al. (2014); Ruru (2018).

24. UNGA (2007).

25. Congreso Constituyente Democrático del Peru (1993).

26. Li (2015:640–647); Millones (2016).

27. For a documentary about Maxima Acuña-Atalaya's life and struggle against one of the world's biggest mining companies see Sparrow (2020).

28. See Merino (2015).

29. Huambachano (2014).

30. For more on the Treaty of Waitangi see Orange (2015); Mutu (2018); Walker (1990). In 1995, New Zealand's government and the Waikato-Tainui iwi signed the first Treaty of Waitangi settlement. The Waikato-Tainui iwi received $170 million in reparation from the New Zealand government, formally acknowledging the wrongful confiscation of 1.2 million acres of Waikato land in the 1860s. See Fisher (2015); Muru-Lanning (2012).

31. See Navdanya International (n.d.).

32. See Slow Food (2023).

33. Whyte (2015).

34. Puckey (2011).

35. Hutchings et al. (2018); Moeke-Pickering et al. (2015).

36. Follow-up interview with Dionisio Foco, Cusco, Ccachin, December, 3, 2018. Translation by author.

37. Interview with Fred Tito (Māori), Whangārei, Aotearoa, June 15, 2016.

38. Interview with Elder Tenaiti Tereo (Māori), Ngāiti Porou, Aotearoa New Zealand, April 16, 2015.

39. Durie M. (1985).
40. Morrison (2011).
41. Royal (2012); Hikuroa (2017); McAllister et al. (2019); L. T. Smith et al. (2016).
42. Apffel-Marglin (1998).
43. Mātāmua (2007).
44. Hutchings et al. (2018); Moeke-Pickering et al. (2015).
45. In this book "traditional Māori" refers to the Māori people prior to the arrival of European settlers.
46. See Walker (1990); Fiso (2020); Durie M. (2001).
47. Interview with Rereata Makiha, Ahipara, Aotearoa New Zealand, July 20 2015.
48. Mātāmua (2007); Hutchings and Smith (2020).
49. Māori scholars have written extensively about the value of mātaurauranga Māori in environmental stewardship, food systems, and climate change in response to the government policies and systems that have marginalized mātauranga and prioritised Western science. For mātauranga Māori see M. Durie (1996); Royal (2012); Hikuroa (2017). Changes to the New Zealand school curriculum proposed in 2021 aimed to position mātauranga Māori on equal footing with other bodies of knowledge. The proposed change to the curriculum led to the publication in the *New Zealand Listener* magazine, an influential news weekly, of a letter by seven non-Indigenous academics from the University of Auckland claiming that mātauranga Māori is "not science." See Dunlop (2021).
50. Saberes in Spanish.
51. Pre-Inka civilizations of Peru also had their own calendars, such as the Moche civilization, which used a lunar-solar calendar based on the moon's phases and the sun's position.
52. Interview with Valentina Avilés (Quechua), Cusco, Pampacorral, October, 24, 2014. Translation by author.
53. Interview with Delia Cocha (Quechua), Cusco, Ccachin, November, 14, 2014. Translation by author.
54. Follow-up interview with Crisostomo Quispe (Quechua), Cusco, Choquecancha, July, 22, 2022. Translation by author.
55. This summary of my visit to Maras Moray was written from field notes. For more info on "Maras" see La Cadena (2001); Earls and Cervantes (2015, 121–48).
56. This summary was written from field notes based on oral traditions told by Quechua research partners while working the land. For more on Andean agriculture see Espinoza (1987); Grillo (1998); Valladolid and Apfell-Marglin (2001).

57. International Potato Center (2021); Espinoza (1987).

58. Uqa (in Quechua) and oca (in Spanish) is a yellow and purple tuber that grows in the Andean highlands.

59. This crop has high nutritional value since its protein content is higher than that of wheat and rice.

60. Maca is a root crop that has its origins in the highlands of Peru; it is relatively unknown in the academic literature on food despite its high levels of proteins.

61. See Kuhnlein and Chan (2000); Te Waka Kai Ora. 2022; Kuhnlein et al. (2013).

62. See Howard (2009, 2021).

63. Waitangi Tribunal (n.d.).

64. Waitangi Tribunal (1991, 2).

65. On April 14, 2011, President Alan García and former Peruvian Minister of Agriculture Rafael Quevedo signed Supreme Decree 003-2011-AG (Sectorial Regulations for Biosafety of Genetically Modified Organisms for Agriculture, Forestry, and Their Derived Products). The decree allows the National Institute of Agricultural Innovation of the Ministry of Agriculture to exercise powers of regulation, risk analysis, and monitoring on applications for agro-genetically modified field testing and production in Peru. See Ministerio de Agricultura (2011).

66. On December 9, 2011, Law No. 29811 banning the production and commercialization of GMOs for ten years was signed by newly appointed Peruvian President Humala (Congreso de la Republica del Peru, 2011).

67. On January 6, 2021, the Peruvian Congress extended the moratorium until the end of 2035 under law number 31111 (Ministerio de Ambiente Peru, 2021).

68. In Spanish, despacho.

69. Interview with Valentina Pillco, Cusco, Rosaspata, August 5, 2018. Translation by author.

70. Marsden (2003).

71. Interview with Percy Tipene, Kaitaia, Aotearoa New Zealand, May 12, 2013.

72. Cariño (2018).

73. However, these claims have contradictions and complexity, as former President of Bolivia Evo Morales continued with a politics of extraction. There was a clear difference between protecting Pachamama in theory and practice in Ecuador. See McNelly (2020); Farthing (2019); Álvarez (2015); Jennings (2022).

74. Statistics New Zealand (2008); Stankovitch (2008).

75. See Andersen and Poppel (2002).

76. Gliessman et al. (2019).

CHAPTER 4

1. Interview with Petronila Quispe (Quechua), Cusco, Choquecancha, July 15, 2014. Translation by author.
2. Interview with Carmen Sicos (Quechua), Cusco, Pampacorral, October 15, 2014. Translation by author.
3. The scientific name of the mashua is tropaeolum tuberosum. It is an Andean tuber from Peru, very similar to potatoes, which is eaten cooked or roasted as a vegetable. Quinoa, which many regard as a "supergrain," is not a grain but a flowering plant in the amaranth family. Quinoa has high nutritional value, including a higher protein content than wheat or rice. For more information on the quinoa see Jacobsen et al. (2003). Amaranth is a herbaceous plant indigenous to the South American Andes that grows widely in the rural Peruvian Andes. Its high nutrient content and drought tolerance have caught the attention of farmers seeking more resilient and adaptable crops amid climate change threats.
4. Interview with Juana Suñiga, (Quechua), Cusco, Ccachin, December 18, 2014. Translation by author.
5. Uqa is a tuber, root vegetable that grows in the Andes and is known in Spanish as oca. Ulluco is a root crop that grows in the Andean region of South America, second only to the potato in prevalence. It contains high levels of protein, calcium, and carotene. In Peru it is known by the hispanized term olluco.
6. Kañihua (Cheopodium pallidicaule), an Andean grain that is similar to quinoa, is widely consumed in the highlands of Peru. The leaves of kañihua contain significant protein and are used in salads, according to my field notes.
7. Interview with Julio Sunco, Cusco, Pampacorral, December 18, 2018. Translation by author.
8. Interview with Lino Mamani, Cusco, Sacaca, October, 31, 2019. Translation by author.
9. Interview with Rosita Huilca, Cusco, Ccachin, October 16, 2014. Translation by author.
10. Interview with Carmen Sicos, Cusco, Pampacorral, January 23, 2015. Translation by author.
11. Espinoza (1987).
12. Interview with Bernandina Ttito, Cusco, Choquecancha, February 3, 2015. Translation by author.
13. Interview with Dionisio Quispe, Cusco, Ccachin, December 2, 2014. Translation by author.
14. Interview with Gomercinda Sutta, Cusco, Pampacorral, January 23, 2015. Translation by author.
15. Interview with Lino Mamani, Cusco, at a community gathering that took place in Chawaytire on March 9, 2015. Translation by author.
16. See Núñez del Prado (2008).

CHAPTER 5

1. Mānuka or kahikātoa (Leptospermum scoparium) is a rather variable plant ranging from flat creeping forms and small shrubs to tall trees of up to 10 meters. It was called the "tea tree" by Captain James Cook, a British explorer who first made contact with Māori in 1796. Mānuka/kahikātoa flowers smell very sweet and they provide an important source of pollen and nectar for native bees, flies, moths, beetles, and geckos. The plant can be found in many different habitats including wetlands, river gravels, and dry hillsides. When mature, it is very tolerant of drought, waterlogging, strong winds, and frost, and it can grow at less fertile, colder, wetter, and more acidic sites than kānuka. Kānuka (Kunzea ericoides) is superficially similar to mānuka, but it can grow into a tree up to 30 meters tall. The trunk and branches are usually clad in long, leathery strips of bark, rather than the short, papery, rather flaky brown bark typical of the tree forms of mānuka/kahikātoa. Kānuka leaves lack the sharp tip of mānuka/kahikātoa. The flowers of this species are usually solitary but occur in clusters. The capsules of kānuka split open to release their seeds. Early settlers battled hard to clear their land and regarded mānuka/kahikātoa and kānuka as invasive shrubs that undid all of their hard work. Today, however, these plants can act as an important tool for re-vegetating bare, eroded slopes. By creating shade and shelter from the wind, they provide an excellent nursery for other, slower-growing native plants. Then, as these other plants get taller and overtop them, the mānuka/kahikātoa and kānuka die away as a result of being shaded. Kereru (kūkupa, kūkū) (Hemiphaga novaeseelandiae) are large arboreal pigeons native to New Zealand.

2. This memory field work to Ngāti Porou is summarized from my notes.

3. Interview with Keri Kaa, Ngāti Porou, Aotearoa New Zealand, April 14, 2015.

4. Interview with Lionel Hotene (Māori), Tāmaki Makaurau (Auckland), Aotearoa New Zealand, July 15, 2014.

5. Roberts et al. (2004).

6. Ngāta (1972, 6).

7. Murphy (2011).

8. Taonui (2011).

9. For more on the whakapapa of Māori food systems see Moeke-Pickering et al. (2015); Hutchings and Smith (2020).

10. Roberts et al. (2004); Taonui (2011).

11. Houkamau and Sibley (2010).

12. See Moko Mead (2003).

13. Metge (1995:21).

14. Durie (1996).

15. Moko Mead (2003).

16. Ibid., 23).

17. Follow-up interview with Rereata Makiha, Ahipara, Aotearoa New Zealand, April 3, 2016.

18. Follow-up interview with Mate Heitia, Whakatāne, Aotearoa New Zealand, July 15, 2021.

19. See Black (2014); Clucas et al. (2012).

20. Walker (1984).

21. Ibid.

22. M. Durie (2005).

23. Moko Mead (2003); Harmsworth and Roskruge (2014); Erueti (1993).

24. There are variations of the term "mana whenua," such as mana ki te whenua and mana o te whenua. See M. Durie (2003).

25. Interview with Elizabeth Ngarimu, Gisborne, Aotearoa New Zealand, April 18, 2014.

26. The late Dr. Apirana Mahuika gave this speech at a Ture Whenua hui (Māori land meeting) in Gisborne in August 2014. This meeting was part of a nationwide hui to amend Te Ture Whenua Māori Act (Māori Land Act) 1993 to better support them to use and develop their whenua. In this meeting Mahuika asserted the mana (authority) and self-determination of Māori peoples to their lands and futures, which has been recognized in the Te Ture Whenua Māori Act (Succession, Dispute Resolution, and Related Matters). The goal of the Te Ture Whenua Māori Act is to enhance the intergenerational wellbeing of owners of Māori land. For more info see Erueti (1993).

27. Interview with Elizabeth Ngarimu, Gisborne, Aotearoa New Zealand, April 18, 2014.

28. Interview with Fred Ttito, Whangārei, Aotearoa New Zealand, July 15, 2016.

29. Salmond (1992); Walker (1984).

30. Moko Mead (2003).

31. For the protests led by Cooper see Harris (2004). Bastion Point is a coastal area of land in Auckland city in the Northern part of Aotearoa. It holds cultural and historical significance for Māori people because of protests that occurred there in the 1970s that highlighted the resilient resistance of Māori against forced land alienation by pākehā (European descendants). The protests started on January 5, 1977, and ended on May 25, 1978, the 507th day, when 222 protesters were evicted and arrested by police. These land protests have bolstered Māori peoples' aspirations to enact their land sovereignty rights up through the current day. See New Zealand History (n.d.).

32. Lucy Mackintosh (2019).

33. Ibid.

34. Jackson (2007).

35. Marsden (1988). For more see Kawharu (2000); Royal (2003); Roberts et al. (1995); Watene (2016).

36. Kawharu (2000).

37. Interview with Buchanan Beech-Cullen, Whangārei, Aotearoa New Zealand, July 15, 2016. Buchanan Beech-Cullen has many tribal affiliations, which span Te Ika-a-Māui (North Island) and Te Waka a Māui (South Island) of Aotearoa such as Te Uri o Hau, a Northland subtribe of Ngāti Whatua.

38. For more on rāhui on environmental conservation see Whaanga and Wehi (2017). For rāhui in the legal system of Aoteroa see Wheen and Ruru (2011).

39. Tapu means sacred. A person, object, or place that is tapu may not be touched or, in some cases, even approached. In Māori food tradition a person must say a karakia (prayer) before eating food to remove the tapu, the sacredness of the food. For a detailed explanation see Shirres (1982).

40. Interview with Rereata Makiha, Tāmaki Makaurau (Auckland), Aotearoa New Zealand, July 22, 2015.

41. Interview with Mate Heitia, Ngāti Awa, Aotearoa New Zealand, July 15, 2021.

42. Aroha Mead, email correspondence, October 10, 2019.

43. Ibid.

44. In 2007, I had my first opportunity to take part in a pōwhiri when a Māori kaumātua (Elder) conducted a pōwhiri for me on my first day of employment at the Tertiary Education Commission/Te Amorangi Mātauranga Matua (Crown Agency). Five years later, another pōwhiri was held at the Waipapa marae at the University of Auckland to welcome me into the cohort of Indigenous doctoral students at the business school. These rituals recognized that not only was I stepping into the realm of Māori; within me, I carry the spirit of my ancestors, and the pōwhiri acknowledges and welcomes both encounters. The pōwhiri as a cultural custom has extended beyond the marae (sacred meeting place) and is now held at the workplace or at the beginning of a conference, though each whānau (family), hapū (sub-tribe), and iwi (tribe) have their own kawa (protocols) and tikanga (rules) for this welcome ritual.

45. See Watene (2016).

CHAPTER 6

1. On March 11, 2020, the World Health Organization declared the coronavirus disease named COVID-19 to be a pandemic. It was originally identified in China at the end of 2019. Coronaviruses are a group of related viruses that cause diseases in mammals and birds. In humans, coronaviruses cause illness ranging from the common cold to more severe diseases such as severe acute respiratory syndrome. In some cases, they result in death, especially in older people and those with underlying health conditions. President Donald Trump declared COVID-19 a national emergency in the United States on March

13, 2020. States like California begin imposing stay-at-home orders six days later. Peruvian President Martín Vizcarra declared the country in a state of national emergency and announced a country-wide lockdown to contain COVID-19 on March 15, 2020. Ten days later Aotearoa moved into Alert Level 4—Lockdown. See Beehive New Zealand (2020); President of Peru (2020); "Coronavirus Disease (COVID-19)" (n.d.). See National Institutes of Health (2021) on the National Cancer Institute study that, for example, "highlights [the] pandemic's disproportionate impact on Black, American Indian/Alaska Native, and Latino adults"; Costa (2021); Villagrán (2019); Holmes (2023).

2. Montag et al. (2021); Sidiq et al. (2021); Price et al. (2022); Spencer et al. (2020); Wittman and James (2022); Kesselman (2023).

3. For more on roadside checkpoints that were set up by Māori to protect communities during the nationwide COVID-19 lockdown in 2020 see Fitzmaurice and Bargh (2021).

4. This is a summary of my notes taken from first-hand experience and conversations with Māori research collaborators, friends, and food growers such as Tina Ngāta, Rereata Makiha, and Lionel Hotene in the regions of Te Tai Tokerau (Northland), Tāmaki-makau-rau (Auckland), Waikato, Te Moana-a-Toi (Bay of Plenty), and Te Tai Rāwhiti (Gisborne) from September 2020 to December 2021. For example, in the Tairāwhiti (East Coast) region, whānau in remote areas were operating checkpoints on roads in and out of the region, working with the police and local councils. The aim was to protect vulnerable communities with minimal healthcare infrastructure. Urban community food gardens such as the Papatūānuku Kōkiri Marae selected a small group of volunteers to organize food packages and reach out to people and local businesses who wanted to donate financial resources and food. Some provided a financial contribution and others contributed in-kind with food products, such as Chef Peter Gordon, owner of Homeland Restaurant in Auckland City, who donated groceries to the Papatūānuku Kōkiri Marae. Armed with face masks and hand sanitizers, volunteers prepared the food packages, and others mobilized makeshift distribution centers and began identifying the vulnerable within their communities.

5. The Universal Declaration of Human Rights (UNGA 1948) recognizes the right to adequate food as a fundamental human right to be upheld by states as duty bearers. It also underscores the indivisibility and interdependency of all human rights. States have the duty, obligation, and responsibility to respect, protect, and fulfill human rights, including the right to food, under international law, as outlined in the 1948 Universal Declaration of Human Rights and Article 11 of the 1966 International Covenant on Economic, Social and Cultural Rights (UNGA 1966).

6. Peru instituted a fifteen-day mandatory quarantine effective from March 16, 2020. During this lockdown, there were curfews and border closures. People

could only leave their homes to obtain essential goods, transit across the national territory was restricted, and international transport by land, air, sea, and river was suspended. For more on Peru's COVID-19 lockdown see Andina (2020).

7. Merino and Gustafsson (2021); Montag et al. (2021).

8. See Salmón (2012); Shiva (2016b); Whyte (2016).

9. Several studies from Turtle Island (North America) and Aotearoa New Zealand focus on Indigenous food sovereignty in the context of treaty-guaranteed rights. See, for example, Moeke-Pickering et al. (2015); Gilbert et al. (2020). The Great Lakes Indian Fish & Wildlife Commission, commonly known by its acronym, GLIFWC, was formed in 1984, representing eleven Ojibwe tribes in Minnesota, Wisconsin, and Michigan who reserved hunting, fishing, and gathering rights in the 1836, 1837, 1842, and 1854 Treaties with the United States government. See Whyte (2017); Lowitt et al. (2019); Raster and Hill (2017).

10. See Mātāmua (2007).

11. Morrison (2011, 100).

12. Watene (2022).

13. Agrobiodiversity, or agricultural biodiversity, results from natural selection processes and the careful selection and innovative developments of farmers, fishers, and herders over millennia, all of which are considered components of a people's biocultural heritage. For a more extensive definition of agrobiodiversity see UNEP (2020); FAO (1999).

14. Roberts et al. (1995).

15. Huambachano (2018).

16. This is a summary of my notes taken from an interview and email correspondence (2014–2022) with Rereata Makiha, a prominent kaumātua (Elder) on the maramataka with tribal affiliations to Ngāti Mahurehure, Te Aupōuri, and Te Arawa. Maramataka is based on the understanding of the moon's phases and the occurrence of the solstices and movements of heavenly bodies across the night sky that acted as indicators of appropriate times for planting, finishing, and harvesting of crops. It is the Māori ability to foretell suitable times for fishing and harvesting crops through the maramataka that enabled traditional Māori to produce adequate food. For more on the Māori maramataka see Mātāmua (2007); Ropiha (2000); Roberts, Weko, and Clarke (2006); Tāwhai (2013).

17. This explanation of the "Inti and Quilla" calendars is summarized from my notes. The Inti calendar is based on the solar cycle and had 365 solar days while the Quilla calendar had 328 days. Andean people consult with the Pleiades and interpret the symbolic expression of the cosmos for agricultural purposes. The Inti calendar was used for economic activities such as agriculture, mining, warfare, and construction. The Quilla calendar is used to mark the festivities of the agricultural cycle. Quechua people continue to consult with the Pleiades and interpret the symbolic expression of the cosmos for agricultural purposes. I

observed that Elders of Choquecancha and Ccachin gather around to observe when the Willkawara (Sacred Star) constellation comes up in the sky in June. I recorded that the Willkawara in Quechua translates to Sacred Star from the composition of two words: willka, sacred and wara, star. When the Willkawara Star, which in the Cusco sky relates to the appearance of the constellation of Sirius that reaches its zenith towards the end of February, appears, this is a sign to harvest the first potatoes from the early sowing. When Willkawara is in the western sky after the peak in March (a few weeks after the equinox), it is a sign that harvest will be larger than the previous season. See Rostworowski (2015); Lajo (2006, 2011).

18. See UNGA (2007). Specifically, in Article 3: Indigenous Peoples' right to self-Determination, in Article 4: Indigenous peoples' right to autonomy, and Article 32, Indigenous Peoples have the right to regulate and establish priorities for the use of their territories for development, and Article 20 Indigenous peoples have the right to maintain and develop their political, economic, and social systems or institutions, to be secure in the enjoyment of their own means of subsistence and development, and to engage freely in all their traditional and other economic activities.

19. See CBD (2010).
20. See UNHRC (2018).
21. See New Zealand Legislature (2018).
22. See WTEP (2013); Rowe (2018).
23. Kothari and Bajpai (2017, 103).
24. Constitución de La República Del Ecuador (2008).
25. Kimmerer (2013, 37).
26. This explanation about "offerings to Pachamama" and the role of a paqo (plural, paqos) is summarized from my notes. "Paqo" is the Quechua name for the healer who has spiritual powers to see the unseen world.
27. Interview with Petronila Quispe (Quechua), Cusco, Choquecancha, July 20, 2014.
28. In Quechua and Aymara ch'uñu means "processed potatoes." It is widely written as "chuño" in Peru.
29. Crisostomo Quispe, Cusco, Choquecancha, November 15, 2014. Translation by author.
30. Interview with Lionel Hotene, Auckland, Aotearoa New Zealand, March 5, 2015.
31. For more on Māori rīwai and horticulture see the extensive work of Dr. Nick Roskruge (Te Ātiawa/Ngāti Porou), including Roskruge, Puketapu, and McFarlane (2010); Roskruge (2011, 2009).
32. Hutchings et al. (2012).
33. See Huambachano (2018, 2020).
34. Personal communications with Rowen White of the Indigenous Seed Keepers Network 2017–2020, especially at the Intertribal Food Summits hosted

by The Intertribal Agriculture Council, which includes panels and sessions by Indigenous Seed Keepers Network members every year. Also see Shiva (2012).

35. Kloppenburg (2010, 165).

36. More recently, I have been working with Slow Food Peru on a campaign entitled "Peru, Free of GMOs" to resist the Peruvian government's intention to allow the use of GMOs in the country. On May 27, 2020, the Ministry of Agriculture and Irrigation released a public consultation of the agricultural biotechnology safety regulation act with the intention to approve Resolution No. 123-2020-MINGRI in support of GMOs (Congreso de la República del Peru 2021). The Slow Food campaign aims to educate people about the importance of preserving Peru's biodiversity and to reach out to the hundreds of smaller-scale rural famers scattered throughout the country, giving them a voice and defending their rights to protect the biological diversity of their plants and food crops.

37. Wisconsin (and Great Lakes) Intertribal Seed Stewardship Cohort (n.d.)

CHAPTER 7

1. This is a summary of my notes from discussions with Quechua research collaborators. In the Quechua language chakitaqlla refers to a foot-plow tool that is usually made of wood and has a blade of stone and bronze metal.

2. The kō, a version of the foot plow made entirely of wood.

3. The concept of buen vivir draws on the wealth of the region's Indigenous traditions to propose a socio-ecological, balanced, and culturally sensitive approach to living well. Buen vivir animates critiques of the development paradigm that relies on a binary and hierarchical classification of nations and peoples as "developed" and "underdeveloped" with roots in the belief that human competence transcends the limitations of Nature and, therefore, higher production and industrialization of goods are keys to economic prosperity and peace. Buen vivir has inspired social movements in disagreement with neoliberal and capitalist ideologies and has stimulated environmentalist campaigns demanding different environmental governance approaches beyond extractivism in Bolivia, Ecuador, and Peru. Buen vivir has even reached its way into two new Constitutions. In the late 2000s, Ecuador and Bolivia institutionalized buen vivir in their constitutions as a main principle for improving food and nutrition security. In Peru, buen vivir has gained popularity in Indigenous movements pushing against governments' support of extractive activities on their ancestral territories that disregard their rights for self-determination and territoriality. Thus, buen vivir is not a static concept but an evolving idea. See Quijano (1992); Walsh (2010); Gudynas (2011); Esteva (1992); Peña (2016); Triveño (2020); Merino (2015).

4. For example, the two most recent Intergovernmental Science-Policy Platform on Biodiversity and Ecosystem Services (IPBES) 2019 and 2022 reports highlighted the contributions of Indigenous and traditional and local knowledge in safeguarding biodiversity and food security, urging humanity to recognize their ways of life, knowledge, and principles. They were about "biodiversity and ecosystems services" and "diverse values and valuation of Nature," respectively. IPBES is an independent intergovernmental body comprising over 130 member governments. Established by 94 national governments in 2012, IPBES provides policymakers with objective scientific assessments about the state of knowledge regarding the planet's biodiversity, ecosystems, and the contributions they make to people, as well as options and actions to protect and sustainably use these vital natural assets.

5. For examples of traditional Indigenous farmers from around the world on how the nurturing of biodiversity and food can counter the alienation caused by displacement see Nazarea and Gagnon (2022). For how Native American communities are reviving Indigenous food sovereignty see Coté (2022); Morrison and Brynne (2016); Nelson (2019). For the role of African Americans driving a food sovereignty movement see White (2018); Love and Pitt (2019). For an overview of the role of Latin American Indigenous and local farmers in safeguarding food security through agroecology see Wittman and James (2022); FAO (2016).

6. Personal communications with Mate Heitia and Sonny Heitia, in the city of Whakatāne on the East Coast of Aotearoa, June 2021. REKA is a charitable trust that in 2008 built a Māori food garden at the back of Rangataua Marae (sacred meeting place) also known as Pahou Pa, located just south of the city of Whakatāne. The goal of REKA is to revive the traditional teachings that Māori once used for growing food, become self-sufficient, and improve the health of many families of Ngāti Rangataua who are suffering from many health problems linked to a lack of traditional foods, such as obesity and type 2 diabetes.

7. The Arts of Foraging workshops offered by Mamakan are one example. (See note 14 in chapter 3.)

8. Another example in Peru is CHIRAPAQ, the Centre for Indigenous Cultures of Peru. For the past thirty years CHIRAPAQ has been promoting the assertion of Indigenous identity and the acknowledgement of Indigenous rights in the exercise of citizenship and food sovereignty with commitment to Indigenous children, youth, and women.

9. For more on Generación con Causa see PromPerú (n.d.). For a critical perspective on the Peruvian gastronomical boom (in the past ten years, Peru has been considered one the world's top gastronomy countries), see García (2021).

10. Interview with Peter Gordon, Auckland, Aotearoa New Zealand, July 20, 2021.

11. This is a summary of my notes taken from a presentation about "Introduction to Seed Saving" and "Seed Banking and Selection" by Rowen

White and Clayton Brascoupe, members of the Indigenous Seed Keepers Network, at Great Lakes Food Sovereignty Summit, Jijak Camp, Michigan, April 2017. For conference information, see IAC Great Lakes (2017).

12. Examples of Indigenous entrepreneurial acumen in support of Indigenous Food Sovereignty include Shiwi, a Peruvian company dedicated to the trade of products from protected areas, and Homeland restaurant with its development of Māori-based food products. Homeland's vegan kawakawa pesto sauce, developed by Chef Peter Gordon and his team, is made from freshly picked kawakawa, Marlborough-grown pine nuts, garlic, olive, and sunflower oils, and parsley, and can be served with wood-roasted kūmara (sweet potato). These examples promote new relationships within our local food systems—producer-consumer, rural-urban—and healthy competition among producers and among consumers, ultimately shaping and reshaping market economies.

13. Coté (2016, 2).

Bibliography

Agrawal, Arun. 1995. "Dismantling the Divide Between Indigenous and Scientific Knowledge." *Development and Change* 26: 413–39.

Alcoff, Linda. 2017. "Philosophy and Philosophical Practice: Eurocentrism as an Epistemology of Ignorance." In *The Routledge Handbook of Epistemic Injustice*, 397–408. London: Routledge.

Altieri, Miguel. 1995. *Agroecology: The Science of Sustainable Agriculture*. 2nd ed. Boulder, CO: Westview Press.

Altieri, Miguel, and Clara Nicholls. 2005. *Agroecology and the Search for a Truly Sustainable Agriculture*. Mexico City: United Nations Environment Programme Environmental Training Network for Latin America and the Caribbean.

———. 2012. "Agroecology Scaling Up for Food Sovereignty and Resiliency." In *Sustainable Agriculture Reviews: Volume 11*, edited by Eric Lichtfouse, 1–29. Dordrecht: Springer Netherlands. https://doi.org/10.1007/978-94-007-5449-2_1.

Álvarez, Santiago García. 2015. "Environmental Policies and Pachamama in Ecuador. Theory and Practice in Rafael Correa's Government (2007–2013)." *International Journal of Environmental Policy and Decision Making* 1 (3): 227. https://doi.org/10.1504/IJEPDM.2015.074299.

Andersen, Thomas, and Birger Poppel. 2002. "Living Conditions in the Arctic." *Social Indicators Research* 58 (1–3): 191–216.

Andina. 2020. "Peru: Government Decrees Mandatory Social Isolation for 15 Days to Combat Coronavirus." https://andina.pe/ingles/noticia-peru-government-decrees-mandatory-social-isolation-for-15-days-to-combat-coronavirus-788411.aspx.

Apffel-Marglin, Frederique, ed. 1998. *The Spirit of Regeneration: Andean Culture Confronting Western Notions of Development*. London: Zed.

Archibald, Jo-ann. 1992. "Editorial: Giving Voice to Our Ancestors." *Canadian Journal of Native Education* 19 (2): 141–44.

———. 2008. *Indigenous Storywork: Educating the Heart, Mind, Body and Spirit*. Vancouver, British Columbia: UBC Press.

Australian Bureau of Statistics. 2015. "Australian Aboriginal and Torres Strait Islander Health Survey: Nutrition Results—Food and Nutrients, 2012–13." Canberra: Australian Bureau of Statistics.

Battiste, Marie. 2000. *Reclaiming Indigenous Voice and Vision*. Vancouver: University of British Columbia Press.

Battiste, Marie, and James Youngblood (Sa'ke'j) Henderson. 2000. *Protecting Indigenous Knowledge and Heritage: A Global Challenge*. Saskatoon, Canada: Purich Publishing.

Beehive New Zealand. 2020. "All of Government Team Press Conference: Tuesday, 24 March 2020." Accessed July 28, 2022. https://www.beehive.govt.nz/sites/default/files/2020-03/240320%20All%20of%20Government%20Press%20Conference.pdf.

Berkes, Fikret. 2012. *Sacred Ecology*. London: Routledge.

Bernstein, H., and P. Woodhouse. 2010. "Productive Forces in Capitalist Agriculture: Political Economy and Political Ecology." *Journal of Agrarian Change* 10 (3): 300–453.

Bezner Kerr, Rachel, Jeffrey Liebert, Moses Kansanga, and Daniel Kpienbaareh. 2022. "Human and Social Values in Agroecology: A Review." *Elementa: Science of the Anthropocene* 10 (1): 00090.

Belay, Million. 2017. "Mapping the Food System's Past, Present and Futures in Ethiopia." https://www.stockholmresilience.org/research/research-news/2017-04-28-mapping-the-food-systems-past-present-and-futures-in-ethiopia.html.

Bishop, Russel. 1991. "Te Ropu Rangahua Tikanga Rua: The Need for Emancipatory Research under the Control of the Māori People for the Betterment of Māori People." *New Zealand Annual Review of Education* 2: 205–23.

———. 2005. "Freeing Ourselves from Neocolonial Domination in Research: A Kaupapa Māori Approach to Creating Knowledge." In *The Sage Handbook of Qualitative Research*, edited by Norman K. Denzin and Yvonna S. Lincoln, 3rd ed., 109–38. Thousand Oaks, CA: SAGE Publications.

Bishop, Russel, and Ted Glynn. 1999. *Culture Counts: Changing Power Relations in Education*. Palmerston North: Dunmore Press.

Black, Taiarahia. 2014. "'Te Koko Ki Ohiwa (the Surge at Ohiwa)." In *Enhancing Mātauranga Māori and Global Indigenous Knowledge*, 12–28. Wellington, New Zealand: New Zealand Qualifications Authority.

Borch, Merete. 2001. "Rethinking the Origins of Terra Nullius." *Australian Historical Studies* 32 (117): 222–39.

Bryman, A., and E. Bell. 2011. *Business Research Methods*. 3rd ed. Oxford: Oxford University Press.

Buntu, Baba. 2013. "Claiming Self: the Role of Afrikology in Social Transformation." *Scriptura: Journal for Contextual Hermeneutics in Southern Africa* 112 (1): 1–12. https://doi.org/10.10520/EJC146680.

Cajete, Gregory. 2000. *Native Science: Natural Laws of Interdependence*. Santa Fe, NM: Clear Light Publishers.

Calvário, Rita, and Annette Aurélie Desmarais. 2023. "The Feminist Dimensions of Food Sovereignty: Insights from La Via Campesina's Politics." *The Journal of Peasant Studies* 50 (2): 640–64. https://doi.org/10.1080/03066150.2022.2153042.

Campbell, Hugh. 2020. *Farming Inside Invisible Worlds: Modernist Agriculture and Its Consequences*. New York: Bloomsbury Academic. https://library.oapen.org/handle/20.500.12657/58834.

Cárdenas, Yenny Vega, and Uapukun Mestokosho. 2023. "Recognizing the Legal Personhood of the Magpie River/Mutehekau Shipu in Canada." In *A Legal Personality for the St. Lawrence River and Other Rivers of the World*, edited by Yenny Vega Cárdenas and Daniel Turp, 1-15. Geneva: Éditions JFD.

Cariño, Joji. 2018. "Introduction." In *Indicators Relevant for Indigenous Peoples: A Resource Book*, edited by Mara Stankovitch, ix–xiii. Baguio City: Tebtebba Foundation.

CBD (Convention on Biological Diversity). n.d. "Peru Main Details." Accessed October 14, 2023. https://www.cbd.int/countries/profile/?country = pe.

———. 2010. Nagoya Protocol on Access to Genetic Resources and the Fair and Equitable Sharing of Benefits Arising from Their Utilization to the Convention on Biological Diversity. https://www.cbd.int/abs.

———. 2016. "Convention on Biological Diversity." https://www.cbd.int/convention/text.

———. 2023. "National Biodiversity Strategies and Action Plans (NBSAPs)." Accessed October 13, 2023. https://www.cbd.int/nbsap/.

Chakrabarty, Dipesh. 2000. *Provincializing Europe: Postcolonial Thought and Historical Difference*. Princeton: Princeton University Press.

Chávez, Vivian. 2022. "Cultural Humility and Social Inclusion." In *Handbook of Social Inclusion: Research and Practices in Health and Social Sciences*, 129–44. Cham: Springer International Publishing.

Chibvongodze, Danford T. 2016. "Ubuntu Is Not Only About the Human! An Analysis of the Role of African Philosophy and Ethics in Environment

Management." *Journal of Human Ecology* 53 (2): 157–66. https://doi.org/10.1080/09709274.2016.11906968.

Chilisa, Bagele. 2012. *Indigenous Research Methodologies*. London: SAGE Publications.

———. 2020. *Indigenous Research Methodologies*. 2nd ed. London: SAGE Publications.

Chirinos Rivera, Andrés. 2010. *Quipus del Tahuantisuyo: Curacas, Incas y su saber matemático en el siglo XVI*. Lima, Peru: Editorial Comentarios.

Claeys, Priscilla. 2015. "Food Sovereignty and the Recognition of New Rights for Peasants at the UN: A Critical Overview of La Via Campesina's Rights Claims over the Last 20 Years." *Globalizations* 12 (4): 452–65. https://doi.org/10.1080/14747731.2014.957929.

Clapp, Jennifer, and Joseph Purugganan. 2020. "Contextualizing Corporate Control in the Agrifood and Extractive Sectors." *Globalizations* 17 (7): 1265–75.

Clapp, Jennifer, William G. Moseley, Barbara Burlingame, and Paola Termine. 2022. "The Case for a Six-Dimensional Food Security Framework." *Food Policy* 106: 102164.

Clucas, R., H. Moller, C. Bragg, D. Fletcher, P. O'B Lyver, and J. Newman. 2012. "Rakiura Māori Muttonbirding Diaries: Monitoring Trends in Tītī (Puffinus Griseus) Abundance in New Zealand." *New Zealand Journal of Zoology* 39 (2): 37–41. https://doi.org/10.1080/03014223.2011.621438.

Collins, Patricia Hill. 1991. "On Our Own Terms: Self-Defined Standpoints and Curriculum Transformation." *The National Women's Studies Association Journal* (3): 367–81.

Collis, Jill, and Roger Hussey. 2003. *Business Research: A Practical Guide for Undergraduate and Postgraduate Students*. Bristol, UK: Palgrave Macmillan.

Congreso Constituyente Democrático del Peru. 1993. "Constitución Política Del Peru." https://www.congreso.gob.pe/Docs/files/constitucion/Constitucion-politica-08-04-19.pdf.

Congreso de la República del Peru. 2011. "Ley N 29811." https://www.minam.gob.pe/wp-content/uploads/2017/04/Ley-N%C2%B0-29811.pdf.

Constitución de La República Del Ecuador. 2008. https://www.oas.org/juridico/pdfs/mesicic4_ecu_const.pdf.

Corntassel, Jeff. 2008. "Toward Sustainable Self-Determination: Rethinking the Contemporary Indigenous-Rights Discourse." *Alternatives* 33: 105–32.

Corntassel, Jeff, and Cheryl Bryce. 2012. "Practicing Sustainable Self-Determination: Indigenous Approaches to Cultural Restoration and Revitalization." *Brown Journal of World Affairs* 18 (3): 151–62.

"Coronavirus Disease (COVID-19)." n.d. World Health Organization. Accessed October 12, 2023. https://www.who.int/emergencies/diseases/novel-coronavirus-2019.

Costa, Daniel. 2021. "The Farmworker Wage Gap Continued in 2020: Farmworkers and H-2A Workers Earned Very Low Wages during the Pandemic, Even Compared with Other Low-Wage Workers." *Working Economics Blog*. 2021. https://www.epi.org/blog/the-farmworker-wage-gap-continued-in-2020-farmworkers-and-h-2a-workers-earned-very-low-wages-during-the-pandemic-even-compared-with-other-low-wage-workers.

Coté, Charlotte. 2016. "'Indigenizing' Food Sovereignty. Revitalizing Indigenous Food Practices and Ecological Knowledges in Canada and the United States." *Humanities* 5 (3): 57.

———. 2022. *A Drum in One Hand, a Sockeye in the Other: Stories of Indigenous Food Sovereignty from the Northwest Coast*. Seattle: University of Washington Press.

Cusicanqui, Silvia Rivera. 2012. "Ch'ixinakax Utxiwa: A Reflection on the Practices and Discourses of Decolonization." *South Atlantic Quarterly* 111 (1): 95–109.

D'Cruz, Heather, Philip Gillingham, and Sebastian Melendez. 2007. "Reflexivity, Its Meanings and Relevance for Social Work: A Critical Review of the Literature." *The British Journal of Social Work* 37 (1): 73–90.

Daigle, Michelle. 2019. "Tracing the Terrain of Indigenous Food Sovereignties." *The Journal of Peasant Studies* 46 (2): 297–315.

Declaration of Nyéléni. 2007. Selingue, Mali: Nyéléni 2007, the World Forum for Food Sovereignty. https://nyeleni.org/spip.php?article290.

Descartes, René. 2000. *Descartes: Philosophical Essays and Correspondence*. New York: Hackett Publishing.

Desmarais, Annette Aurelie, and Jim Handy. 2014. "Food Sovereignty, Food Security: Markets and Dispossession." In *Controversies in Science and Technology: From Sustainability to Surveillance*, edited by Daniel Lee Kleinman, Karen A. Cloud-Hansen, and Jo Handelsman. Oxford, UK: Oxford University Press.

Desmarais, Annette Aurelie, Priscilla Claeys, and Amy Trauger, eds. 2017. *Public Policies for Food Sovereignty: Social Movements and the State*. Routledge.

DiPrete Brown, Lori, Sumudu Atapattu, Valerie Stull, Claudia Irene Calderón, and Mariaelena Huambachano. 2020. "From a Three-Legged Stool to a Three-Dimensional World: Integrating Rights, Gender and Indigenous Knowledge into Sustainability Practice and Law"." *Sustainability* 12: 1–22. https://doi.org/10.3390/su12229521.

Duarte, Marisa Elena. 2017. *Network Sovereignty: Building the Internet Across Indian Country*. Seattle: University of Washington Press.

Duncan, Jessica, and Priscilla Claeys. 2018. "Politicizing Food Security Governance through Participation: Opportunities and Opposition." *Food Security* 10 (6): 1411–24.

Dunlop, Mani. 2021. "University Academics' Claim Mātauranga Māori 'Not Science' Sparks Controversy." *RNZ*, July 28, 2021, sec. Te Ao Māori. https://www.rnz.co.nz/news/te-manu-korihi/447898/university-academics-claim-matauranga-maori-not-science-sparks-controversy.

Durie, Edward Taihakurei. 1996. "Will the Settlers Settle-Cultural Conciliation Law?" *Otago L. Rev.* 8: 449.

Durie, Mason. 1985. "A Māori Perspective of Health." *Social Science & Medicine* 20 (5): 483–86.

———. 1996. *Mātauranga Māori: Iwi and the Crown: A Discussion Paper*. Palmerston North: Department of Māori Studies, Massey University.

———. 2001. *Mauri Ora: The Dynamics of Māori Health*. Oxford: Oxford University Press.

———. 2003. *Ngā Kāhui Pou Launching Māori Futures*. Auckland: Huia Publishers.

———. 2005. *Nga Tai Matatu: Tides of Māori Endurance*. Oxford: Oxford University Press.

Earls, John C., and Gabriela Cervantes. 2015. "Inka Cosmology in Moray: Astronomy, Agriculture, and Pilgrimage." In *The Inka Empire*, edited by Izumi Shimada, 121–48. Austin: University of Texas Press.

Erueti, Andrew. 1993. "Te Ture Whenua Māori 1993." LLM research paper, Law Faculty, Victoria University of Wellington. https://researcharchive.vuw.ac.nz/bitstream/handle/10063/7221/thesis.pdf.

Escobar, Arturo. 2019. *Autonomía y Diseño: La Realización de Lo Comunal*. Popayán: Editorial Universidad del Cauca.

Espinoza, Soriano. 1987. *Los Incas. Economía, Sociedad y Estado En La Era Del Tahuantinsuyo*. Lima: Amaru editores.

Esteva, Gustavo. 1992. "Development." In *The Development Dictionary: A Guide to Knowledge as Power*, edited by Sachs Wolfgang. London: Zed Books.

———. 2015. "The Hour of Autonomy." *Latin American and Caribbean Ethnic Studies* 10 (1): 134–45. https://doi.org/10.1080/17442222.2015.1034436.

FAO (Food and Agriculture Organization of the United Nations. 2001. "The State of Food Insecurity in the World 2001: Food Insecurity—When People Live with Hunger and Fear Starvation." https://www.fao.org/3/y1500e/y1500e00.htm.

———. 2016. *Contributing to Food Security and Nutrition for All*. The State of World Fisheries and Aquaculture 2016. https://www.fao.org/3/i5555e/i5555e.pdf.

———. 2019. "The State of the World's Biodiversity for Food and Agriculture." http://www.fao.org/3/CA3129EN/CA3129EN.pdf.

———. 2021. "The State of Food Security and Nutrition in the World 2021. Transforming Food Systems for Food Security, Improved Nutrition and

Affordable Healthy Diets for All." Rome: FAO, IFAD, UNICEF, WFP, and WHO. https://doi.org/10.4060/cb4474en.

———. 2022. "The State of the World's Forests 2022: Forest Pathways for Green Recovery and Building Inclusive, Resilient and Sustainable Economies." https://doi.org/10.4060/cb9360en.

FAO, IFAD, UNICEF, WFP and WHO (2022). "The State of Food Security and Nutrition in the World 2022: Repurposing Food and Agricultural Policies to Make Healthy Diets More Affordable." https://doi.org/10.4060/cc0639en.

FAO, IFAD, PAHO, UNICEF, and WFP. 2023. *Regional Overview of Food Security and Nutrition—Latin America and the Caribbean 2022: Towards Improving Affordability of Healthy Diets*. Rome: FAO, IFAD, UNICEF, PAHO, WFP.

Farthing, Linda. 2019. "An Opportunity Squandered? Elites, Social Movements, and the Government of Evo Morales." *Latin American Perspectives* 46 (1): 212–29. https://doi.org/10.1177/0094582X18798797.

Grillo, Eduardo Fernández. 1998. "Development or Decolonization in the Andes?" In *The Spirit of Regeneration: Andean Culture Confronting Western Notions of Development*, edited by Frédérique Apffel-Marglin, 221–43. London: Zed.

Fisher, Martin. 2015. "Balancing Rangatiratanga and Kawanatanga: Waikato-Tainui and Ngāi Tahu's Treaty Settlement Negotiations with the Crown." PhD diss., Victoria University of Wellington. http://researcharchive.vuw.ac.nz/handle/10063/4642.

Fiso, Monique. 2020. *Hiakai*. Wellington: Penguin Books New Zealand.

Fitzmaurice, Andrew. 2014. *Sovereignty, Property and Empire, 1500–2000*. Cambridge, UK: Cambridge University Press.

Fitzmaurice, Luke, and Maria Bargh. 2021. *Stepping Up: COVD-19 Roadside Checkpoints and Rangatiratanga*. Wellington, NZ: Huia Publishers.

Freire, Paulo. 2018. *Pedagogy of the Oppressed*. London: Bloomsbury.

Fresno-Calleja, Paloma. 2017. "Fighting Gastrocolonialism in Indigenous Pacific Writing." *Interventions* 19 (7): 1041–55. https://doi.org/10.1080/1369801X.2017.1401938.

Gadgil, Madhav, Fikret Berkes, and Carl Folke. 1993. "Indigenous Knowledge for Biodiversity Conservation." *Ambio*, 151–56.

García, María Elena. 2021. *Gastropolitics and the Specter of Race: Stories of Capital, Culture, and Coloniality in Peru*. Oakland: University of California Press.

GARN. 2023. "Universal Declaration for the Rights of Mother Earth—Global Alliance for the Rights of Nature (GARN)." March 9, 2023. https://www.garn.org/universal-declaration-for-the-rights-of-mother-earth.

Gilbert, Jonathan, Jennifer Krueger-Bear, and Catherine Techtmann. 2020. "Nourishing Our Seeds of Shared Leadership: Great Lakes Indian Fish &

Wildlife Comission (GLIFWC) Biological Services Division ReCharge 5." https://data.glifwc.org/reports/.

Gilgun, Jane. 2010. "Reflexivity and Qualitative Research: Current Issues in Qualitative Research." *An Occasional Publication for Field Researchers from a Variety of Disciplines* 1 (2). https://www.scribd.com/document/35787948/Reflexivity-and-Qualitative-Research.

Gliessman, Stephen. 2007. *Agroecology: The Ecology of Sustainable Food Systems*. Boca Raton, FL: CRC Press.

Gliessman, Steve, Harriet Friedmann, and Philip H. Howard. 2019. "Agroecology and Food Sovereignty." https://opendocs.ids.ac.uk/opendocs/handle/20.500.12413/14606.

Gonzales, Tirso. 2015. "An Indigenous Autonomous Community-Based Model for Knowledge Production in the Peruvian Andes." *Latin American and Caribbean Ethnic Studies* 10 (1): 107–33. https://doi.org/10.1080/17442222.2015.1034433.

Grey, Sam, and Raj Patel. 2015. "Food Sovereignty as Decolonization: Some Contributions from Indigenous Movements to Food System and Development Politics." *Agriculture and Human Values* 32 (3): 431–44.

Grillo, Eduardo. 1991. "El Lenguaje En Las Culturas Andina y Occidental Moderna." In *Cultura Andina Agrocéntrica, Proyecto Andino de Tecnologías Campesinas*, 67–98. Lima, Peru: PRATEC.

Gudynas, Eduardo. 2011. "Buen Vivir: Today's Tomorrow." *Development* 54 (4): 441–47. https://doi.org/10.1057/dev.2011.86.

Halperin, Sandra. 2018. "Development Theory." *Encyclopedia Britannica*. https://www.britannica.com/money/topic/development-theory.

Harmsworth, Garth, and Nick Roskruge. 2014. *Indigenous Māori Values, Perspective, and Knowledge of Soils in Aotearoa-New Zeland*. London: CRC Press.

Harris, Aroha. 2004. *Hīkoi: Forty Years of Māori Protest*. Welington: Huia Publishers.

Harvey, David. 2005. *A Brief History of Neoliberalism*. Oxford: Oxford University Press.

Henry, Ella, and Hone Pene. 2001. "Kaupapa Māori: Locating Indigenous Ontology, Epistemology and Methodology in the Academy." *Organization* 8 (2): 234–42.

Hikuroa, Daniel. 2017. "Mātauranga Māori—the Ūkaipō of Knowledge in New Zealand." *Journal of the Royal Society of New Zealand* 47 (1): 5–10. https://doi.org/10.1080/03036758.2016.1252407.

HLPE. 2019. "Agroecological and Other Innovative Approaches for Sustainable Agriculture and Food Systems That Enhance Food Security and Nutrition." Report by the High Level Panel of Experts on Food Security and Nutrition of

the Committee on World Food Security, Rome. https://www.fao.org/documents/card/en/c/ca5602en.
———. 2020. "Food Security and Nutrition: Building a Global Narrative Towards 2030." Report by the High Level Panel of Experts On Food Security and Nutrition of the Committee on World Food Security, Rome. http://www.fao.org/3/ca9731en/ca9731en.pdf.
Holling, C. S., Fikret Berkes, and Carl Folke. 2000. "Science, Sustainability and Resource." In *Linking Social and Ecological Systems: Management Practices and Social Mechanisms for Building Resilience*, edited by Fikret Berkes and Carl Folke, 342–62. Cambridge, UK: Cambridge University Press.
Holmes, Seth M. 2023. *Fresh Fruit, Broken Bodies: Migrant Farmworkers in the United States*. Oakland: University of California Press.
Holt-Giménez, Eric. 2017. *A Foodie's Guide to Capitalism: Understanding the Political Economy of What We Eat*. New York: NYU Press.
Holt-Giménez, Eric, and Annie Shattuck. 2011. "Food Crisis, Food Regimes, and Food Movements: Rumblings of Reform or Tides of Transformation?" *The Journal of Peasant Studies* 38 (1): 109–44.
Holt-Giménez, Eric, Annie Shattuck, and Ilja Van Lammeren. 2021. "Thresholds of Resistance: Agroecology, Resilience and the Agrarian Question." *The Journal of Peasant Studies* 48 (4): 715–33.
Houkamau, Carla A., and Chris G. Sibley. 2010. "The Multi-Dimensional Model of Māori Identity and Cultural Engagement." *New Zealand Journal of Psychology* 39 (1): 8–28.
Howard, Philip. 2009. "Visualizing Consolidation in the Global Seed Industry: 1996–2008." *Sustainability* 1 (4): 1266–87.
———. 2021. *Concentration and Power in the Food System: Who Controls What We Eat?* Vol. 3. London: Bloomsbury.
Huambachano, Mariaelena. 2012. "Carbon Emissions Scheme: Analysis of the Impact of the New Zealand Emission Trading Scheme on the Agribusiness Value Chain." *The International Journal of Environmental Sustainability* 8 (1): 51–62.
———. 2014. "Business and Sustainability: The Camisea Project in the Peruvian Amazon Basin." In *Corporate Social Responsibility and Sustainability: Emerging Trends in Developing Economies*, edited by Gabriel Eweje, 215–40. London: Emerald Group Publishing Limited.
———. 2015a. "Food Security and Indigenous Peoples Knowledge: El Buen Vivir-Sumaq Kawsay in Peru and Tē Atānoho, New Zealand, Māori-New Zealand." *Food Studies* 5 (3): 33–47.
———. 2015b. "The Ayni Principle: An Indigenous Theory of Value Creation." In *Indigenous Spiritualities at Work: Transforming the Spirit of Enterprise*, by C. Spiller, edited by R. Wolfgramm, 99–117. Charlotte: Information Age Publishing.

———. 2016. "Through an Indigenous Lens Food Security Is Food Sovereignty: Case Studies of Māori of Aotearoa New Zealand and Andeans People of Peru." PhD diss., The University of Auckland.

———. 2018. "Enacting Food Sovereignty in Aotearoa New Zealand and Peru: Revitalizing Indigenous Knowledge, Food Practices and Ecological Philosophies." *Agroecology and Sustainable Food Systems* 42 (9): 1003–28. https://doi.org/10.1080/21683565.2018.1468380.

———. 2019. "Indigenous Food Sovereignty: Reclaiming Food as Sacred Medicine in Aotearoa New Zealand and Peru." *New Zealand Journal of Ecology* 43 (3): 1–6.

———. 2020. "Indigenous Good Living Philosophies and Regenerative Food Systems in Aotearoa New Zealand and Peru." In *Routledge Handbook of Sustainable and Regenerative Food Systems*, edited by Jessica Duncan Wiskerke, Michael Carolan, and S. C. Johannes, 38–49. London: Routledge.

Hutchings, Jessica. 2023. "Sovereignty, Kai, and the Land Where We Grow." Interview by Dan Kelly. Accessed October 13, 2023. https://stonesoupsyndicate.com/articles/sovereignty-kai-and-the-land-where-we-grow.

Hutchings, Jessica, and Jo Smith. 2020. *Te Mahi Oneone Hua Parakore: A Māori Soil Sovereignty and Well-Being Handbook*. Christchurch: Freerange Press.

Hutchings, Jessica, Jo Smith, and Garth Harmsworth. 2018. "Elevating the Mana of Soil through the Hua Parakore Framework." *MAI Journal* 7 (1): 92–102.

Hutchings, Jessica, Percy Tipene, Gretta Carney, Angeline Greensill, Pounamu Skelton, and Mahinarangi Baker. 2012. "Hua Parakore: An Indigenous Food Sovereignty Initiative and Hallmark of Excellence for Food and Product Production." *MAI Journal* 1 (2): 131–45.

IAC Great Lakes. 2017. "Great Lakes Intertribal Food Summit." 2017. https://iacgreatlakes.com/events/great-lakes-intertribal-food-summit.

Iles, Alastair. 2005. "Learning in Sustainable Agriculture: Food Miles and Missing Objects." *Environmental Values* 14 (2): 163–83.

Illich, Ivan. 1973. "Tools for Conviviality. London: Calder and Boyers." *Science, Technology, and Social Movements* 493: 13625–28.

Indigenous Foundations. 2023. "Global Actions." July 28, 2023. https://indigenousfoundations.arts.ubc.ca/global_actions.

INEI (National Institute of Statistics and Informatics). 2017. "Peruvian Population and Housing Census." https://www.inei.gob.pe.

Instituto Nacional de Salud. 2018. "El mestizo peruano tiene el 60% de genes nativos." https://web.ins.gob.pe/es/prensa/noticia/el-mestizo-peruano-tiene-el-60-de-genes-nativos.

International Potato Center. 2021. "Potato." February 5, 2021. https://cipotato.org/potato/.

IPBES. 2019. "Global Assessment Report on Biodiversity and Ecosystem Services of the Intergovernmental Science-Policy Platform on Biodiversity and Ecosystem Services." Bonn, Germany: Zenodo. https://doi.org/10.5281/zenodo.6417333.

———. 2022. "Methodological Assessment of the Diverse Values and Valuation of Nature of the Intergovernmental Science-Policy Platform on Biodiversity and Ecosystem Services." Bonn, Germany: Zenodo. https://doi.org/10.5281/zenodo.7687931.

IPES-Food. 2023. "Who's Tipping the Scales? The Growing Influence of Corporations on the Governance of Food Systems, and How to Counter It." http://www.ipes-food.org/pages/tippingthescales.

Jackson, Moana. 2007. "Globalisation and the Colonising State of Mind." In *Resistance: An Indigenous Response to Neoliberalism*, edited by M. Bargh, 167–182. Wellington: Huia Publishers.

Jacobsen, S. E., A. Mujica, and R. Ortiz. 2003. "The Global Potential for Quinoa and Other Andean Crops." *Food Reviews International* 19 (1-2): 139–48.

Jennings, Victoria Claire. 2022. "Rights of Pachamama: More Like Poetry Than Law? Assessing the Strength and Impact of Nature's Constitutional Rights in Ecuador." Master's Thesis, University of Oslo. https://www.duo.uio.no/bitstream/handle/10852/101368/1/HUMR5200_Candidate-7006.pdf.

Jiménez Estrada, Vivian. 2005. "The Tree of Life as a Research Methodology." *The Australian Journal of Indigenous Education* 34 (1): 44–52. https://doi.org/10.1017/S1326011100003951.

Karla, Peña. 2016. "Social Movements, the State, and the Making of Food Sovereignty in Ecuador." *Latin American Perspectives* 43 (1): 221–37.

Kawharu, Merata. 2000. "Kaitiakitanga: A Māori Anthropological Perspective of the Māori Socio-Environmental Ethic of Resource Management." *The Journal of the Polynesian Society* 109 (4): 349–70.

Kayira, Jean. 2015. "'(Re)Creating Spaces for uMunthu: Postcolonial Theory and Environmental Education in Southern Africa.'" *Environmental Education Research* 21 (1): 106–28. https://doi.org/10.1080/13504622.2013.860428.

Kesselman, Brittany. 2023. "Transforming South Africa's Unjust Food System: An Argument for Decolonization." *Food, Culture & Society*. https://doi.org/10.1080/15528014.2023.2175483.

Kimmerer, Robin Wall. 2015. *Braiding Sweetgrass: Indigenous Wisdom, Scientific Knowledge, and the Teachings of Plants*. Minneapolis: Milkweed Editions.

Kloppenburg, Jack. 2010. "Seed Sovereignty: The Promise of Open Source Biology." In *Food Sovereignty: Recconnecting Food, Nature, and Community*, edited by Hannah Wittman, Annette Aurelie Desmarais, and Nettie Wiebe, 165. Halifax, NS: Fernwood Publishing.

Knuth, Lidija, and Margaret Vidar. 2011. "Constitutional and Legal Protection of the Right to Food around the World." The Right to Food Studies. Food and Agriculture Organization of the United Nations (FAO). https://www.fao.org/3/ap554e/ap554e.pdf.

Kothari, Ashish, and Shrishtee Bajpai. 2017. "We Are the River, the River Is Us." *Economic & Political Weekly* 52 (37): 103.

Kovach, Margaret. 2009. *Indigenous Methodologies: Characteristics, Conversations and Contexts*. Toronto: University of Toronto Press.

Kuhnlein, Harriet. 2017. "Gender Roles, Food System Biodiversity, and Food Security in Indigenous Peoples' Communities." *Maternal & Child Nutrition* 13: e12529.

Kuhnlein, Harriet, and Hing Man Chan. 2000. "Environment and Contaminants in Traditional Food Systems of Northern Indigenous Peoples." *Annual Review of Nutrition* 20 (1): 595–626.

Kuhnlein, Harriet, Bill Erasmus, Dina Spigelski, and Barbara Burlingame. 2013. *Indigenous Peoples' Food Systems and Well-Being: Interventions and Policies for Healthy Communities*. Rome: Food and Agriculture Organization of the United Nations (FAO). https://www.cabdirect.org/cabdirect/abstract/20133239133.

La Cadena, Marisol. 2001. "Reconstructing Race: Racism, Culture and Mestizaje in Latin America." *NACLA Report on the Americas* 34 (6): 16–23. https://doi.org/10.1080/10714839.2001.11722585.

La Via Campesina. (2017). "Agroecology Is a Way of Life." https://viacampesina.org/en/agroecology-is-a-way-of-life-an-in-depth-interview-with-students-of-agroecologic-school-educar.

Ladson-Billings, Gloria. 2000. "Fighting for Our Lives: Preparing Teachers to Teach African American Students." *Journal of Teacher Education* 51 (3): 206–14.

LaDuke, Winona. 1999. *All Our Relations: Native Struggles for Land and Life*. Minnesota: South End Press.

———. 2005. *Recovering the Sacred: The Power of Naming and Claiming*. Cambridge: South End Press.

Lajo, Javier. 2011. "Un model Sumaq Kawsay de gobierno." América Latina en movimiento. http://alainet.org/active/49164&lang = es.

———. 2006. *Qhapaq Ñan: La Ruta Inka de Sabiduría*. Quito, Ecuador: Editorial Abya Yala.

Latouche, Serge. 2004. "Degrowth Economics." *Le Monde Diplomatique* 11 (1–5).

———. 2007. "De-Growth: An Electoral Stake." *The International Journal of Inclusive Democracy* 3 (1): 14–18.

Le Grange, Lesley. 2012. "Ubuntu, Ukama, Environment and Moral Education." *Journal of Moral Education* 41 (3): 329–40. https://doi.org/10.1080/030572 40.2012.691631.

LeCompte, Margaret Diane, Judith Preissle, and Renata Tesch. 1993. *Ethnography and Qualitative Design in Educational Research*. San Diego: Academic Press.

Lefa, B. 2015. "The African Philosophy of Ubuntu in South African Education." *Studies in Philosophy and Education* 1 (1).

Li, Fabiana. 2015. *Unearthing Conflict: Corporate Mining, Activism, and Expertise in Peru*. Durham, NC: Duke University Press.

Love, Catherine. 2004. "Extensions on Te Wheke." Working Papers No. 6–04, The Open Polytechnic of New Zealand.

Love, Shivon Pearl, and Khaliah D. Pitt. 2019. "Our Kitchen." *Our Mothers' Kitchens*. 2019. https://www.ourmotherskitchens.org/our-kitchen.

Lowitt, Kristen, Charles Z. Levkoe, Ryan Lauzon, Kathleen Ryan, and Dean Sayers. 2019. "Indigenous Self-Determination and Food Sovereignty through Fisheries Governance in the Great Lakes Region." In *Civil Society and Social Movements in Food System Governance*, edited by Peter Andrée, Jill K. Clark, Charles Z. Levkoe, and Kristen Lowitt, 145-164. New York: Routledge.

Lugones, María. 2008. "Coloniality and Gender." *Tabula Rasa*, no. 9: 73–102.

Mackintosh, Lucy. 2019. "Unearthing the History of Ihumātao, Where the Land Tells Stories." RNZ. 18 August 2019. https://www.rnz.co.nz/news/on-the-inside/396954/unearthing-the-history-of-ihumatao-where-the-land-tells-stories.

Maia, Filipe. 2022. *Trading Futures: Toward a Theological Critique of Financialized Capitalism*. Durham, NC: Duke University Press.

Manohar, Swetha, Shauna Downs, Sabina Shaikh, Sithirith Mak, Serey Sok, Elizabeth Graham, Lais Miachon, and Jessica Fanzo. 2023. "Riverine Food Environments and Food Security: A Case Study of the Mekong River, Cambodia." *Bulletin of the World Health Organization* 101 (2).

Mariátegui, José Carlos. 1988. *Seven Interpretative Essays on Peruvian Reality*. Austin: University of Texas Press.

Mātāmua, Rangi. 2007. *Matariki: The Star of the Year*. Wellington: Huia Publishers.

Mburu, Gathuru. 2007. "The African Biodiversity Network (ABN): Building a Grassroots Momentum for Protection of African Heritage." *Revista Brasileira de Agroecologia* 2 (2): 1765–69.

Marsden, M. 1988. "The Natural World and Natural Resources, Māori Values Systems and Perspectives, Resource Management Law Reform." Working paper 29, Part A. Wellington: Ministry of Environment.

———. 2003. *The Woven Universe: Selected Readings of Rev. Māori Marsden*. Ōtaki: The Estate of Rev. Māori Marsden.

Martens, Tabitha Robin. "Responsibilities and Reflections: Indigenous Food, Culture, and Relationships." *Canadian Food Studies/La Revue Canadienne des études sur l'alimentation*, 5(2): 9–12. https://doi.org/10.15353/cfs-rcea.v5i2.216.

Matta, Raúl. 2019. "Celebrity Chefs and the Limits of Playing Politics from the Kitchen." In *Globalized Eating Cultures*, edited by Jörg Dürrschmidt and York Kautt, 183–201. Cham: Springer International Publishing.

Merino, Roger. 2015. "The Politics of Extractive Governance: Indigenous Peoples and Socio-Environmental Conflicts." *The Extractive Industries and Society* 2 (1): 85–92.

McAllister, Tara G., Jacqueline R. Beggs, Shaun C. Ogilvie, Rauru Kirikiri, Amanda Black, and Priscilla M. Wehi. 2019. "Kua Takoto Te Mānuka: Mātauranga Māori in New Zealand Ecology." *New Zealand Journal of Ecological Society* 43 (3): 1–7.

McFarlane, Turi. 2007. "The Contribution of Taewa (Māori Potato) Production to Māori Sustainable Development." Master's thesis, Massey University, Palmerston North. https://researcharchive.lincoln.ac.nz/server/api/core/bitstreams/001f2aa7-e61b-4510-b441-f24eadb8e9cc/content.

McGregor, Deborah. 2004. "Coming Full Circle: Indigenous Knowledge, Environment, and Our Future." *The American Indian Quarterly* 28 (3): 385–410.

———. 2018. "Mino-Mnaamodzawin: Achieving Indigenous Environmental Justice in Canada." *Environment and Society* 9 (1): 7–24.

McMichael, Philip. 2009. "A Food Regime Analysis of the 'World Food Crisis.'" *Agriculture and Human Values* 26 (4): 281–95. https://doi.org/10.1007/s10460-009-9218-5.

McMichael, Philip, and Ian Scoones. 2011. "Biofuels, Land and Agrarian Change." *Special Issue of Journal of Peasant Studies* 37 (4): 575–92.

McNelly, Angus. 2020. "Neostructuralism and Its Class Character in the Political Economy of Bolivia Under Evo Morales." *New Political Economy* 25 (3): 419–38. https://doi.org/10.1080/13563467.2019.1598962.

Medrano, Manuel. 2021. "Testimony from Knotted Strings: An Archival Reconstruction of Early Colonial Andean Khipu Readings." *History and Anthropology* 32 (3): 289–311. https://doi.org/10.1080/02757206.2020.1854749.

Menser, Michael. 2014. "The Territory of Self-Determination: Social Reproduction, Agroecology, and the Role of the State." In *Globalization and Food Sovereignty: Global and Local Change in New Politics of Food*, edited by Jeffrey McKelvey Ayres, Peter Andrée, Bossia, and Maria-Josee Massicotte, 53–83. Toronto: University of Toronto Press.

Merino, Roger. 2016. "An Alternative to 'Alternative Development': Buen Vivir and Human Development in Andean Countries." *Oxford Development Studies* 44 (3): 271–86.

———. 2020. "The Cynical State: Forging Extractivism, Neoliberalism and Development in Governmental Spaces." *Third World Quarterly* 41 (1): 58–76. https://doi.org/10.1080/01436597.2019.1668264.

Merino, Roger, and Maria-Therese Gustafsson. 2021. "Localizing the Indigenous Environmental Steward Norm: The Making of Conservation and Territorial Rights in Peru." *Environmental Science and Policy* 124 (July): 627–34.

Metge, Joan. 1995. *New Growth from Old: The Whānau in the Modern World.* Wellington: Victoria University Press.

Mignolo, Walter. 1999. "Coloniality at Large: Knowledge at the Late Stage of the Modern/Colonial World System." 5 (2): 1–10.

Millones, Jorge. 2016. "Conga Mines: Development as Conflict in Peru." *South Atlantic Quarterly* 115 (3): 640–47.

Ministerio de Agricultura. 2011. "Decreto Supremo 003-2011-AG." https://www.midagri.gob.pe/portal/download/pdf/marcolegal/normaslegales/decretossupremos/2011/ds03-2011-ag.pdf.

Ministerio de Ambiente Peru. 2021. "Minam avanza en el proceso de reglamentación de la Ley de Moratoria sobre transgénicos." https://www.gob.pe/institucion/minam/noticias/502194-minam-avanza-en-el-proceso-de-reglamentacion-de-la-ley-de-moratoria-sobre-transgenicos%20.

Ministerio de Cultura, Peru. 2023. "Indicadores Sociales | BDPI." July 15, 2023. https://bdpi.cultura.gob.pe/indicadores-sociales.

Moeke-Pickering, Taima, Mate Heitia, Sonny Heitia, Rolinda Karapu, and Sheila Cote-Meek. 2015. "Understanding Māori Food Security and Food Sovereignty Issues in Whakatāne." *Mai Journal* 4 (1): 29–42.

Mohanty, Chandra Talpade. 1984. "Under Western Eyes: Feminist Scholarship and Colonial Discourses." *Boundary 2:* 333–58.

Moko Mead, Hirini. 2003. *Tikanga Māori: Living by Māori Values.* Wellington: Huia Publishing.

Montag, Doreen, Marco Barboza, Lizardo Cauper, Ivan Brehaut, Isaac Alva, Aoife Bennett, and José Sanchez-Choy. 2021. "Healthcare of Indigenous Amazonian Peoples in Response to COVID-19: Marginality, Discrimination and Revaluation of Ancestral Knowledge in Ucayali, Peru." *BMJ Global Health* 6 (1): e004479.

Montenegro de Wit, Maywa. 2021. "What Grows from a Pandemic? Toward an Abolitionist Agroecology." *The Journal of Peasant Studies* 48 (1): 99–136.

Morgan, Kepa. 2006. "Decision-Support Tools and the Indigenous Paradigm." *Proceedings of the Institution of Civil Engineers. Engineering Sustainability* 159 (4): 169–77.

Morrison, Dawn. 2011. "Indigenous Food Sovereignty: A Model for Social Learning." *Food Sovereignty in Canada: Creating Just and Sustainable Food Systems* 97: 99.

Morrison, Dawn, and Abra Brynne. 2016. "Responsibilities and Relationships: Decolonizing the BC Food Systems Network." https://www.indigenousfoodsystems.org/sites/default/files/resources/BCFSN%20CFICE%20report%20FINAL%20(1).pdf.

Mudombi-Rusinamhodzi, Grace, and Leonard Rusinamhodzi. 2022. "Food Sovereignty in Sub-Saharan Africa: Reality, Relevance, and Practicality." *Frontiers in Agronomy* 4: 1–7. https://doi: 10.3389/fagro.2022.957011.

Murphy, Ngahuia. 2011. "Te Awa Atua." M.A. thesis, University of Waikato. https://researchcommons.waikato.ac.nz/handle/10289/5532.

Muru-Lanning, Marama. 2012. "The Key Actors of Waikato River Co-Governance: Situational Analysis at Work." *AlterNative: An International Journal of Indigenous Peoples* 8 (2): 128–36.

———. 2016. *Tupuna Awa: People and Politics of the Waikato River*. Auckland, NZ: Auckland University Press.

Mutu, Margaret. 2018. "Behind the Smoke and Mirrors of the Treaty of Waitangi Claims Settlement Process in New Zealand: No Prospect for Justice and Reconciliation for Māori Without Constitutional Transformation." *Journal of Global Ethics* 14 (2): 208–21.

Mzukisi, Qobo, and Nceku Nyathi, eds. 2016. "Ubuntu, Public Policy Ethics and Tensions in South Africa's Foreign Policy." *South African Journal of International Affairs* 23 (4): 421–36. https://doi.org/10.1080/10220461.2017.1298052.

Navdanya International. n.d. "Our Staff: Vandana Shiva." http://www.vandanashiva.com/ and https://navdanyainternational.org/our-staff/vandana-shiva.

Nazarea, Virginia D., and Terese V. Gagnon, eds. 2022. "Moveable Gardens: Itineraries and Sanctuaries of Memory." *Journal of Latin American Geography* 21 (1): 215–17.

Naess, Arne. 1973. "The Shallow and the Deep: The Long-Range Ecology Movement: A Summary." *Inquiry* 16: 95–100.

National Institutes of Health. 2021. "NCI Study Highlights Pandemic's Disproportionate Impact on Black, American Indian/Alaska Native, and Latino Adults." October 4, 2021. https://www.nih.gov/news-events/news-releases/nci-study-highlights-pandemics-disproportionate-impact-black-american-indian-alaska-native-latino-adults.

Nelson, Melissa K. 2019. "Wrestling with Fire: Indigenous Women's Resistance and Resurgence." *American Indian Culture and Research Journal* 43 (3): 69–84.

Nelson, Melissa K., and Daniel Shilling, eds. 2018. *Traditional Ecological Knowledge: Learning from Indigenous Practices for Environmental Sustainability*. Cambridge: Cambridge University Press.
Nestle, Marion. 2019. *Food Politics: How the Food Industry Influences Nutrition and Health*. Oakland: University of California Press.
New Zealand Legislature. 2017. Te Awa Tupua (Whanganui River Claims Settlement) Act. https://www.legislation.govt.nz/act/public/2017/0007/latest/whole.html.
New Zealand Ministry of Health—Manatū Hauora. 2023. "New Zealand Ministry of Health—Manatū Hauora." https://www.health.govt.nz/our-work/populations/Māori-health/tatau-kahukura-Māori-health-statistics/nga-mana-hauora-tutohu-health-status-indicators/diabetes.
New Zealand History. n.d. "Bastion Point." https://nzhistory.govt.nz/keyword/bastion-point.
Ngāta, Apirana. 1972. "Rauru-Nui-a-Toi Lectures." Department of Anthropology, Victoria University of Wellington.
Norgaard, K., R. Reed, and C. Van Horn. 2011. "A Continuing Legacy: Institutional Racism, Hunger and Nutritional Justice on the Klamath." In *Cultivating Food Justice: Race, Class, and Sustainability*, edited by Alison Hope Alkon and Julian Agyeman, 23–46. Boston: MIT Press.
Núñez del Prado, Daisy. 2008. "Yanantin y Masintin: La Cosmovisión Andina." Universidad Andina del Cusco. https://www.academia.edu/10401973/YANANTIN_Y_MASINTIN_LA_COSMOVISION_ANDINA.
Orange, Claudia. 2015. *An Illustrated History of the Treaty of Waitangi*. Wellington, NZ: Bridget Williams Books.
Patel, Raj. 2012. *Stuffed and Starved: The Hidden Battle for the World Food System*. Rev. ed. New York: Melville House.
Patel, Raj, and Jason W. Moore. 2017. *A History of the World in Seven Cheap Things: A Guide to Capitalism, Nature, and the Future of the Planet*. Oakland: University of California Press.
Perfecto, Ivette, John Vandermeer, and Angus Wright, eds. 2019. *Nature's Matrix: Linking Agriculture, Biodiversity Conservation and Food Sovereignty*. New York: Routledge.
Perrault, Thomas. 2005. "Why Chacras (Swidden Gardens) Persist: Agrobiodiversity, Food Security, and Cultural Identity in the Ecuadorian Amazon." *Human Organization* 64 (4): 327–39.
Pierotti, Raymond, and Daniel Wildcat. 2000. "Traditional Ecological Knowledge: The Third Alternative (Commentary)." *Ecological Applications* 10 (5): 1333–40.
Pihama, Leonie. 2010. "Kaupapa Māori Theory: Transforming Theory in Aotearoa." *He Pukenga Korero: A Journal of Māori Studies* 9 (2): 5–14.

———. 2015. "Kaupapa Māori Theory: Transforming Theory in Aotearoa." In *He Pukenga Korero*, edited by Leonie Pihama, S. Tiakiwai, and K. Southey, 5–15. Hamilton: Te Kotahi Institute, University of Waikato-Tainui College for Research and Development and Ngā Pae o te Māramatanga.

Pilling, Dafydd, and Julie Bélanger. 2019. "The State of the World's Biodiversity for Food and Agriculture." Rome: FAO Commission on Genetic Resources for Food and Agriculture.

Pimbert, Michael P. 2017. "Democratizing Knowledge and Ways of Knowing for Food Sovereignty, Agroecology and Biocultural Diversity." In *Food Sovereignty, Agroecology and Biocultural Diversity*, edited by Michael Pimbert, 259–321. London: Taylor & Francis Group.

Pimbert, Michael, and Tomáš Uhnák. 2019. "Agroecology and Food Sovereignty: Charting a Way to a Radical Transformation of the Food System." In *Politics of Food*, edited by Dani *Burrows* and Aaron *Cezar*, 88–99. Berlin: Sternberg Press.

Pinstrup-Andersen, Per. 2003. "Challenges to Agricultural Production in Asia in the 21st Century." In *Proceedings of a CARDI International Conference on Research on Water in Agricultural Production in Asia for the 21st Century, Phnom Penh, Cambodia, 25–28 November 2003. Canberra:* The Australian Centre for International Agricultural Research (ACIAR).

Pohatu, Taina Whakaatere. 2005. "Āta: Growing Respectful Relationships—Kaupapa Māori." *Ata: Journal of Psychotherapy Aotearoa New Zealand* 17, no. 1: 13–26.

President of Peru. 2020. "State of Emergency Decree, March 2020." Accessed October 12, 2023. http://busquedas.elperuano.pe/dispositivo/NL/1907451-1.

Price, Mindy Jewell, Alex Latta, Andrew Spring, Jennifer Temmer, Carla Johnston, Lloyd Chicot, Jessica Jumbo, and Margaret Leishman. 2022. "Agroecology in the North: Centering Indigenous Food Sovereignty and Land Stewardship in Agriculture 'Frontiers.'" *Agriculture and Human Values* 39 (4): 1191–1206.

PromPerú: Comisión de Promoción del Perú para la Exportación y el Turismo. n.d. "¿Qué es Generación con Causa? | Perú Info." Accessed August 12, 2023. https://sites.peru.info/es-pe/generacionconcausa.

Publicación Oficial—Diario Oficial El Peruano. 2020. "LEY Nº 31111: Ley que modifica la ley 29811, ley que establece la moratoria al ingreso y producción de organismos vivos modificados al territorio nacional por un período de 15 años, a fin de establecer la moratoria hasta el 31 de diciembre de 2035." https://bioseguridad.minam.gob.pe/wp-content/uploads/2021/02/Ley-31111.pdf.

Puckey, Adrienne. 2011. *Trading Cultures: A History of the Far North*. Wellington: Huia Publishers.

Quijano, Aníbal. 1992. "Colonialidad y Modernidad/Racionalidad." *Perú Indígena* 13 (29): 11–20.
———. 1995. "Raza, Etnia y Nación En Mariátegui: Cuestiones Abiertas." *Estudios Latinoamericanos* 2 (3): 3–19.
———. 2000. "Coloniality of Power and Eurocentrism in Latin America." *International Sociology* 15 (2): 215–32.
Rangimarie, Rose Pere. 1982. "AKO Concepts And Learning In The Māori Tradition." Working Paper. University of Waikato.
Raster, Amanda, and Christina Gish Hill. 2017. "The Dispute Over Wild Rice: An Investigation of Treaty Agreements and Ojibwe Food Sovereignty." *Agriculture and Human Values* 34 (2): 267–81.
Ricciardi, V., Z. Mehrabi, H. Wittman, D. James, and N. Ramankutty. 2021. "Highers Yields and More Biodiversity on Smaller Farms." *Nature Sustainability* 4 (7): 651–57.
Rist, Gilbert. 2007. "Development as Buzzword." *Development in Practice* 17: 485–91.
———. 2009. *The History of Development: From Western Origins to Global Faith*. London: Bloomsbury.
Roberts, M., F. Weko, and L. Clarke. 2006. *Maramataka: The Māori Moon Calendar*. Christchurch, New Zealand: Lincoln University Agribusiness and Economics Research Unit.
Roberts, Mere, Brad Haami, Richard Benton, Terre Satterfield, Melissa L. Finucane, Mark Hēnare, and Manuka Hēnare. 2004. "Whakapapa as a Māori Mental Construct: Some Implications for the Debate over Genetic Modification of Organisms." *The Contemporary Pacific* 1: 1–28.
Roberts, Mere, Waerete Norman, Nganeko Minhinnick, Del Wihongi, and Carmen Kirkwood. 1995. "Kaitiakitanga: Māori Perspectives on Conservation." *Pacific Conservation Biology* 2 (1): 7–20.
Ropiha, J. 2000. "Traditional Ecological Knowledge of the Maramataka—Māori Lunar Calendar." Master's thesis, Victoria University of Wellington.
Roskruge, Nick. 1999. "Taewa Māori: Their Management, Social Importance and Commercial Viability," Diploma research report, Massey University.
———. 2011. "Traditional Māori Horticultural and Ethnopedological Praxis in the New Zealand Landscape." *Management of Environmental Quality: An International Journal* 22 (2): 200–12.
———. 2009. "The Foods of Rongo-Marae-Roa; Sustaining the Māori of New Zealand. In *Tropical Roots and Tubers in a Changing Climate: A Convenient Opportunity for the World*," edited by International Society for Tropical Root Crops (ISTRC), 34–37. Lima, Peru: ISTRC-Peru Branch.
Roskruge, Nick, Aleise Puketapu, and Turi McFarlane. 2010. "Nga Porearea Me Nga Matemate o Nga Mara Taewa. Pests and Diseases of Taewa (Māori

Potato) Crops." Palmerston North, NZ: Massey University Institute of Natural Resources.

Roskruge, Nick, and Semese, Sai. 2020. *Ngā Pōrearea Me Ngā Matemate o Ngā Māra Kūmara: Pests and Diseases of Kūmara (Sweet Potato) Crops*. Palmerston North, New Zealand: Tahuri Whenua.

Rosset, Peter Michael, Braulio Machín Sosa, Adilén María Roque Jaime, and Dana Rocío Ávila Lozano. 2011. "The Campesino-to-Campesino Agroecology Movement of ANAP in Cuba: Social Process Methodology in the Construction of Sustainable Peasant Agriculture and Food Sovereignty." *The Journal of Peasant Studies* 38 (1): 161–91.

Rostworowski, María. 1988. *Historia Del Tahuantinsuyu*. Lima, Peru: Instituto de Estudios Peruanos.

Rowe, Tia. 2018. "The Fight for Ancestral Rivers: A Study of the Māori and the Legal Personhood Status of the Whanganui River and Whether Māori Strategies Can Be Used to Preserve the Menominee River." *Michigan State International Law Review* 27 (3): 593–627.

Royal, Te Ahukaramū Charles. 2003. *The Woven Universe: Selected Writings of Rev. Māori Marsden*. Otaki: Estate of Rev. Māori Marsden. https://cir.nii.ac.jp/crid/1130282272746443776.

——. 2012. "Politics and Knowledge: Kaupapa Māori and Mātauranga Māori." *New Zealand Journal of Educational Studies* 47 (2): 30–37.

——. 2014. "Indigenous Ways of Knowing." In "The University Beside Itself," *Argos Aotearoa* 1.

Ruckstuhl, Katharina, Michelle Thompson-Fawcett, and Hauauru Rae. 2014. "Māori and Mining: Indigenous Perspectives on Reconceptualising and Contextualising the Social Licence to Operate." *Impact Assessment and Project Appraisal* 32 (4): 304–14.

Ruru, Jacinta. 2018. "Listening to Papatūānuku: A Call to Reform Water Law." *Journal of the Royal Society of New Zealand* 48 (2–3): 215–24.

Salmón, Enrique. 2012. *Eating the Landscape: American Indians' Stories of Food, Identity, and Resilience*. Tucson: University of Arizona Press.

Salmond, Anne. 1992. *Two Worlds: First Meetings between Māori and Europeans, 1642–1772*. Honolulu: University of Hawai'i Press.

Salomon, Frank. 2001. "How an Andean 'Writing Without Words' Works." *Current Anthropology* 1 (42): 1–27.

Schutter, Olivier de. 2012. "Report Submitted by the Special Rapporteur on the Right to Food, Olivier de Schutter: Women's Rights and the Right to Food." A/HRC/22/50. Geneva, Switzerland: United Nations.

Segrest, Valerie. 2013. "Revitalizing Northwest Coastal Indian Food Culture through Food Sovereignty." Presented at the World Issues Forum, Fairhaven College and Western Washington University. https://vimeo.com/58113157.

Shirres, Michael P. 1982. "Tapu." *The Journal of the Polynesian Society* 91 (1): 29–51.
Shiva, Vandana. 2005. *Earth Democracy: Justice, Sustainability, and Peace.* Cambridge, MA: South End Press.
———. 2012. "The Seed Emergency: The Threat to Food and Democracy." *Al Jazeera English.* February 6, 2012. https://www.aljazeera.com/opinions/2012/2/6/the-seed-emergency-the-threat-to-food-and-democracy.
———. 2016a. *Seed Sovereignty, Food Security: Women in the Vanguard of the Fight against GMOs and Corporate Agriculture.* Berkeley: North Atlantic Books.
———. 2016b. *The Violence of the Green Revolution: Third World Agriculture, Ecology, and Politics.* Lexington: University Press of Kentucky.
Sidiq, Fathir Fajar, David Coles, Carmen Hubbard, Beth Clark, and Lynn J. Frewer. 2021. "Sago and the Indigenous Peoples of Papua, Indonesia: A Review." *Journal of Agriculture and Applied Biology* 2 (2): 138–49.
Slow Food. 2023. "Red de Terra Madre." https://www.slowfood.com/es/nuestra-red/red-de-terra-madre.
Smith, Graham Hingangaroa. 1997a. "The Development of Kaupapa Māori: Theory and Praxis." PhD diss., University of Auckland.
———. 1997b. "The Dialectic Relation Theory and Practice in the Development of Kaupapa Māori Praxis." In *Kaupapa Rangahau: A Reader,* edited by Leonie Pihama, Sarah-Jane Tiakiwai, and Kim Southey, 17-27. 2nd ed. Hamilton: Te Kohati Research Institute, University of Waikato. https://www.waikato.ac.nz/__data/assets/pdf_file/0009/339885/Kaupapa-Rangahau-A-Reader_2nd-Edition.pdf.
———. 2003. "Indigenous Struggle for the Transformation of Education and Schooling." Keynote address, Alaskan Federation of Natives (AFN) convention, Anchorage, Alaska, October 2003. https://www.nelsontasmankindergartens.com/uploads/1/4/4/2/14426744/indigenous_struggle.pdf.
———. 2005. "The Problematic of Indigenous Theorizing: A Critical Reflection." Paper presented at the AERA Annual Conference.
Smith, Linda Tuhiwai. 2012. *Decolonizing Methodologies: Research and Indigenous Peoples.* London: Bloomsbury.
———. 2005. "On Tricky Ground: Researching the Native in the Age of Uncertainty." In *Handbook of Qualitative Research,* edited by N. Denzin and Y. Lincoln, 85–107. London: SAGE.
Smith, Linda Tuhiwai, Te Kahautu Maxwell, Haupai Puke, and Pou Temara. 2016. "Indigenous Knowledge, Methodology and Mayhem: What Is the Role of Methodology in Producing Indigenous Insights? A Discussion from Mātauranga Māori." *Knowledge Cultures: A Multidisciplinary Journal* 4 (3): 131–56.

Sousa Santos, Boaventura de. 1977. "The Law of the Oppressed: The Construction and Reproduction of Legality in Pasargada." *Law & Society Review* 12: 5–126.

Sparrow, Claudia. 2020. "Stand with Maxima." https://www.standwithmaxima.com.

Spencer, Michael S., Taurmini Fentress, Ammara Touch, and Jessica Hernandez. 2020. "Environmental Justice, Indigenous Knowledge Systems, and Native Hawaiians and Other Pacific Islanders." *Human Biology* 92 (1): 45–57.

Stankovitch, Mara, ed. 2008. *Indicators Relevant for Indigenous Peoples: A Resource Book*. Baguio City, Philippines: Tebtebba Foundation.

Statistics New Zealand. 2008. *Māori Statistics Framework: A Discussion Document*. Wellington: Statistics New Zealand.

Stiglitz, Joseph E. 2002. *Globalization and Its Discontents*. New York: W. W. Norton.

Swaminathan, M. S. 2012. "Role of Genetic Modification in Developing Climate Smart Agriculture to Ensure Sustained Food Security." *Agricultural Research* 1 (4): 295–98.

Swantz, Marja Liisa. 2008. "Participatory Action Research as Practice." In *The Sage Handbook of Action Research: Participative Inquiry and Practice*, edited by Peter Reason and Hilary Bradbury, 31–48. Thousand Oaks, CA: SAGE.

TallBear, Kim. 2013. *Native American DNA: Tribal Belonging and the False Promise of Genetic Science*. Minneapolis: University of Minnesota Press.

Taonui, Rāwiri. 2011. "Whakapapa—Genealogy." *Te Ara, The Encyclopedia of New Zealand*. https://teara.govt.nz/en/whakapapa-genealogy/page-1.

Tauli-Corpuz, Victoria. 2015. "UN Special Rapporteur: Indigenous Peoples Rights Must Be Respected in Global Climate Change Agreement." United Nations Special Rapporteur on the Rights of Indigenous Peoples. http://unsr.vtaulicorpuz.org/site/index.php/en/press-releases/61-clima-change-hrc.

Tawhai, Wiremu. 2013. *Living by the Moon: Te Maramataka a Te Whānau-ā-Apanui*. Wellington, NZ: Huia Publishers.

Triveño, Karen Crespo. 2020. "Can Food Sovereignty Practice Intersect with Bolivia's Process of Decolonizing Its Plurinational State? The Politics of Decolonizing Food Systems." *Honors Thesis*, University of San Francisco, https://repository.usfca.edu/honors/31.

Truman, Harry. 1949. "Inaugural Address." Harry S. Truman Library and Museum. https://www.trumanlibrary.gov/library/public-papers/19/inaugural-address.

UN News. 2020. "As Famines of 'Biblical Proportion' Loom, Security Council Urged to 'Act Fast.'" 21 April 2020. https://news.un.org/en/story/2020/04/1062272.

UNDEA (United Nations Department of Economic and Social Affairs). 2020. "Sustainable Development Goals Report 2020." https://unstats.un.org/sdgs/report/2020/The-Sustainable-Development-Goals-Report-2020.pdf.

———. 2021. "The State of the World's Indigenous Peoples 2021: Rights to Land, Territories, and Resources." https://www.un.org/development/desa/indigenouspeoples/wp-content/uploads/sites/19/2021/03/State-of-Worlds-Indigenous-Peoples-Vol-V-Final.pdf

———. 2015. Transforming Our World: The 2030 Agenda for Sustainable Development." https://sdgs.un.org/2030agenda.

UNEP (United Nations Environment Programme). 2000. "Cartagena Protocol on Biosafety to the Convention on Biological Diversity: Text and Annexes." https://www.cbd.int/doc/legal/cartagena-protocol-en.pdf.

UNGA (United Nations General Assembly). 2007. "United Nations Declaration on the Rights of Indigenous Peoples." https://www.un.org/development/desa/indigenouspeoples/wp-content/uploads/sites/19/2018/11/UNDRIP_E_web.pdf.

———. 1966. "International Covenant on Economic, Social and Cultural Rights." https://www.refworld.org/docid/3ae6b36c0.html.

———. 1948. "Universal Declaration of Human Rights." https://www.ohchr.org/EN/Issues/Education/Training/Compilation/Pages/UniversalDeclarationofHumanRights(1948).aspx.

UNHCR (United Nations High Commissioner for Human Rights). 2010. "The Right to Adequate Food." OHCR Fact Sheet No. 34. www.ohchr.org/Documents/Publications/FactSheet34en.pdf.

UNHRC (United Nations Human Rights Council). 2018. "United Nations Declaration on the Rights of Peasants and Other People Working in Rural Areas." https://digitallibrary.un.org/record/1650694?ln=en.

UNWCED (United Nations World Commission on Environment and Development). 1987. "Report of the World Commission on Environment and Development: Our Common Future." https://digitallibrary.un.org/record/139811?ln=en.

Urton, Gary. 1998. "From Knots to Narratives: Reconstructing the Art of Historical Record Keeping in the Andes from Spanish Transcriptions of Inka Khipus." *Ethnohistory* 45, no. 3 (1998): 409–38. https://doi.org/10.2307/483319.

———. 2003. *Signs of the Inka Khipu: Binary Coding in the Andean Knotted-String Records*. Austin: University of Texas Press.

Valcárel, Luis. 2015. *El Virrey Toledo, Gran Tirano Del Perú*. Lima, Peru: Universidad Inca Garcilaso de la Vega.

Valladolid, J., and F. Apffel-Marglin. 2001. "Andean Cosmovision and the Nurturing of Biodiversity." In *Indigenous Traditions and Ecology: The Interbeing of Cosmology and Community*, edited by John Grim and E. Tucker, 620–39. Cambridge, MA: Harvard University Press.

Villagrán, José Guadalupe. 2019. "Revisiting the 'Midwest Stream': An Ethnographic Account of Farmworkers on the Texas-Michigan Circuit." PhD diss., University of Texas at Austin.

Waitangi Tribunal. 1991. "Wai 262 Claim." https://irp.cdn-website.com/855a29e4/files/uploaded/26102021094502.pdf.

———. n.d. "Waitangi Tribunal." Accessed September 29, 2023. https://waitangitribunal.govt.nz/.

Walker, Ranginui. 1984. "The Genesis of Māori Activism." *The Journal of the Polynesian Society* 93 (3): 267–81.

———. 1990. *Struggle without End*. Auckland: Penguin Books.

Walsh, Catherine. 2010. "Development as Buen Vivir: Institutional Arrangements and (de)Colonial Entanglements." *Development* 53 (1): 15–21. https://doi.org/10.1057/dev.2009.93.

Walter, Maggie, and Chris Andersen. 2013. *Indigenous Statistics: A Quantitative Research Methodology*. London: Routledge.

Watene, Krushil. 2016. "Valuing Nature: Māori Philosophy and the Capability Approach." *Oxford Development Studies* 44 (3): 287–96. https://doi.org/10.1080/13600818.2015.1124077.

———. 2022. "Reimagining the Human-Environment Relationship: Indigenous Philosophy and Intergenerational Justice." Stockholm: UNU-UNEP. http://collections.unu.edu/eserv/UNU:8829/UNUUNEP_Watene_RHER.pdf.

Weber-Pillwax, Cora. 2004. "Indigenous Researchers and Indigenous Research Methods: Cultural Influences or Cultural Determinants of Research Methods." *Pimatisiwin: A Journal of Aboriginal and Indigenous Community Health* 2 (1): 78–90.

Whaanga, Hēmi, and Priscilla Wehi. 2017. "Rāhui and Conservation? Māori Voices in the Nineteenth Century Niupepa Māori." *Journal of the Royal Society of New Zealand* 47 (1): 100–6. https://doi.org/10.1080/03036758.2016.1252408.

Wheen, Nicola, and Jacinta Ruru. 2011. "Providing for Rāhui in the Law of Aotearoa New Zealand." *The Journal of the Polynesian Society* 120 (2): 169–82.

The White House. 2022. "White House Releases First-of-a-Kind Indigenous Knowledge Guidance for Federal Agencies." December 1, 2022. https://www.whitehouse.gov/ceq/news-updates/2022/12/01/white-house-releases-first-of-a-kind-indigenous-knowledge-guidance-for-federal-agencies.

Te Waka Kai Ora. 2022. "He kai te rongoā he rongoā te kai: report into the evidence presented by te waka kai ora to the Waitangi Tribunal's inquiry to the wai 262 claim." Papawhakaritorito trust: Kaitoke.

White, Monica M. 2018. *Freedom Farmers: Agricultural Resistance and the Black Freedom Movement*. Chapel Hill: The University of North Carolina Press.

Whitbourne, Robert. "Agricultural Development & Indigenous Ways-of-Knowing: Māori & Quechuan Experiences of Participatory Development." Ph.D. diss., The University of Auckland, 2017.

Whyte, Kyle Powys. 2015. "Food Justice and Collective Food Relations." SSRN Scholarly Paper ID 2555303. Rochester, NY: Social Science Research Network. https://doi.org/10.2139/ssrn.2555303.

———. 2016. "Food Justice and Collective Food Relations." In *The Ethics of Food: An Introductory Textbook*, edited by A. Barnhill, M. Budolfson, and T. Doggett, 1–21. Oxford: Oxford University Press.

———. 2017. "Our Ancestors' Dystopia Now: Indigenous Conservation and the Anthropocene." In *The Routledge Companion to the Environmental Humanities*, edited by Ursula Heise, John Christensen, and Michelle Nieman, 208–15. London: Routledge.

———. 2021. "Time as Kinship." In *The Cambridge Companion to Environmental Humanities*, edited by J. Cohen and S. Foote, 39–55. Cambridge: Cambridge University Press.

Wilson, Sean. 2001. "What Is Indigenous Research Methodology?" 25 (1): 175–79.

———. 2009. *Research Is Ceremony: Indigenous Research Methods*. Black Point, NS: Fernwood Publications.

Wisconsin (and Great Lakes) Intertribal Seed Stewardship Cohort. n.d. Accessed October 12, 2023. https://iacgreatlakes.com/2019/01/07/wisconsin-and-great-lakes-intertribal-seed-stewardship-cohort/.

Wittman, Hannah. 2011. "Food Sovereignty: A New Rights Framework for Food and Nature?" *Environment and Society* 2 (1): 87–105.

Wittman, Hannah, and Dana James. 2022. "Land Governance for Agroecology." *Elementa: Science of the Anthropocene* 10 (1): 00100.

Wittman, Hannah, Annette Aurelie Desmarais, and Nettie Wiebe. 2010. "The Origins and Potential of Food Sovereignty." In *Food Sovereignty: Reconnecting Food, Nature and Community*, edited by Annette Aurélie Desmarais, Nettie Wiebe and Hannah Wittman, 1–14. Nova Scotia: Fernwood Publishing.

Wolfe, Patrick. 1999. *Settler Colonialism and the Transformation of Anthropology*. London: A&C Black.

———. 2006. "Settler Colonialism and the Elimination of the Native." *Journal of Genocide Research* 8 (4): 387–409.

WTEP (Waikato-Tainui Te Kauhanganui Incorporated). 2013. "Tai Tumu, Tai Pari, Tai Ao: Waikato-Tainui Environment Plan." https://www.epa.govt.nz/assets/Uploads/Documents/Fast-track-consenting/Ohinewai/Application-documents/Appendix-26-WTEP-Obs-Pols-assessment.pdf.

Yen, Douglas. 1961. "The Adaptation of Kumara by the New Zealand Māori." *The Journal of the Polynesian Society* 70 (3): 338–48.

———. 1971. "Construction of the Hypothesis for Distribution of the Sweet Potato." In *Man Across the Sea*, 328–42. Austin: University of Texas Press.

Yin, Roger. 2009. *Case Study Research: Design and Methods*. 4th ed. Thousand Oaks, CA: SAGE.

Zambrano, Patricia, Ulrike Wood-Sichra, Remidius D. Ruhinduka, Dayo Phillip, Alejandro Nin Pratt, John Komen, Enoch Mutebi Kikulwe, José Falck Zepeda, Fred M. Dzanku, and Judith A. Chambers. 2022. "Opportunities for Orphan Crops: Expected Economic Benefits from Biotechnology." *Frontiers in Plant Science* 13: 825930.

Index

Page numbers in italics indicate illustrations and maps.

Aboriginal peoples. *See* Indigenous peoples
Acarí (Arequipa), 1, 172*n*4
Acuña-Atalaya, Máxima (Newmont Mining Corp case), 82, 181*n*27
Agenda for Sustainable Development, 17–18, 175*n*20
agribusiness (capitalist/industrial food systems): agrochemical companies, 94; capitalist economic development, 14–16; commercial practices, 85, 87; as food injustice, 16–17, 25; genetically modified (GM) crops, 94; monoculture agriculture, 87, 108; vs traditional ecological knowledge, 6–10, 127–28, 133, 154
agricultural practices and rituals: ayni (reciprocity), 75–76, 110–12; chakitaqlla and kō (foot plow tools), 157, 191*nn*1–2; mink'a (labor exchange), 111–12; sata qallta (sowing time), 114; seasonal harvesting, 51, 138, 158, 164; sun and moon calendars, 76, 90–91, 114, 137–38, 157–58, 182*n*51, 189*n*17; "warmi-qhari" (woman-man) activities, 113; yunza (celebrations), 1–2, 172*n*6

agrobiodiversity: about, 173*n*11, 174*n*2, 189*n*13; agroecological knowledge, 23, 132–33, 146–47, 153; agroecological zones, 106–7, 146–47; chakra (agricultural fields), 1, 73, 172*n*5; climate change, 23, 47, 59, 61, 107, 112–13; environmental well-being, 137–38; food crops, 1–2, 12, 93, 107, 157–58, 182*nn*58–59, 183*n*60, 184*n*5; food sovereignty celebration, 163–*66*; non-governmental organizations (NGOs), 60–64, 191*n*36
allin kawsay (well-being): about, 73–74, 159, 180*n*6; ayllu system (communal governance land system), 104–9; ayni/ayninakuy (reciprocity), 41, 75–76, 110–12; holistic/collective philosophy, 18–21, 73–76, 155, 159, 180*n*6; language variants, 74, 180*n*6; mink'a (labor exchange), 111–12; yanantin-masintin (complementarity and equality), 113–14. *See also* well-being
Altieri, Miguel, 23
amaranth plant, 106, 184*n*3

221

Andean Khipu (Quipu) cord: about, 5, 35–36, 173n19, 177n7, 177n9; horizontal cord, *33*, *35*, 38–*39*; khipukamayuq (Khipu-Master), *33*; knots, *35*, *43*; vertical pendants, *35*, *40*
Andersen, Chris, 69
Andersen, Thomas, 100
Anglo-Eurocentrism. *See* Eurocentrism
Anishinaabe language, 18–19
Aotearoa (New Zealand): about, 2; climate, 88; climate change and biodiversity loss, 59; food insecurity and pandemic impacts, 131, 187n1; genetically modified (GM) crops, 94–95; Indigenous gastronomy champions, 164–65, 192n9; kānuka trees, 117, 185n1; kereru (kūkupa, kūkū) birds, 117, 128, 185n1; mānuka/kahikātoa trees, 117, 185n1; map, *46*; public libraries, 50; rivers, 20, 117, 139; towns, 2, 173n9. *See also* Māori people
Association for Nature and Sustainable Development (ANDES), 60, 61, 64
Australia, 16
Avilés, Valentina, 90–91
Aviles, Valeria, 112
Awajún people, 59, 61, 63, 179n44
ayllu system (communal governance land system), 104–9, 145–46
Aymara language, 16, 18, 74, 172n4, 190n28
ayni/ayninakuy (reciprocity), 41, 75–76, 110–12

Bastion Point occupation, 126, 186n31
Beech-Cullen, Buchanan, 44, 128, 187n37
Berkes, Fikret, 22
Biden, President Joe, 23
BioCuencas watershed management project, 60
biodiversity. *See* agrobiodiversity
Bolivia, 50, 100, 178n28, 183n73, 191n3
Brundtland Report, 17
Bryce, Cheryl (Songhees), 27

Cáceres, Braulio, 61
Camisea Natural Gas Project, 83
camote (sweet potatoes), 1, 2, 4, 7, 9, 171n1
Canada (rivers), 20
CAPEMA coffee cooperative, 61, 63–64
capitalist food system. *See* agribusiness (capitalist/industrial food systems)
capulí trees, 172n6

cchaninchay (solution), 104, 112–13
Ccoyo, Aniceto, 74–75
Ceiba (tree of life), 177n9
Centre for Indigenous Cultures of Peru (CHIRAPAQ), 28, 156, 192n8
Chakana/Māhutonga (Southern Cross Constellation) framework: about, 29, 134–*35*, 160–61; cultural/spiritual well-being quadrant, 30, 136–37, 141–45, 147, 149–50; economies of well-being quadrant, 31, 139–40; environmental well-being quadrant, 30–31, 137–38, 152–53; as food insecurity solution, 133–34; as metaphor, 135; political well-being quadrant, 31, 138–39, 145–46; Southern Cross constellation, 29, 134. *See also* Indigenous Food Sovereignty; Pachamama/Papatūānuku (Mother Earth)
chanikuy waqekuy (hospitality), 111
Chávez, Vivian, 57
Choquecancha village (Peru), 141–42
Chorrillos (Peru), 1, 32, 172n2
chuño/ch'uñu (potato), 146–47, 190n28
climate change, 23, 47, 59, 61, 107, 112–13
collective well-being. *See* holistic/collective well-being
colonialism. *See* settler colonialism
community-based participatory action research (CBPAR), 42, 63
Condori, Amauta, 71, 180n3
Conservation International (CI)-Peru, 60, 61
Convention on Biological Diversity, 100
Cooper, Whinia, 126, 186n31
Corntassel, Jeff (Tsalagi), 26, 27
Coté, Charlotte, 165–66
COVID-19 pandemic, 131–32, 187n1, 188n6, 188nn3–4
Cruz, Marisol, 76
cultural identity, 58, 83–84, 118–20, 125–26
cultural/spiritual well-being, 52, 83–84, 86–87, 136–37, 141–45, 149–50, 154–56
Cusco village (Peru), 5, 44–*45*, 61–64, 73–74, 142–45, 178n28
Cuy al palo traditional food (Peru), 63

Daigle, Michelle (Cree), 28
de Dios Cruz, Juan (Paqo), 142–45
Dell, Hinetu, 78
Dell, Kiri, 116, 117
Doctrine of Discovery (DoD), 13, 85
Duarte, Marisa, 58

Durie, Edward Taihakurei, 121
Durie, Mason, 78–79, 86–87

Ecuador, 100, 139, 183n73, 191n3
English language (academic dominance), 33, 177n4
Espino, Huamán, 60, 64
Espinoza, Waldemar, 110
Eurocentrism: academic language, 33, 177n4; colonial research methodology, 34–35, 55–56, 69, 177nn5–6; development theory, 14–15; research practices, 35, 42; timekeeping, 89; well-being measurement, 100. *See also* settler colonialism

Fisko, Monique, 164
Fletcher Residential housing development, 126–27
Foco, Dionisio, 85–86
Food and Agriculture Organization (FAO), 29
food insecurity: climate change impacts, 23, 47, 59, 61, 107, 112–13; famine, 29; industrial food systems impacts, 15–17, 25; pandemic impacts, 131, 187n1; rates, 29; traditional ecological knowledge solutions, 133–34
food security: about, 24–25; as human right, 22, 26–27, 132, 175n35, 188n5. *See also* Indigenous Food Sovereignty
food sovereignty, 25–27, 176n51; Khipu Model research, 54–68. *See also* Indigenous Food Sovereignty
food systems (terminology), 7. *See also* Māori traditional food systems; Quechua traditional food systems
foodways (terminology), 172n8
Freire, Paolo, 57
Friedman, Harriet, 101

Generación con causa (Generation with a cause) movement, 164, 192n9
genetically modified (GM) crops, 94, 95–96, 150–52, 191n36
Genetically Modified Organisms (GMOs), 96, 183nn65–67
Gliessman, Steve, 101
global food systems, 6–10, 131
Gordon, Chef Peter, 164–65, 188n4, 193n12

Harris, Pauline, 77
He kai te rongoā he rongoā te kai (food is medicine, medicine is food) report, 94–95

Heitia, Mate, 71, 78, *79*, 128
Heitia, Sonny, *79*
Helimo, Ulla, 60
Hēnare, Mānuka, 66, 179n47
holistic/collective well-being: about, 19–21, 72, 159; allin kawsay (well-being), 73–76, 155, 159, 180n6; Indigenous Food Sovereignty, 159–62, 165–66; Māori and Quechua commonalities, 19–21, 81, 140, 154–56, 159–62. *See also* well-being
Homeland restaurant, 164–65, 193n12
Hotene, Lionel, 44, 66, 116, 118–19, *129*, 147, 149–50, 152
Hoturoa, Chief, 118
Howard, Philip, 94, 101
Hua Parakore Certification principles, 150–52
Huambachano, Elena, 63
Huambachano, Mariaelena: academic background, 4; ancestry, 32–33; childhood and family, 1–2, 172n6; experiential learning approach, 103; field trips and community relationships, 3–4, 58–64, 73–75, 76, 102–9, 141–47, 179n44; food security workshop, 112–13; genetically modified (GMO) activism against, 191n36; Hua Parakore Certification, *151*–152; māra kai (food garden) work, 116; pandemic impacts, 132–33; as participant observer, 49–50; pōwhiri (formal welcome), 187n44; Quechua language fluency, 33–34; research presentations, 62; research volunteer, 64; seed rematriation project, 156
Huambachano, Patty, 2

Ihumātao land dispossession, 126–27
India, 84, 139
Indigenous Food Sovereignty, 12–31; about, 12–13, 27–28; ayni/ayninakuy (reciprocity), 110–12; celebration and visibility of, 163–66, 192n5; community-based projects, 64; education and workshops, 54, 164, 192n7; food as human right, 22, 132, 175n35, 188n5; global development agenda, 162, 192n4; heritage seeds, 155–56; holistic/collective well-being, 159–62, 165–66; Indigenous gastronomy entrepreneurs, 164–65, 192n9, 193n12; markers of, 103–4; reclamation and resurgence, 6–10, 24–28, 157–66; relational ethics approach, 136–37;

Indigenous Food Sovereignty *(continued)*
  rematriation, 28–31, 84, 140, 154–56, 161–62, 176*n*62, 190*n*34; restaurant chefs, 164–65, 193*n*12; scholarship on, 5–6, 27–28; seed rematriation and seed-saving, 84, 112–13, 155–56, 165, 190*n*34, 192*n*11; solutions, 112–13; treaty-gauranteed food gathering sites, 133, 189*n*9; youth empowerment, 164, 192*n*8. *See also* Chakana/Māhutonga framework; food security; food sovereignty; sustainable food systems; traditional ecological knowledge (TEK)

Indigenous peoples: cultural identity, 58, 83–84, 118–20, 125–26; diseases, 5; environmental justice movements, 85–86; food insecurity, 4–5, 16–17, 131–32, 173*n*14, 187*n*1; gastronomy champions, 164–65, 192*n*9; knowledge holders (Elders), 36, 178*n*10; land dispossession, 14, 20, 66, 84–85, 126–27, 129, 179*n*48, 186*n*31; land ontologies, 84–87, 125; pandemic impacts, 131–32, 187*n*1; research decolonization, 55–56, 68; self-determination and decolonizaton, 39, 41, 42, 55–56, 68–69, 138, 190*n*18; terminology, 172*n*3. *See also* Māori people; Quechua (Runakuna) people

Indigenous Seed Keepers Network, 28, 156, 165, 176*n*61, 190*n*34, 192*n*11

industrial food systems. *See* agribusiness (capitalist/industrial food systems)

Inka lunar calendar, 90–91, 182*n*51

Inkan counting device (Yupana), *33*

Intergovernmental Science-Policy Platform on Biodiversity and Ecosystem Services (IPBES), 192*n*4

International Covenant on Economic, Social and Cultural Rights (1966), 175*n*35, 188*n*5

International Indigenous Forum on Biodiversity, 100

Inti (sun) agricultural calendar, 76, 114, 137–38, 157–58, 189*n*17

Kaa, Keri, 118, 119

kaitiakitanga (land guardianship), 127–28

kañihua (grain), 107, 184*n*6

kānuka trees, 117, 185*n*1

Kaupapa Māori movement, 36–37, 55, 65–67, 178*n*11

kereru (kūkupa, kūkū) birds, 117, 128, 185*n*1

Khipu cord. *See* Andean Khipu (Quipu) cord

Khipu Model (Indigenous-based research methodology), 32–70; about, *3, 5*, 55, 173*n*19; accountability, 34, 69, 99; being/ontology phase, *40–42, 43*; community gatherings, 44–48; community relationships and decolonization, 34–38, 56, 68, 161, 177*nn*5–6; doing phase, 42–*43*, 44; elements, 34; ethics of engagement, 57–58; food justice/sovereignty, 55–68; goals, 37–38; Indigenous voice, 69, 161; intellectual sovereignty, 69; interrelations, *43*; Kaupapa Māori concepts, 36–37, 178*n*11; knowing phase, 38–*39, 43*; mātauranga (Māori) and yachay (Quechua), 38; as metaphor for Khipu cord, 36, 177*n*9; origins, 55; participant compensation, 47, 178*nn*19–20; reflexivity and cultural humility, 34, 58; self-determination, 68–69; storytelling and metaphors, 49; study location and data collection methods, 44–50; talking circles, 48–49; theoretical framework phases, 38–44, 68–69; traditional ecological knowledge, 22; transformative research, 68; transparency, 34. *See also* research methodology

khipukamayuq (Khipu-Master), *33*

Kimmerer, Robin Wall, 17, 140

kinship philosophy, 4, 20–21, 99, 119–20

Kloppenburg, Jack, 155

Knight, Mere, 147

kūmara (sweet potatoes), 1, 2, 88, 120, *129, 149*–150, 171*n*1, 173*n*10

kūmara tipu (sweet potato seedlings), 79

La Via Campesina movement, 25–26, 176*n*51

Lajo, Javier, 73

land ontologies, 84–87, 125

Lares Valley (ayllu Lares), 47, 64, 73, 102–*3*, 106–7

Latin American Congress of Young Farmers (SISAY), 164

Law on Sustainable Investment in the Amazon: Decree 27037, 82

living well. *See* well-being

maca root crop, 93, 183*n*60

Magpie River (Canada), 20

Mahuika, Dr. Apirana, 124–25, 186*n*26

Makiha, Rereata, 77, 88–90, 121–23, 128, 189*n*16

Mamakan botanical artist, 77, 181n14
Mamani, Lino, 107, 108, 112
mana whenua and mana moana (authority over the land), 124-27, 130, 186n24
manaakitanga (generosity and care for others), 65, 128-30
mānuka/kahikātoa trees, 117, 185n1
Māori land: cultural-spiritual relationship, 84-87; hikoi (political protest movements), 126-27, 186n31; kaitiakitanga (land guardianship), 127-28; land dispossession, 14, 20, 66, 84-85, 126-27, 129, 179n48, 186n31; land ontologies, 84-87, 125; mana whenua and mana moana (authority over the land), 124-27, 130, 186n24; Quechua ontology commonalities, 84-87; rivers and legal rights of, 20, 139; Wai 262 (flora and fauna) claim, 94-95; waiata (song), 129; as whenua (placenta), 86-87, 125
Māori people: cultural identity, 83-84, 118-20, 125-26; diseases, 5, 16; food insecurity, 12, 16-17, 131, 187n1; iwi (tribes), 44, 46-47, 77-78, 116-18, 128-29; language, 78, 123; origin and creation stories, 86-87; pandemic impacts, 131, 187n1; research participants, 39-44, 119; settler colonialism treaties, 14, 20; tangata whenua (people of the land), 83, 85, 86, 95, 120; tino rangatiratanga (sovereignty and self-determination), 55, 81-84, 95, 124-27, 150-53, 181n30. See also Aotearoa (New Zealand)
Māori philosophy and worldview: atuas (gods), 118; burial practices, 87; holistic/collective well-being, 19-21, 81, 140, 154-56, 159-62, 166; intergenerational equity and justice practices, 98-99; kaumātua (male Elders), 77, 116, 130, 149, 189n16; Kia mau ki to Māoritanga (hold fast to your Māoritanga (being Māori)), 166; kuia (female Elders), 116, 147; manaakitanga (generosity and care for others), 65, 128-30; maramataka (Māori lunar calendar), 52, 65, 67, 77, 88-90, 138, 153, 189n16; mātauranga (Māori knowledge), 36-37, 65, 88-90, 123, 182n49; mauri ora (well-being and harmony), 18-21, 77-80, 155, 159; mauri (essence) practices, 97-98; origin and creation stories, 86-87; proverb, 32, 177n1; Quechua commonalities, 4, 6-10, 18-21, 72-73; Ranginui (Sky Father)/Papatūānuku (Earth Mother), 119-20; Rongomātāne (god of cultivation), 147; science curriculum, 89, 123, 182n49; tikanga (ethical practices), 65-67, 120-30; tūrangawaewae (belonging), 87, 125-26, 150; whakapapa (genealogical connections), 117-21, 124-25; Whareponga marae (sacred meeting place), 117-18; whenua (placenta), 86-87, 125. See also Pachamama/Papatūānuku (Mother Earth)
Māori traditional food systems: agrobiodiversity guardians, 138, 189n13; community relationships, 46, 66; creation stories, 120; crop types, 71, 180n2; eel drying practice, 122; environmental justice movements, 85-86; environmental well-being, 152-53; food as human right, 22, 132; food sovereignty education, 164, 192n7; genetically modified (GM) crops threat, 94-95; hākari (ceremonial feast), 128-29; kai (food) boxes, 132, 188nn3-4; kaitiakitanga (land guardianship), 127-28; kereru (pigeons), 117, 128, 185n1; knowledge holders, 88-90; kō (foot plow tools), 157, 191n2; kūmara (sweet potatoes), 1, 2, 88, 120, 149-150, 171n1, 173n10; manaakitanga (generosity and care for others), 65, 128-30; māra kai (food garden), 116, 132, 188n4; maramataka (lunar calendar), 51-52, 65, 67, 77, 88-90, 138, 153, 189n16; mātauranga (traditional ecological knowledge), 6-10, 22-23, 88-90, 94-95, 153; medicinal plants, 71, 121; oral traditions, 88; vs organic food production, 53; pātaka kai (communal store house), 88-89, 90, 150; peruperu potatoes, 116, 149-150; pōwhiri (welcome ritual), 65, 130, 187n44; pre settler colonialism, 88, 182n45; Quechua cultural connections, 2-3, 7-10, 18-21, 87-96; rāhui (restriction), 128, 187n38; Rapua E te Iwi nga Kai o nga Atua (People, look for the food of the gods for wellness (REKA)), 163-64, 192n6; revitalization, 28, 67, 77; rongoā Māori (plant healing knowledge), 77, 181n14; Rongomātāne (god of agriculture), 137; tapu (sacredness), 128, 187n39; tikanga (ethical practices), 121-22, 123, 187n39. See also Papatūānuku Kōkiri Marae (urban organic community garden)

māra kai (food garden), 44, 116, 147–49, 153
maramataka (Māori lunar calendar), 52, 65, 67, 77, 88–90, 138, 189n16
Marsden, M., 97, 127
mashua (tuber), 106, 107, 184n3
Mātāmua, Rangi, 77, 89
Matariki lunar festivals, 90
mātauranga (Māori knowledge), 36–37, 65, 88–90, 182n49
mauri (essence), 78, 80, 95, 97–98, 120, 123, 152
mauri ora (well-being and harmony), 18–21, 78, 155, 159
Máxima Acuña-Atalaya v. Newmont Mining Corp case, 82, 181n27
McGregor, Deborah, 22
McMichael, Philip, 25
Mead, Aroha, 129
Menser, Michael, 26
Merino, Lourdes Villegas, 61
mestiza (female) / mestizo (male), 32, 177n3
Metge, Joan, 121
millenium development goals (MDGs), 100, 175n20
mink'a (labor exchange), 111–12
mino-mnaamodzawin (good life), 18, 175n24
Moko Mead, Hirini, 121
Montoya, Cesar, 64
Morgan, Dr. Te Kīpa Kēpa, 80
Morrison, Dawn, 27, 87, 136–37
Mother Earth. See Pachamama/Papatūānuku (Mother Earth)
Murphy, Ngahuia, 119

Native Land Court, 124–25, 186n26
Nature: accountability, 98–99; agricultural rituals, 114; Chakana/Māhutonga framework, 29–31, 134–40; climate justice and rivers, 20, 138–39; constellations, 29, 134, 189n17; ethical relationships, 74, 120; harmony cosmovision, 19–21, 71–72; kaitiakitanga (land guardianship), 127–28; kinship philosophy, 119–20; lunar calendars, 76, 88–91, 138, 182n51, 189nn16–17; rakinakuy (equilibrium), 41; reciprocity, 99; rights, 4, 173n13; social and environmental justice movements, 85–86; sustainable principles, 128, 187nn38–39; tenets, 74–75; well-being, 20–21, 83–84. See also Pachamama/Papatūānuku (Mother Earth)

Navdanya International, 84
Nelson, Melissa, 26
neoliberalism, 15–16, 25–26, 108
New Zealand. See Aotearoa (New Zealand)
New Zealand Settlements Act, 126
Newmont Mining Corp case, 82, 181n27
Newton, Pania, 127
Ngā Pae o te Māramatanga (Māori Centre of Research Excellence), 54
Ngārimu, Elizabeth, 124, 125
Ngāta, Āpirana Turupa, 119
Nuu-chah-nulth (nuučaan̓) language, 18–19, 175n25

ora (embodied mauri), 18–21, 78, 155, 159

Pachamama/Papatūānuku (Mother Earth): about, 20–21; agricultural connection to, 71–72, 83–84; ch'alla (food) offerings, 97, 142–44, 145, 190n26; climate justice rights, 20, 138–39; cultural/spiritual well-being, 52, 83–84, 86–87, 136–37, 154–56; equilibrium (rakinakuy), 41; as nourishment, 20–21, 85–86; origin and creation stories, 86–87; reciprocity, 99, 110–12; sun and moon calendars, 76, 90–91, 114, 137–38, 157–58, 182n51, 189n17; warmi-pacha (fertility), 114; as whenua (placenta), 86–87, 125. See also Chakana/Māhutonga (Southern Cross Constellation) framework; Māori philosophy and worldview; Nature; Quechua philosophy and worldview
Papatūānuku Kōkiri Marae (urban organic community garden): aims, 147; certification, 54, 66; community services, 152–53; entrance, 147–48; environmental well-being, 152–53; Hua Parakore Certification, 150–53; māra kai (food garden), 44, 147–49, 153; pandemic response, 188n4; restaurant food grower, 164–65; tino rangatiratanga (self-determination), 150–53; workshops, 147. See also Māori traditional food systems
Paqo (mystic), 142–44, 145, 190n26
paracay (yellow corn), 92
pātaka kai (communal store house), 88–89, 90, 150
Peru: agrobiodiversity, 12, 60–64, 93, 107, 182nn58–59, 183n60, 184n5, 191n36; agrochemical companies, 94; buen vivir movement, 191n3; capulí trees, 172n6; climate change, 59, 61; coffee

cooperative, 61; first settlements, 172*n*2; genetically modified (GM) crops protests and moratoriums, 96, 183*nn*65–67; Indigenous free, prior, and informed consent (FPIC), 82–83; Indigenous gastronomy champions, 164, 192*n*9; Indigenous legal recognition, 82; mining projects, 82; native vs improved potatoes, *105*, 107–8; natural gas reserves, 83; natural resources protests, 82–83, 181*n*27; neoliberal agrarianism, 108; pandemic response, 132, 188*n*6; public libraries, 50, 178*n*28; rebellions, 172*n*7; towns, 1, 5, 172*n*2, 172*n*4; watershed management project, 60
Pillco, Valentina, 97
Pimbert, Michael, 23
Pohatu, Taina Whakaatere, 37
Poppel, Birger, 100
Potato Park, 61, 63, 64
Potato Park biocultural protocol (PPBC), 63
Puckey, Adrienne, 85

Qocha, Delia, 91
Quechua language: discrimination against, 33–34; disenfranchisement, 109; mestiza (female) / mestizo (male), 32, 177*n*3; as Runakuna, 71, 180*n*3; sumak kawsay as bien vivir, 74, 159–60, 191*n*3; variations and distinctions between, 74
Quechua (Runakuna) people: charangos and quena (musical instruments), 143–44; communities, 73–76, 102–14, 141–47, 180*n*7; community leaders, 112; cultural identity, 41, 83–84, 125–26; discrimination against, 33–34; diseases, 5; environmental justice movements, 85–86; food insecurity, 12, 16–17; human rights abuses, 172*n*7; intergenerational equity and justice, 98–99; kinship tradition with Māori, 20–21; land dispossession, 14, 84–85; land ontologies, 84–87; legal instruments, 82–83; natural resources threats and protests, 82–83, 181*n*27; origins, 32–33, 177*n*3; pandemic impact, 132–33; research participants, 39–*45*, 59–64, *75*; self-determination, 81–84; settler colonialism effects, 14; traditional clothing, *93*, 141–*42*
Quechua philosophy and worldview: allin kawsay (well-being and harmony), 18–21, 73–76, 155, 159; ayninakuy (reciprocity), 41; buen vivir (living well), 74, 159–60, 191*n*3; chanikuy waqekuy (hospitality), 111; festivals, 97; intergenerational equity and justice practices, 98–99; land relationship, 84–87; Māori commonalities, 4, 6–10, 18–21, 72–73; rakinakuy (equilibrium), 41; sumak kawsay vs allin kawsay (philosophy of life), 62, 159, 191*n*3; talking circles rituals, 48–49; warmi-pacha (fertility), 114; warmi-qhari (woman-man), 113–14; yanantin-masintin (complementarity), 41. *See also* Pachamama/Papatūānuku (Mother Earth)
Quechua traditional food systems: agricultural calendar rituals, 76, 90–91, 114, 137–38, 157–58, 182*n*51, 189*n*17; agrobiodiversity, 12, 60–64, 93, 107, 182*nn*58–59, 183*n*60, 184*n*5, 191*n*36; agrobiodiversity guardians, 138, 189*n*13; amaranth, 106, 184*n*3; ayllu system (communal governance land system), 104–9, 145–46; ayni/ayninakuy (reciprocity), 110–12; camote (sweet potatoes), 1, 2, 4, 7, 9, 171*n*1; chakra (agricultural fields), 1, 73, 172*n*5; chanikuy waqekuy (hospitality), 111; chiri uchu (traditional dish), 111–12; chuño/ch'uñu (potato), 146–47, 190*n*28; Cuy al palo (traditional dish), 63; food rituals, 111–12, 141–*44*, 145, 190*n*26; foot plow tools (chakitaqlla), 157, 191*n*1; Inka lunar calendar, 90–91, 182*n*51; Inti (sun) and Quilla (lunar) calendars, 137–38, 189*n*17; kañihua (grain), 107, 184*n*6; maca (root crop), 93, 183*n*60; Māori cultural connections, 2–3, 7–10, 18–21, 87–96; mashua (tuber), 106, 107, 184*n*3; medicinal plants, 61; native vs improved potatoes, *105*, 107–8; pachamanca (traditional dish), 143; paracay (yellow corn), *92*; potato varieties, *166*; precolonial crop species, 91–*93*; preservation techniques, 146–47; quinoa, 93, 106, 183*n*59, 184*n*3; reclamation, 28, 164; seed keepers, *92–93*; spiritual well-being, 141–45; traditional dishes, *143*–144; traditional foods, 1, 2, 4, 7, 9, 63, 111–12, 141, 171*n*1; ulluco (root crop), 107, 184*n*5; uqa (corn tubers), 93, 107, 183*n*58, 184*n*5; values and principles, 102–15; welcome food, 141; yachay (traditional ecological knowledge), 22–23, 90–*93*, 94, 96, 182*nn*50–51; yacón (root vegetable), 61; yunza (agicultural celebrations), 1–2, 172*n*6

Quijano, Aníbal, 56
Quilla (moon) agricultural calendar, 76, 114, 138, 157-58, 189*n*17
Quispe, Crisostomo, 76, 91, *105*, 146
Quispe, Dionisio, 110
Quispe, Marisol, *92*, 112
Quispe, Petronila, 64, 104, 112, 141, 145
Quispe, Sonia, 64, 92, 104, 132
Quispe, Valentina, 64

Rapua E te Iwi nga Kai o nga Atua (People, look for the food of the gods for wellness (REKA)), 163-64, 192*n*6
Reátegui, Víctor Mardonio Del Castillo, 61
reciprocity, 41, 75-76, 99, 110-12
rematriation, 28-31, 84, 140, 154-56, 176*n*62, 190*n*34
research methodology: coding, 50-51; community gatherings and relationships, 34-35, 40-*43*, 44, *45-46*, 47-48, 60-64, 177*nn*5-6; community-based participatory action research (CBPAR), 42; compensation, 47, 178*nn*19-20; cultural humility, 57-58; data analysis stages, 50-54; data corpus/data extract/data item/data sets, 51; decolonizaton, 34-35, 39, 41, 42, 68, 177*nn*5-6; experiential learning approach, 103; field trips, 3-4, 59-64, 73-*75*, 76, 102-9, 141-47, 179*n*44; Indigeneity terminology, 58; Indigenous based, 62-63, 67-70; Indigenous research partners, 39-44, *45-46*, 47, 75, 104-9; Indigenous voice, 39-*43*, 68-69; interviews, 49; meta-themes, 51-52; mind-map analysis, 52; participant observers, 49-50; positionality, 57-58; presentations, 54, 62; qualitative data analysis, 53; relational accountability, 57-58; relational-ethics approach, 41, 67-68; results validation, 54; secondary data, 50, 53, 178*n*28; social justice, 42; storytelling and metaphors, 49; study locations and data collection, 44-50; talking circles, 48-49, 112; thematic analysis method, 50-54; theoretical framework phases, 38-44; three R's, 41. *See also* Khipu Model
Rivera Zea, Tarcila, 28
rongoā Māori (traditional Māori plant healing knowledge), 77, 181*n*14

sata qallta (sowing time), 114
Save Our Unique Landscape (SOUL), 126-27

Schneider, Dr. Claudio, 60
seed keepers, 28, *92-93*, 156, 165, 176*n*61, 190*n*34, 192*n*11
self-determination: autonomy, 55-56, 124-27; decolonizaton, 39, 41, 42, 55-56, 68-69, 81-84, 138, 190*n*18; research model, 68-69; urban organic community garden, 150-53; well-being, 81-84
settler colonialism: about, 13-14; capitalism and Indigenous food insecurity, 4-5, 173*n*14; coloniality definition, 55-56; Indigenous language suppression, 34; land dispossession, 14, 20, 66, 84-85, 126-27, 129, 179*n*48, 186*n*31; vs self-determination and decolonization, 81-84; vs traditional food systems and food sovereignty, 6-10. *See also* Eurocentrism; Treaty of Waitangi (Te Tiriti o Waitangi)
Shampuyaco people, 60-61
Shiva, Vandana, 84
Shiwi food company, 193*n*12
Sicos, Carmen, 106, 109
Silva, Juan de Dios Cruz, 64
Slow Food Peru, 60, 84, 155-56, 164, 191*n*36
Smith, Graham Hingangaroa, 55
Southern Cross constellation, 29, 134, 160-61
spirituality. *See* cultural/spiritual well-being
Stenner, Tammy, 61, 64
suma qamaña (living well), 18, 74
sumak/allin kawsay (living well): as buen vivir, 74, 159-60, 191*n*3; holistic/collective philosophy, 73, 155, 159, 180*n*6
Sunco, Julio, 107
Suñiga, Juana, 106
sustainable development goals (SDGs), 17-18, 175*n*20
sustainable food systems: vs agribusiness, 6-10, 154; ayllu system (communal governance land system), 105-6, 145-46; ayni/ayninakuy (reciprocity), 110-12; cchaninchay (solution), 112-13; crop types, 71, 106-7, 180*n*2, 184*n*3, 184*nn*5-6; intergenerational equity and justice, 98-99; mink'a (labor exchange), 111-12; values and principles (Māori), 116-30; values and principles (Quechua), 102-15; yields, 21. *See also* Māori traditional food systems; Quechua traditional food systems

Sutta, Gomercinda, 74, 111
sweet potatoes. See camote (sweet potatoes); kūmara (sweet potatoes)

taewa (Maori potatoes), 71, 88, 180n2
tangata whenua (people of the land (Māori)), 83, 85, 86, 95, 120
Tauli-Corpuz, Victoria, 18
Te Awa Tupua (Whanganui River), 20, 139
Te Hemara, Hana, 123
Te Pou Tupua guardian, 139
Te Tiriti o Waitangi (Treaty of Waitangi), 14, 20, 65–66, 83, 85, 95, 126, 138, 181n30
Te Ture Whenua Māori Act (Māori Land Act), 186n26
Te Waka Kai Ora (the National Māori Organics Authority of Aotearoa), 66, 94
Te Whare Tapa Whā (House of Four Sides) model, 79–80
Te Wheke (octopus model), 79–80
Teraitua, Valerie, 44, 66, 147, 150
Tereo, Tenaiti, 86
tikanga (ethical values and practices): application of, 121–22, 123–29, 130; definitions, 121; food system role, 121–22; karakia (prayer), 122–23, 149, 187n39; respect, 122–23
tino rangatiratanga (Māori sovereignty and self-determination), 55, 95, 150–53
Tipene, Uncle Percy, 54, 66, 98, 152
Tito, Fred, 44, 86, 125
Titto, Maria, 92–93
Tokoroa town (Te Kaokaoroa o Pātetere), 2, 173n9
traditional ecological knowledge (TEK): about, 4; vs agribusiness, 133; agriculture sustainability, 6–9; agroecological practices, 21–24, 146–47, 153; agroecological zones, 106–7, 146–47; food as human right, 22, 132, 175n35, 188n5; as food insecurity solution, 133–34; guidance (to government), 23; intergovernmental policy practices, 162, 192n4; scholarship on, 22–23; seed system and seed keepers, 28, 92–93, 156, 165, 176n61, 190n34, 192n11; Western view of, 21–22. See also Indigenous Food Sovereignty
traditional food systems. See Māori traditional food systems; Quechua traditional food systems; sustainable food systems
traditional food systems (terminology), 172n8
Treaty of Waitangi (Te Tiriti o Waitangi), 14, 20, 65–66, 83, 85, 95, 126, 138, 181n30

Treaty of Waitangi Act, 66, 179n48
trees (capulí), 172n6
Truman, President Harry S., 15
Ttito, Bernardina, 110
Ttito, Maria, 141
Ttito, Sonia, 75–76, 141
tūrangawaewae (belonging), 87, 125–26, 150
Turtle Island (North America), 18–19, 54, 84, 156, 175nn24–25, 189n9

ulluco (root crop), 107, 184n5
United Nations: millennium development goals (MDGs), 175n20; sustainable development goals (SDGs), 17–18, 175n20
United Nations Declaration on the Rights of Indigenous Peoples (UNDRIP), 82, 138, 190n18
United Nations Permanent Forum on Indigenous Issues, 100
United Nations World Food Program, 29
United States: seed-saving organizations, 165, 192n11; traditional ecological knowledge guidelines, 23
Universal Declaration of Human Rights (1948), 132, 175n35, 188n5
Universal Declaration of the Rights of Mother Earth, 173n13
uqa (corn tubers), 93, 107, 183n58, 184n5

Villafuerte, Sofia, 64

Wai 262 (flora and fauna) claim, 94–95
Wai A Ariki Onerahirahi (Food Forest) garden, 44, 86, 125, 128
Waiapu (Waiapu Koka huhua) River, 117
Waitangi Tribunal, 66, 67, 94–95, 179n48
Walter, Maggie, 69
warmi-pacha (fertility), 114
warmi-qhari (woman-man), 113–14
Watene, Krushil, 137
Weber-Pillwax, Cora, 41
well-being: as buen vivir, 74, 159–60, 191n3; cultural/spiritual, 52, 83–84, 86–87, 136–37, 141–45, 149–50, 154–56; economies of, 139–40; environmental, 137–38, 152–53; Indigenous vs non-Indigenous scholarship on, 72, 100–101; intergenerational, 137; mauri ora (well-being and harmony (Māori)), 18–21, 78, 155, 159; measurement of, 100–101; philosophies, 18–21, 77–80,

well-being *(continued)*
 175nn24–25; political, 138–39, 145–46; rematriation, 28–31, 84, 140, 154–56, 176n62, 190n34; self-determination, 81–84; sustainable food systems, 71–101, 116–30. *See also* allin kawsay (well-being); holistic/collective well-being
whakapapa (genealogical connections), 117–21, 124–25
Whareponga marae (sacred meeting place), 117–*18*
whenua: mana whenua (authority over the land), 124–27, 186n24; placenta, 86–87, 125

White, Rowan, 165, 176n62, 192n11
Whyte, Kyle, 16, 20, 54
Wilson, Shawn, 40, 57

yachay (Quechua traditional ecological knowledge), 90–*93*, 94, 96, 182nn50–51
yacón (root vegetable), 61
yanantin-masintin (complementarity and equality), 41, 76, 104, 113–14, 145–46
Yupana (Inkan counting device), *33*

Zulu language, 19

www.ingramcontent.com/pod-product-compliance
Lightning Source LLC
Chambersburg PA
CBHW020809230426
43666CB00007B/928